THE CARLTON **SPORTS** GUIDE

FORMULA ONE 2018

This edition published in 2018
by Carlton Books Limited
20 Mortimer Street
London W1T 3JW

A CIP catalogue record for this book is available from the British Library.

The publisher has taken reasonable steps to check the accuracy of the facts contained
herein at the time of going to press, but can take no responsibility for any errors.

ISBN 978-1-78739-050-8

Editorial Director: Martin Corteel
Design Manager: Luke Griffin
Designer: RockJaw Creative
Picture Research: Paul Langan
Production: Lisa Cook
Assistant Editor: David Ballheimer

Printed in Spain

Opposite: Lewis Hamilton does a celebratory doughnut after his
ninth-place finish in the 2017 Mexican GP was enough to clinch his
fourth Drivers' World Championship title.

THE CARLTON SPORTS GUIDE

FORMULA ONE 2018

BRUCE JONES

CARLTON
BOOKS

CONTENTS

4

Right: Max Verstappen laps up the applause from the grandstands after winning the Mexican GP. His outstanding performance was overshadowed by the clash between title rivals Lewis Hamilton and Sebastian Vettel who he will surely challenge again in 2018.

Celebrations all around as Lewis Hamilton is carried shoulder-high after scoring his fifth British GP win at Silverstone on a day when he slashed 19 points out of Ferrari driver Sebastian Vettel's 20-point championship lead.

ANALYSIS OF THE 2018 SEASON

Whenever Formula One appears to have achieved a balance, something seems to crop up to threaten the status quo. For 2018, with F1's owners Liberty Media starting to alter things, the teams are becoming restless as changes are proposed, chief among which are moves to make engines cheaper. For 19 drivers, though, the big question is how to topple the 20th from the top of their ranks: Mercedes' Lewis Hamilton.

A pattern across the decades of what happens whenever the people who run the World Championship - the FIA and Liberty Media - try to change Formula One, is that there is no consensus. For example, with Liberty Media pushing to make engines cheaper from 2021 and thus F1 more affordable, the well-heeled teams have voted against it, as they're keen to preserve their performance advantage...

One change that the teams and drivers have all had to agree on is the fitting of a wishbone-shaped protective halo around the top of the cockpit opening above helmet height to improve driver safety (see the Talking Point feature on pages 58-59).

Other changes to the rulebook include drivers having to make do with three engines all year rather than four. To limit how much the teams can gain engine performance by burning oil, the amount of oil that they will be allowed to burn has been halved to 0.6 litres per 100km. The number of official test days has been cut to seven.

The most obvious change is that Pirelli will extend the range of tyre compounds it supplies to seven, with the softest of the range now being denoted by pink sidewall markings.

Most desired of all, however, will be anything that can reduce the number of grid penalties as they jumbled too many grids last year when penalties were applied after qualifying.

Away from politics and negotiation, the F1 playing field is likely to be more on the level as, unlike in 2017, there are no technical changes that threaten to upset the order. What that means is that

Mercedes will start as favourites to make it a fifth constructors' championship title in five years, and potentially a fifth drivers' title for Lewis Hamilton, with the team keen that Valtteri Bottas keeps moving forwards in the Finn's second year with the team.

However, Ferrari's Sebastian Vettel is sure to be a real threat again this year as the team bearing the prancing horse was at its best for years in 2017. Kimi Raikkonen will again be the support act.

Red Bull Racing will be seeking to topple Ferrari at the very least, and Daniel Ricciardo knows that he will have his hands full keeping Max Verstappen back.

Force India performed brilliantly last year, on an infinitely smaller budget than the teams finishing ahead of them and smaller too than some of those that it outstripped. Sergio Perez and Esteban Ocon will provide the fireworks.

Williams welcome Lance Stroll back, and he will be joined by Russian Sergey Sirotkin as they try to help the team go forward again.

Scuderia Toro Rosso took an unusual course through 2017, as it used four drivers. With Carlos Sainz Jr being coaxed away by Renault and Daniil Kvyat being pushed to the sidelines after continuing to disappoint the management, the door was opened for Pierre Gasly and Brendon Hartley. Impressed by their performances in the late-season races, it has kept them on for 2018. As this pair faces its first full season in F1, the team will be hoping that Honda can live up to its close-season promises that it would find more power

and greater reliability from the V6 engines that McLaren chose not to use again. The deal to take them on rather than stick with Renault V6s has more to do with boosting future engine options for Red Bull's senior partner, Red Bull Racing, than with a likely performance breakthrough for Toro Rosso, but you never know...

Renault ought to be on the way back up the championship table as it continues its task to re-establish itself in the midfield and, hopefully, on towards the front. In Nico Hulkenberg and 2017 transfer Sainz Jr, it has two excellent drivers. The big question is whether the French-built engines will be able to offer both power and reliability in 2018, as it was unable to offer both at the same time last year.

Haas F1 continued to get stuck in last year and has retained its driver line-up of Romain Grosjean and Kevin Magnussen who will deliver as many points as the car can achieve.

Don't expect McLaren to run around at the back of the pack in 2018 as it did through much of the past three years when it was hampered by weak Honda engines. With Renault power, Fernando Alonso and Stoffel Vandoorne ought to be scoring points on a regular basis if the Woking outfit's ranks of designers and engineers have still got what it takes.

It's hard to see Sauber not remaining at the tail of the field in 2018, as the Swiss team is still short on both money and design clout. However, engine-supplier Ferrari has been pushing to introduce greater driving talent to its line-up.

MERCEDES GP PETRONAS F1

After three years of domination, Mercedes found its challengers closer last year. With the mettle of a great team, though, it struck back and pulled clear again. Don't be surprised if it manages to make it five constructors' titles in a row in 2018.

Lewis Hamilton had a new team-mate in Valtteri Bottas last year. Expect the Finn to be closer to his pace more of the time in 2018.

Mercedes races in silver but it really is the gold standard in Formula 1, and has been for four years in succession. Yet, just to emphasise that no team stays on top forever in the competitive cauldron of the World Championship, what is now Mercedes had actually closed its doors at the end of the 2008 season when Honda pulled the plug on Honda Racing. It took an 11th hour rescue package to bring it back to life, as Brawn, and the rest is history.

Yet, this was just one of the kinks in the road for a team that has known many names.

Back in 1999, having bought the Tyrrell team's championship entry, the team burst into life from a new base at Brackley. With backing from British American Tobacco, it would race as British American Racing, with 1997 World Champion Jacques Villeneuve as the lead driver. Foolishly, it made grandiose claims before its cars had even turned a wheel and fell flat on its face as even finishing a race proved to be something of a struggle.

Great strides were made for 2000, when the team landed Honda engines and ranked equal fourth with Benetton. Villeneuve then scored its first podium finishes in 2001. However, as Ferrari dominated in 2002, BAR fell backwards, to eighth. So changes needed to be made and David Richards brought his Prodrive concern in to sort

THE POWER AND THE GLORY

NIKI LAUDA

Anyone with three F1 drivers' titles to his name is worth listening to and this Austrian who rose through the formulae without too much success but then galvanised Ferrari and got it winning again deserves respect. This was in 1975 and he was world champion again in 1977 after bouncing back from a fiery accident that nearly killed him at the Nurburgring in 1976. Lured back from starting his own airline, Niki won his third F1 title with McLaren in 1984 but since then has been involved in management, helping Mercedes to progress.

STILL TOP DESPITE A GREATER CHALLENGE

That Lewis Hamilton stormed to last year's drivers' title wasn't a surprise. That Mercedes was able to make it four constructors' titles on the trot was, as it was caught on the hop when Nico Rosberg announced his retirement after landing the 2016 crown. Valtteri Bottas was bought out of his Williams contract and did a decent job, but a temporary dip in form in the second half of the season was a worry as the team looked to maximise its points haul.

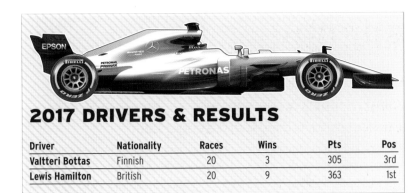

2017 DRIVERS & RESULTS

Driver	Nationality	Races	Wins	Pts	Pos
Valtteri Bottas	Finnish	20	3	305	3rd
Lewis Hamilton	British	20	9	363	1st

FOR THE RECORD

Country of origin:	England
Team base:	Brackley, England
Telephone:	(44) 01280 844000
Website:	www.mercedes-amg-f1.com
Active in Formula One:	As BAR 1999-2005, Honda Racing 2006-08, Brawn GP 2009, Mercedes 2010 onwards
Grands Prix contested:	344
Wins:	75
Pole positions:	88
Fastest laps:	50

THE TEAM

Non-executive chairman:	Niki Lauda
Head of Mercedes-Benz Motorsport:	Toto Wolff
Technical director:	James Allison
MD, Mercedes-AMG High Performance Powertrains:	Andy Cowell
Technology director:	Geoff Willis
Engineering director:	Aldo Costa
Performance director:	Mark Ellis
Sporting director:	Ron Meadows
Chief designer:	John Owen
Chief race engineer:	Andrew Shovlin
Chief track engineer:	Simon Cole
Test driver:	George Russell
Chassis:	Mercedes F1 W09
Engine:	Mercedes V6
Tyres:	Pirelli

things out in 2003, with Jenson Button as lead driver. Improvements came, and Button raced to four second places in 2004, to give BAR a high point of second overall that year.

Doing well in F1 demands constant improvement and BAR couldn't manage that, so fell to sixth in 2005 before Honda upped its involvement and it morphed into Honda Racing for 2006. It picked up the reward of Button claiming its and his first win, at Hungary, but form fell away in 2007 and 2008, forcing Honda to withdraw as the global economic slump hit.

Technical director Ross Brawn saved the team and, timed with a clever interpretation of the rulebook, its use of a double-diffuser created the pick of the pack for 2009 when Button won six of the first seven races to race on to the title, with Rubens Barrichello adding two more to give the team the constructors' title too despite rival teams having even moved ahead once they too introduced double-decked diffusers. Having supplied the team with engines, Mercedes saw the publicity gains and duly wanted a greater involvement so took over the team for 2010. Yet, without that key technical advantage, it didn't achieve the same results with Rosberg and returning World Champion Michael Schumacher. Indeed, it took until 2012 for the team to win again when Rosberg was first home in China.

Despite being expected to play second fiddle to his illustrious compatriot, Rosberg had proved himself to be the more effective driver and so it was decided that Schumacher should retire from F1 for a second time and this opened the door for Lewis Hamilton to join from McLaren. Then, with Brawn and the strong technical line-up of Paddy Lowe and Rob Bell, the team began to make solid progress and the team ranked second behind Red Bull with three wins on the board.

That was nothing, though, compared with what followed in 2014 when Hamilton raced to four wins in the first five races after Rosberg had won the opening round. From there, no other team won a race until the 11th round, in Hungary, when Red Bull came good and did so in the 12th too before Mercedes won the rest for a runaway constructors' title success. Mercedes had certainly made its mark and Hamilton would go on to win the 2015 title as well before Rosberg pipped him to the crown in 2016.

11

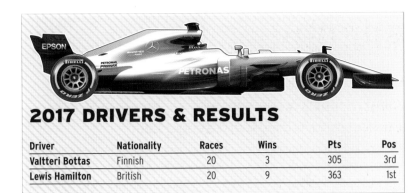
Ross Brawn is flanked by Rosberg and Schumacher when Mercedes returned to F1 in 2010.

"For our team, the bonus factors are the respect and sportsmanship that have grown between our two drivers. The chemistry and dynamic between Valtteri and Lewis work and are what we need to take the fight to our competitors." **Toto Wolff**

LEWIS HAMILTON

Lewis is now in the pantheon, his fourth F1 title moving him alongside Alain Prost and Sebastian Vettel, but he was still learning as he went along, having to develop the Mercedes to keep ahead of the double challenge from Ferrari and Red Bull.

Only two World Champions have now taken more F1 titles than Lewis, with Michael Schumacher top on seven and Juan Manuel Fangio following on five. Had anyone said when Lewis was taken under McLaren's wing as a promising young kart racer that he might have a shot at those, there may not have been too many people who reckoned that this could be on.

As it is, Lewis's spectacular passage through karting was always going to attract attention. It did, and this was fortunate, as Lewis's father Anthony certainly didn't have the funds to take him further. So, McLaren's backing was imperative and Lewis used it well, as he won the British Formula Renault Championship in 2003 then the European F3 crown, also at his second attempt, in dominant form in 2005.

GP2 came next and Lewis got the job done at the first time of asking. So, with no further ado, no messing around with a tail-end team, Lewis stepped into F1 with McLaren in 2007. He won four times and came within an ace of winning the title in his rookie year, but scraped home in 2008. That was one on the board and more

Lewis enjoyed last year's scrap and reckons it helped him improve even more as a driver.

would surely follow. Except they didn't as McLaren slipped off the pace.

For 2013, Lewis moved to Mercedes, then rattled out two more F1 titles, in 2014 and 2015, before being pipped by team-mate Nico Rosberg to the 2016 crown.

TRACK NOTES

Nationality:	BRITISH
Born:	7 JANUARY 1985, STEVENAGE, ENGLAND
Website:	www.lewishamilton.com
Teams:	McLAREN 2007-12, MERCEDES 2013-18

CAREER RECORD

First Grand Prix:	2007 AUSTRALIAN GP
Grand Prix starts:	208
Grand Prix wins:	62

2007 Canadian GP, United States GP, Hungarian GP, Japanese GP, 2008 Australian GP, Monaco GP, British GP, German GP, Chinese GP, 2009 Hungarian GP, Singapore GP, 2010 Turkish GP, Canadian GP, Belgian GP, 2011 Chinese GP, German GP, Abu Dhabi GP, 2012 Canadian GP, Hungarian GP, Italian GP, United States GP, 2013 Hungarian GP, 2014 Malaysian GP, Bahrain GP, Chinese GP, Spanish GP, British GP, Italian GP, Singapore GP, Japanese GP, Russian GP, United States GP, Abu Dhabi GP, 2015 Australian GP, Chinese GP, Bahrain GP, Canadian GP, British GP, Belgian GP, Italian GP, Japanese GP, Russian GP, United States GP, 2016 Monaco GP, Canadian GP, Austrian GP, British GP, Hungarian GP, German GP, United States GP, Mexican GP, Brazilian GP, Abu Dhabi GP, 2017 Chinese GP, Spanish GP, Canadian GP, British GP, Belgian GP, Italian GP, Singapore GP, Japanese GP, United States GP

Poles:	72
Fastest laps:	38
Points:	2,610
Honours:	2008, 2014, 2015 & 2017 F1 WORLD CHAMPION, 2006 GP2 CHAMPION, 2005 EUROPEAN F3 CHAMPION, 2003 BRITISH FORMULA RENAULT CHAMPION, 2000 WORLD KART CUP CHAMPION, 1995 BRITISH CADET KART CHAMPION

HITTING TOP GEAR FOR NUMBER FOUR

The challenge was greater than before in 2017: less so from within the team, as Valtteri Bottas struggled to keep up, but more so from outside as Ferrari and Red Bull Racing were right on the pace. Perhaps because of this, F1 experts feel that Lewis rose to new heights as the year progressed. Indeed, after weathering the great start to the year made by Ferrari's Sebastian Vettel across the first six races, Lewis went up a level to deliver consistently. Some wins were by small margins, other by demoralising ones, with his run to glory at Silverstone being one of his most impressive. Improved form in qualifying in the second half of the year really helped Lewis's cause as he chased after that fourth title. Able to land the title with two rounds to spare gave Lewis reason to smile when leaving Mexico, although being hit and knocked down the order by Vettel on the opening lap certainly wasn't part of the plan and it meant that he wasn't able to celebrate on the podium.

VALTTERI BOTTAS

It must have been a shock last year to suddenly find himself driving for the most competitive team after a career spent aiming to get to the top. Although he had his first three wins, Mercedes' number two still has form to find.

Finland is a large country with a lot of lakes and an awful lot of trees, but very few people. Its landscape is tailor-made for raising rally stars on its thousands of kilometres of dirt road, all offering ample opportunity to hone car control. However, the nation has also boxed above its weight in producing Formula 1 World Champions. There was Keke Rosberg in 1982, then Mika Hakkinen in 1998 and 1999, Kimi Raikkonen in 2007 and Keke's son Nico in 2016, although he was half German and raced under the German flag.

Valtteri was thus not aiming for something that might be unobtainable when he started showing good form in Formula Renault. In his second season at this level, in 2008, Valtteri won the European Championship ahead of Daniel Ricciardo, with a further 12 wins in the Northern European series.

Two solid seasons of F3 followed, with Valtteri winning the F3 Masters race in both 2009 and 2010, and ranking third in the European series in both years as well.

Then, while his better-heeled rivals moved up to GP2, the last step before F1, Valtteri's budget would stretch only

Valtteri was amazed last year by how hard Hamilton works and learnt a lot from him.

to GP3, so he tried that and did what he absolutely had to do to keep his single-seater dreams alive: he won the title.

What would prove to be a career lifeline followed, as the champion was given two days' F1 testing with Williams. Valtteri

went on to do such a good job that he was signed to run in the first Friday practice session at grands prix in 2012.

A full race seat followed for 2013, but the team was uncompetitive and he scored just four points as the Williams team managed to rank only ninth out of the 11 teams. Six podiums and 186 points in 2014 was far better as Valtteri ranked fourth. Then, in 2015, Valtteri was a podium visitor again and ended up fifth.

At this point, he was being tipped to replace Raikkonen at Ferrari, but his compatriot stayed on and it started looking as though his moment of joining one of F1's top teams had passed, until Nico retired...

PITCHED INTO THE BIG TIME

The close-season leading into 2017 must have been a time of considerable examination of Valtteri's self-belief. For, instead of aiming to do everything to earn promotion to the best team, Nico Rosberg's sudden decision to quit after winning the 2016 drivers' title landed him a drive with Mercedes. Released by Williams to chase his dreams of becoming a grand prix winner and more, he leapt at the opportunity and impressed the team with his no-nonsense dedication to the job in hand. No one has ever doubted Valtteri's speed, but he was coming into Lewis Hamilton's camp. Early signs were good as the Finn started with third in Australia, then took pole in Bahrain. He then took his maiden win in Russia. Five races later, in Austria, Valtteri added another. However, as the season advanced, he struggled to keep up, something that was exacerbated by Red Bull Racing coming on strong but, most notably, by Hamilton shifting up a gear as the title battle hotted up.

TRACK NOTES

Nationality:	FINNISH
Born:	28 AUGUST 1989, NASTOLA, FINLAND
Website:	www.valtteribottas.com
Teams:	WILLIAMS 2013-16, MERCEDES 2017-18

CAREER RECORD

First Grand Prix:	2013 AUSTRALIAN GP
Grand Prix starts:	97
Grand Prix wins:	3
2017 Russian GP, Austrian GP, Abu Dhabi GP	
Poles:	4
Fastest laps:	3
Points:	716
Honours:	2011 GP3 CHAMPION, 2009 & 2010 FORMULA 3 MASTERS WINNER, 2008 EUROPEAN & NORTHERN EUROPEAN FORMULA RENAULT CHAMPION

Formula One transporters have come a long way since they were simple trucks or trailers, with contemporary ones extending vertically to provide office space.

SCUDERIA FERRARI

There were times last year when Ferrari set the pace. Yet, and this was a cause for concern, it couldn't live with the pressure. The *tifosi* will be praying that lessons have been learnt so that Mercedes might be toppled in 2018.

For much of last year, Ferrari was able to claim one or more podium finishes, but it knows that it needs to advance to beat Mercedes in 2018.

Ferrari has the most wins, most pole positions, fastest laps, points scored and constructors' titles, as you would expect from a team that has been in the hunt since the inaugural World Championship in 1950. Yet, the success hasn't been spread uniformly across the decades, and history shows that Ferrari has had lows as well as highs, something that the management sometimes has forgotten when reacting after a failure. Last year was a time when technical frailty just as the team was pushing Mercedes led to many on the team looking over their shoulders nervously.

The team, of course, used to have one man at the helm who wasn't ever going to be fired. This was the man himself, Enzo Ferrari. He was a racer who was given the job of running the Alfa Romeo works grand

THE POWER AND THE GLORY

SIMONE RESTA
Born within earshot of the Imola circuit, Simone graduated in mechanical engineering from the University of Bologna. Moving directly into motor racing, Simone joined the Minardi team in 1998 and worked in its research and development department for three years. Since joining Ferrari in 2001 as senior design engineer, he advanced to the post of head of research and development in 2006 and he has subsequently risen to become deputy chief designer. Then, on Pat Fry's departure in late 2014, Simone was promoted to chief designer.

A YEAR OF SPEED BUT FAILURE TOO
When Sebastian Vettel won the opening race in Australia, things looked good for Ferrari. Mercedes wasn't going to have things its own way under the new technical regulations. When that speed was repeated for wins in Bahrain and Monaco, things still looked good. Yet Ferrari was unable to stop the Hamilton/Mercedes juggernaut once it got up to speed, although Vettel threw away potential wins in both Azerbaijan and Singapore before his car failed in Japan.

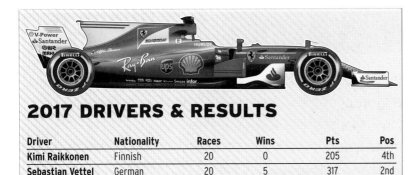

2017 DRIVERS & RESULTS

Driver	Nationality	Races	Wins	Pts	Pos
Kimi Raikkonen	Finnish	20	0	205	4th
Sebastian Vettel	German	20	5	317	2nd

FOR THE RECORD

Country of origin:	Italy
Team base:	Maranello, Italy
Telephone:	(39) 536 949111
Website:	www.ferrari.com
Active in Formula One:	From 1950
Grands Prix contested:	930
Wins:	229
Pole positions:	213
Fastest laps:	243

THE TEAM

President:	Sergio Marchionne
Team principal:	Maurizio Arrivabene
Technical director:	Mattia Binotto
Chief designer:	Simone Resta
Chief designer, power unit:	Lorenzo Sassi
Head of aerodynamics:	Dirk de Beer
Director of aerodynamics:	Loic Bigois
Sporting director:	Massimo Rivola
Operations director:	Diego Ioverno
Test driver:	Antonio Giovinazzi
Chassis:	Ferrari F18T
Engine:	Ferrari V6
Tyres:	Pirelli

prix team in the 1930s and then established his own team in 1946. Although Alfa Romeo dominated in the first two years of the World Championship, Ferrari's team was gaining ground and scored its first win at this level in the 1951 British GP. Then Alfa Romeo withdrew and the stage was all Ferrari's, with its lead driver, Alberto Ascari, dominating as he won eight races in a row across the two seasons.

Mercedes' arrival midway through 1954 showed that Ferrari had to raise its game, which it did for Juan Manuel Fangio to become champion in 1956 and then for Mike Hawthorn to just do enough to land the 1958 crown. However, it was now clear that the British teams were on the rise and Ferrari was slow to react to the trend of moving the engine from the cars' nose to behind the drivers' shoulders.

What followed over the decades was that the manufacturer of some of the world's most desirable sports cars – well, it helped to pay for the racing – was seldom the leader in introducing technical breakthroughs. Enzo dismissed the British

teams as "garagistes" as they adopted the Ford Cosworth DFV and yet had the audacity to beat his cars. However, he had to acknowledge that they were delivering superior results on far smaller budgets.

Ferrari was also hampered, especially in the 1960s, by being an exceptionally political team and it took two men of steely resolve to try and make it operate like a proper racing team. The first was John Surtees who raced to the 1964 title. The second was Niki Lauda who forced the management to focus on the things that might make it competitive and raced to the 1975 and 1977 titles. In Lauda's time, at least, there was a strong flow of money to be invested in making the cars go faster, as Fiat had bought Ferrari in 1969 and put in a serious amount of money to ensure Ferrari wins that they hoped would add allure by association to the Fiat road car range.

Although Ferrari was slow to adopt ground effect technology, it won both the drivers' and constructors' titles in 1979 when Jody Scheckter outscored team-mate Gilles Villeneuve. Yet what showed

how Ferrari was no longer at the cutting edge was the fact that even though it was competitive enough to take the constructors' crown in 1982 and 1983, it failed to produce a car fast enough for any of its drivers to win the driver's title until 2000. As with Surtees and Lauda before him, it took considerable force of personality for Michael Schumacher to be World Champion. That he did it again each year through until 2004 showed how he, team principal Jean Todt and technical boss Ross Brawn made the team "less Italian" and more pragmatic.

To F1 fans the world over, being Ferrari means being Italian, but its best years tend to come with the team operating in a more cosmopolitan and level-headed way.

"Losing the championship was a combination, especially in the second half of the season, of technical issues and driver misjudgements."
Sergio Marchionne

Jody Scheckter was champion in 1979. Here, he leads team-mate Gilles Villeneuve at Monza.

Sebastian started last year well and gave it his best shot, although losing his cool from time to time, but a fifth F1 world title wasn't to be. For 2018, the German ace will be hoping for another crack as Ferrari tries again.

When one looks at the unbelievably rapid rise from karts to F1 that Max Verstappen had - just one year, spent in F3 - it makes Sebastian's four-and-a-half-year approach seem tardy. Yet, he didn't hang around. He was a multiple winner in his first year of cars, coming second in the German Formula BMW ADAC series. This landed him backing from Red Bull and he stayed on for another tilt, and 2004 was remarkable as Sebastian won 18 of the 20 races.

He then spent two years in the European F3 Championship, finishing as runner-up in that second campaign.

Having starred in two outings in more powerful Formula Renault 3.5 at the end of 2006, taking a win and a second, Sebastian kicked off in that series in 2007, hoping it would take him to F1 in 2008. He was leading the way, when an F1 seat was made available with BMW Sauber after Robert Kubica was injured in the Canadian GP.

Sebastian then finished the year with Toro Rosso and made the F1 establishment sit up when he qualified on pole at a wet Monza in 2008 then controlled the race for both his and the team's F1 breakthroughs.

Red Bull Racing promoted him for 2009

Sebastian drove exceptionally hard last year, sometimes too hard, but took five wins.

and Sebastian came through at the last round in 2010 to land the drivers' title, a crown that he would keep until 2014 when Mercedes moved ahead.

Since joining Ferrari, Sebastian has had good years in 2015 and 2017.

TAKING HIS HORSE BY THE REINS

Three wins and three second places in the opening six races set Sebastian fair for a title attack, as he and Ferrari responded best to the change in rules that blessed the cars with wider tyres and broader wings. Then Mercedes and Lewis Hamilton got up to speed. Sebastian boiled over in Baku when he swerved into Hamilton before a restart. To make matters tougher still, Ferrari didn't always get its tyre strategy right and then Red Bull Racing found its form in the races, led most notably by Max Verstappen. And it was to counter the young Dutchman that Vettel added to his reputation for being aggressive by blocking him at the start in Singapore and taking both out, along with his own team-mate Kimi Raikkonen. Then, in Mexico, where Hamilton could claim the title, he slipped up again, hitting Hamilton's car. The pressure really got to Sebastian in 2017 and the petulance he showed made his happy-go-lucky demeanour of old seem a distant memory.

TRACK NOTES

Nationality:	GERMAN
Born:	3 JULY 1987, HEPPENHEIM, GERMANY
Website:	www.sebastianvettel.de
Teams:	BMW SAUBER 2007, TORO ROSSO 2007-08, RED BULL RACING 2009-14, FERRARI 2015-18

CAREER RECORD

First Grand Prix:	2007 UNITED STATES GP
Grand Prix starts:	199
Grand Prix wins:	47

2008 Italian GP, 2009 Chinese GP, British GP, Japanese GP, Abu Dhabi GP, 2010 Malaysian GP, European GP, Japanese GP, Brazilian GP, Abu Dhabi GP, 2011 Australian GP, Malaysian GP, Turkish GP, Spanish GP, Monaco GP, European GP, Belgian GP, Italian GP, Singapore GP, Korean GP, Indian GP, 2012 Bahrain GP, Singapore GP, Japanese GP, Korean GP, Indian GP, 2013 Malaysian GP, Bahrain GP, Canadian GP, German GP, Belgian GP, Italian GP, Singapore GP, Korean GP, Japanese GP, Indian GP, Abu Dhabi GP, United States GP, Brazilian GP, 2015 Malaysian GP, Hungarian GP, Singapore GP, 2017 Australian GP, Bahrain GP, Monaco GP, Hungarian GP, Brazilian GP

Poles:	50
Fastest laps:	33
Points:	2,425
Honours:	2010, 2011, 2012 & 2013 F1 WORLD CHAMPION, 2009 & 2017 F1 RUNNER-UP, 2006 EUROPEAN FORMULA THREE RUNNER-UP, 2004 GERMAN FORMULA BMW ADAC CHAMPION, 2003 GERMAN FORMULA BMW ADAC RUNNER-UP, 2001 EUROPEAN & GERMAN JUNIOR KART CHAMPION

KIMI RAIKKONEN

Will this be Kimi's last year as a Ferrari, or even an F1, driver? Pressure is on from the _tifosi_ for a young hotshot to fill Ferrari's second seat to bring a little more excitement into the mix as other top teams constantly look to youth.

It seems strange now that Kimi is approaching 40 that he was once motor racing's shooting star. Sure, he didn't hit F1 as a teenager, but he made the steps from karting so quickly that few even saw him coming. In fact, his was a 23-race ascent, easing the way for later tyros.

Kimi's talent had been spotted in karting and racer-turned-driver manager Steve Robertson gambled by financing his rise. Starting in Formula Renault at the end of 1999, he immediately won the British winter series. In 2000, he added the full British Formula Renault Championship title and tradition dictated that the Robertsons would place him in British F3 for 2001.

They, though, had other plans and convinced Peter Sauber to give him an F1 trial and Kimi did enough to earn a race seat. His debut came at Melbourne and he raced to sixth. That and a handful of other great drives earned Kimi a ride with McLaren for 2002 and a third place podium finish first time out proved them right.

It took until 2003 for his first win and Kimi ended the year as runner-up to Michael Schumacher, a position he matched in 2005 in a year that yielded seven wins.

Kimi has always been a driver who can score points, but he would love one more win.

A Ferrari driver from 2007, he snatched the title in a last round shoot-out with McLaren's Fernando Alonso and Lewis Hamilton. After 2009, he preferred to go rallying, in a world that required few of the PR duties that he so dislikes.

Yet, F1 drew Kimi back for 2012, with Lotus. A win in each of 2012 and 2013 proved that he still had the speed, so Ferrari signed him and he has performed the support role ever since.

TRACK NOTES

Nationality:	FINNISH
Born:	17 OCTOBER 1979, ESPOO, FINLAND
Website:	www.kimiraikkonen.com
Teams:	SAUBER 2001, McLAREN 2002-06, FERRARI 2007-09, LOTUS 2012-13, FERRARI 2014-18

CAREER RECORD

First Grand Prix:	2001 AUSTRALIAN GP
Grand Prix starts:	273
Grand Prix wins:	20
	2003 Malaysian GP, 2004 Belgian GP, 2005 Spanish GP, Monaco GP, Canadian GP, Hungarian GP, Turkish GP, Belgian GP, Japanese GP, 2007 Australian GP, French GP, British GP, Belgian GP, Chinese GP, Brazilian GP, 2008 Malaysian GP, Spanish GP, 2009 Belgian GP, 2012 Abu Dhabi GP, 2013 Australian GP
Poles:	17
Fastest laps:	45
Points:	1,565
Honours:	2007 FORMULA ONE WORLD CHAMPION, 2003 & 2005 FORMULA ONE RUNNER-UP, 2000 BRITISH FORMULA RENAULT CHAMPION, 1999 BRITISH FORMULA RENAULT WINTER SERIES CHAMPION, 1998 EUROPEAN SUPER A KART RUNNER-UP, FINNISH & NORDIC KART CHAMPION

A SHADOW OF HIS FORMER SELF

Sebastian Vettel is a huge fan of Kimi's, finding him to be the perfect team-mate for three reasons. The first is because Kimi is so anti-establishment, which he finds entertaining. The second is because he is apolitical, not interested in trying to engineer an advantage for his side of the garage. The third is because, like all racers, Sebastian wants to be the faster one of the pairing, which he is. While Kimi was as quick and as consistent as ever, he was always that little bit slower than Sebastian. He was the support driver who simply turned up, drove and then went home again. Last year, however, was the first time that Kimi had been so weak in comparison, failing to earn the right to stand on the top step of the podium to extend a winless streak that stretches back to the opening race of the 2013 season. Of course, there were flashes of the old brilliance, like taking pole at Monaco, but Vettel won five grands prix and was on the podium more than twice as many times.

RED BULL RACING

The drivers felt that the team's Renault-built engines held them back, but Red Bull Racing kept raising its game as its exciting young chargers went out there and raced hard in an attempt to keep Mercedes in sight. Expect more of the same in 2018.

Daniel Ricciardo leads the way into the first corner on the streets of Baku, heading for one of the team's three wins last year.

Getting to the front in F1 is one thing, and staying there is quite another, which is why Red Bull Racing's continued push to topple Mercedes has been admirable since the team in silver took over its place at the top of the pile in 2014.

That this team from Milton Keynes is able to keep on challenging owes as much to the calibre and consistency of its personnel as it does to the budget from Red Bull energy drink creator Dietrich Mateschitz.

The team's DNA was created decades ago when three-time World Champion Jackie Stewart decided, in conjunction with his older son Paul, to create a ladder through the single-seater formula to help young drivers, and perhaps Paul, towards the top. After F3000, though, Paul moved aside and so the decision was taken to make that final step, into F1.

Typical of Jackie, standards of presentation were equal to the best as the team's white cars with suitably Scottish

tartan flashes hit the grids in 1997. Second place for Rubens Barrichello at Monaco was a dream result, but regular success proved hard to come by. Its third year in racing's

top category yielded a first win on a day of rain and sun at the Nurburgring, with Johnny Herbert triumphant and Barrichello third, but it had been an unusual race and

THE POWER AND THE GLORY

DAN FALLOWS
The team's chief engineer on the aerodynamics side studied the same aeronautical degree course at Southampton University as its chief technical officer Adrian Newey did before him. He then went to work for Lola Cars as an aerodynamicist before swapping IndyCars for F1 when he joined Jaguar Racing in 2002. Dan then had a spell based in Italy with Dallara before returning to the team in Milton Keynes once it had morphed into Red Bull Racing. He has been there ever since and been promoted to head of aerodynamics.

COMING ON STRONG WITH GREAT DRIVERS
One glance at a results table for 2017 tells a tale of Red Bull Racing's campaign, for it is filled with way more retirements than rivals Mercedes and Ferrari suffered. Renault simply couldn't offer sufficient power for the team's TAG Heuer-badged engines and, when they pushed, reliability became a problem. The team developed its chassis, though, and this gave both drivers an outside chance of victory which they took whenever they were in with a shout.

2017 DRIVERS & RESULTS

Driver	Nationality	Races	Wins	Pts	Pos
Daniel Ricciardo	Australian	20	1	200	5th
Max Verstappen	Dutch	20	2	168	6th

FOR THE RECORD

Country of origin:	England
Team base:	Milton Keynes, England
Telephone:	44) 01908 279700
Website:	www.redbullracing.com
Active in Formula One:	
	As Stewart GP 1997-99,
	Jaguar Racing 2000-04,
	Red Bull Racing 2005 onwards
Grands Prix contested:	360
Wins:	53
Pole positions:	59
Fastest laps:	48

THE TEAM

Chairman:	Dietrich Mateschitz
Team principal:	Christian Horner
Chief technical officer:	Adrian Newey
Chief engineering officer:	Rob Marshall
Chief engineer, aerodynamics:	Dan Fallows
Chief engineer, car engineering:	
	Paul Monaghan
Chief engineer, performance engineering:	
	Pierre Wache
Team manager:	Jonathan Wheatley
Chief engineer:	Guillaume Roquelin
Test driver:	tba
Chassis:	Red Bull RB14
Engine:	TAG Heuer V6
Tyres:	Pirelli

was never in danger of being repeated.

The Stewarts then succumbed to pressure from Ford to sell up and the team came back in metallic dark green as Jaguar Racing in 2001. This was the start of some dark days as, despite the best efforts of Eddie Irvine and then Mark Webber in the cockpit, the team was hampered by interference from automotive bigwigs, something that Ferrari team chiefs have long had to cope with.

With success having proved elusive, the team came out in 2005 with a new identity, as Ford had sold it to Mateschitz who was looking to advance from just being a team sponsor.

Red Bull Racing started solidly under the guidance of former F3000 racer turned team chief Christian Horner, but then advanced once David Coulthard coaxed Adrian Newey across from McLaren to design the cars. Webber returned as well and then Sebastian Vettel joined the line-up in 2009 and other teams started to have another serious rival to consider, as Red Bull Racing closed out the campaign almost as strongly as Brawn had started it to finish the year as runners-up.

Then came the sort of run that all teams dream of, for not only did Red Bull Racing reach the top in 2010 in a tense finale to land the constructors' title as victory for Vettel landed him the drivers' crown, with Webber ending the year third, but it was the start of years of being the top team, making the most of two cracking drivers, a great

chassis and strong engines from Renault.

Vettel and Webber would rank first and third overall again in 2011, with Vettel adding two more titles in 2012 and 2013. However, Mercedes was coming up on the rails and, with Lewis Hamilton as its lead challenger, would prove too strong in 2014.

Daniel Ricciardo kept the Australian theme going in 2014 when he took over from Webber and did something that Webber didn't manage in outscoring Vettel.

For 2015, Vettel moved on to Ferrari. Russian racer Daniil Kvyat didn't prove to be an equal replacement, and Red Bull fell to fourth, but another driver stepped up from its feeder team Scuderia Toro Rosso at the fifth race of 2016, swapping seats with Kvyat. This was Max Verstappen and he won first time out, helping Red Bull back to rank second overall.

"Max is a pure racer, with a rare instinct for what it takes to compete at this level." Christian Horner

Christian Horner gives Mark Webber a hug after he triumphed in the 2012 Monaco GP.

DANIEL RICCIARDO

This will be a season in which the Red Bull Racing drivers will pray that they are given a chance to take the battle to Mercedes' Lewis Hamilton, as both have proved to be among the fiercest Formula 1 racers when the lights turn green.

Business people like collecting airmiles, but young Daniel and his family collected them simply because they had to travel great distances in order to go racing. Being born and brought up in Perth, Western Australia meant that they were thousands of miles away from where most people went racing.

This guided their hand after Daniel tried Formula Ford as a 16-year-old, and so the move was made in 2006 to race not on the Australian scene but instead in the Asian Formula BMW. This had the advantage that it gained greater exposure, as well as letting him learn several grand prix tracks as he finished third overall.

The next step was an even bigger one as Daniel headed to Europe. In two years of Formula Renault, boosted by Red Bull backing in the second year, he peaked by finishing as runner-up in the 2008 European series behind Valtteri Bottas.

His third year away from home brought not just increased maturity but the British F3 Championship crown easily for top team Carlin. Then, had he scored just three more points, he would have added the Formula Renault 3.5 title in 2010; as it was, the title went to Russian racer Mikhail Aleshin.

Daniel outscored team-mate Verstappen last year, but will find that harder in 2018.

Life changed again midway through his second year of Formula Renault 3.5 when backers Red Bull moved Daniel into F1 midway through the year after Narain Karthikeyan left HRT. This gave him the chance to show what he could do and so

Scuderia Toro Rosso gave him a ride in 2012 and Daniel did well enough in the second of these to beat team-mate Jean-Eric Vergne to be promoted to Red Bull Racing for 2014.

Everyone expected that Daniel would be kept in the shade by then four-time world champion Sebastian Vettel, but he outscored the German by three wins to none in 2014 and so his reputation was made. Having finished third that year and again in 2016 proved that Daniel was good enough to become world champion with the right car.

TRACK NOTES

Nationality:	AUSTRALIAN
Born:	1 JULY 1989, PERTH, AUSTRALIA
Website:	www.danielricciardo.com
Teams:	HRT 2011, TORO ROSSO 2012-13, RED BULL RACING 2014-18

CAREER RECORD	
First Grand Prix:	2011 BRITISH GP
Grand Prix starts:	129
Grand Prix wins:	5
	2014 Canadian GP, Hungarian GP, Belgian GP, 2016 Malaysian GP, 2017 Azerbaijan GP
Poles:	1
Fastest laps:	9
Points:	816
Honours:	2010 FORMULA RENAULT 3.5 RUNNER-UP, 2009 BRITISH FORMULA THREE CHAMPION, 2008 EUROPEAN FORMULA RENAULT RUNNER-UP & WESTERN EUROPEAN FORMULA RENAULT CHAMPION

SOME GREAT PASSING MOVES

Liberty Media, recent purchasers of F1, must love Daniel, for he is the embodiment of a racing driver, a very rapid and clean but determined racer. More than that, he is a dream out of the car, seemingly ever smiling and willing to perform the PR duties that the sport and the team require as it tries to spread F1's message. Yet, through 2017, we also saw Daniel having to push harder even than in 2014 when he arrived at Red Bull Racing and outscored his team-mate, Sebastian Vettel. Last year, he found increased pressure from within the Red Bull Racing camp as Max Verstappen not only kept improving his speed but then started to be given the latest development engines after he had signed a contract extension to keep him at the team. Even though Daniel won the Azerbaijan GP and showed great speed at other venues to end the year as the team's higher-placed driver, it seemed that his time as the team leader has come to an end.

MAX VERSTAPPEN

Here is a driver feared by others, a driver with a racer's instinct, who will try moves that others might only consider. Now signed to stay at Red Bull Racing until 2020, he will be desperate for a car that can make him World Champion.

It's not just natural speed that can take a driver all the way to the top of the sport. It's knowing how to maximise every moment that they are in the car, whether it's simply in testing, practice or qualifying. The race is another challenge all over again and race craft can make the difference between being first and not. However, to get all the way to the pinnacle of the sport, a driver needs to push to gain experience.

With not one but two parents steeped in racing, in 1990s Benetton-driving father Jos and karting star mother Sophie, Max had all the advice that he needed as he rose through the karting ranks. The titles stacked up until he landed the world crown in 2013 at the age of 15.

Then came car racing and Max dipped his toe in the water with a couple of wins in the Ferrari-backed Florida Winter Series before stepping straight to F3.

Racing in the European F3 Championship, Max was far from cowed by the more experienced opposition and starting winning for Van Amersfoort Racing by only the second round. Esteban Ocon would go on to take the title, but nine wins were good enough for Max to rank third overall.

Max really started to deliver last year and has even Hamilton worried by his pace.

Talent spotter Helmut Marko had seen enough and signed up Max to make his F1 debut with Scuderia Toro Rosso in 2015 at the age of 17. He was soon rattling the establishment and Max peaked with a pair of fourth-place finishes.

That was enough to prove that he could hack it in F1. Then, with just four races of his second F1 season run, he was suddenly promoted into Daniil Kvyat's seat at Red Bull Racing. Amazingly, on that debut in the Spanish GP, he came home victorious, becoming the youngest ever F1 winner at 17 years and 228 days.

Backed up by four second-place finishes, Max ended the year fifth overall, proving that he was very much part of the establishment by the tender age of 20.

TRACK NOTES

Nationality:	DUTCH
Born: 30 SEPTEMBER 1997, HASSELT, BELGIUM	
Website:	www.verstappen.nl
Teams:	TORO ROSSO 2015-16,
	RED BULL RACING 2016-18

CAREER RECORD

First Grand Prix:	2015 AUSTRALIAN GP
Grand Prix starts:	60
Grand Prix wins:	3
	2016 Spanish GP, 2017 Malaysian GP,
	Mexican GP
Poles:	0
Fastest laps:	2
Points:	421
Honours:	2013 WORLD & EUROPEAN KZ
	KART CHAMPION, 2012 WSK MASTER SERIES
	KF2 CHAMPION, 2011 WSK EURO SERIES
	CHAMPION, 2009 BELGIAN KF5 CHAMPION,
	2008 DUTCH CADET KART CHAMPION, 2007
	& 2008 DUTCH MINIMAX CHAMPION, 2006
	BELGIAN ROTAX MINIMAX CHAMPION

FAST BUT NO LONGER FURIOUS

There were times last year when the Red Bull Racing drivers had reason to feel less than happy, when they were powerless in the face of another masterclass from the Mercedes racers and they were also left in the wake of the more powerful Ferraris. Their TAG Heuer-branded Renault engines were no match. But both the team and Renault pressed on and certainly both drivers did, with Max winning the final Malaysian GP at Sepang and starring on numerous other occasions. His never-give-in attitude was shown most plainly on his last lap pass of Kimi Raikkonen for third place at the United States GP. Everyone thought that it was an amazing move, except for the race stewards... At least he was offered a gift of a chance to make amends in the Mexican GP the following weekend when Vettel clattered into Hamilton on the opening lap just after Max had taken the lead ahead of them, offering Max a free run towards his second win of the campaign.

FORCE INDIA

Force India looks all set to challenge F1's giants again in 2018 and there's no obvious reason why it won't be able to match the impressive fourth-place ranking it achieved last year as it continues to fight lean and punch above its weight.

Force India couldn't match Mercedes, Ferrari or Red Bull Racing for pace, so its drivers spent 2017 fighting against each other, literally.

While not everyone thinks of pink as a sporty colour, there was no problem at all with the Force Indias last year as the extra investment from BWT that made the cars be painted pink injected a welcome stream of finance that enabled the team to at least keep developing through the season. In fact, BWT owner Andreas Weissenbacher has increased his shareholding in the team as Indian businessman Subrata Roy's was diminished as he sold up to pay his tax bill.

Budgetary constraint has always been a factor in this team since it broke into F1 in 1991 as the Jordan team. Masterminded by F3000 team owner Eddie Jordan, it seemed always to be one financial sidestep away from financial disaster. Yet, in its early days, this gave the team a bit of a rock 'n' roll image, a David taking on the Goliaths.

After a stunning debut season in which Jordan ranked fifth overall, the team lost ground when it tried to save money by accepting a Yamaha engine deal for 1992, but bounced back when it elected to pay for

its engines again and used Hart power. This helped it to rank fourth in 1994 and, after landing a Peugeot deal for 1995, got both Rubens Barrichello and Eddie Irvine onto the podium at the Canadian GP.

A deal with Benson & Hedges had the cars painted gold in 1996, then yellow in 1997, and that is how people remember

THE POWER AND THE GLORY

ANDY STEVENSON
This team that was once Jordan has a history of staff retention, which is no mean feat through years of financial difficulty, and a testimony to the loyalty it evokes. One of these long-stayers is Andy Stevenson, who joined Jordan as a mechanic back in 1987, when it was running cars in the British F3 Championship. He stayed on through F3000 and was part of the original Jordan F1 crew in 1991, rising to become chief mechanic in 2002, then team manager in 2005 and on to become sporting director.

GIVING A BIG BANG FOR THE BUCKS
There were no podium finishes last year, but it wasn't for want of trying by Sergio Perez or Esteban Ocon. A top-three finish was always unlikely, as three teams had faster cars, so anything above a seventh place finish was special. Perez took a fourth in Spain and Ocon peaked with a pair of fifth places, but the pink cars had a tendency to get very close to each other, with Perez becoming increasingly upset by the burgeoning pace of his junior team-mate.

2017 DRIVERS & RESULTS

Driver	Nationality	Races	Wins	Pts	Pos
Esteban Ocon	French	20	0	87	8th
Sergio Perez	Mexican	20	0	100	7th

them when Damon Hill held off team-mate Ralf Schumacher in the 1998 Belgian GP to take the team's first win in a one-two finish. This came using Mugen power and the team did better still the following year when Heinz-Harald Frentzen gave the team a pair of victories and Jordan was able to rank third overall behind Ferrari and McLaren. Jordan kept plugging away and Giancarlo Fisichella gave it a surprise victory at Interlagos in 2003, but the team couldn't often match Ferrari, McLaren, Williams and Renault.

The cost of being competitive in F1 then mushroomed and Jordan simply couldn't keep up with the top teams as each team's design department grew from dozens of people to a hundred or more.

Eddie Jordan eventually admitted defeat and sold the team to Russian industrialist Alex Shnaider in 2005. This led to a name change, to Midland, but the team remained at its base across the road from Silverstone, keeping its personnel. Indeed, many stayed on through the next name change, to Spyker in 2007, and the

following one to Force India in 2008. The last of these changes came when the team was bought by wealthy Indian racing fan and former racer Vijay Mallya, with the cars carrying the names of the various drink and food companies he distributes in India.

Landing a competitive engine was the team's number one priority and getting Mercedes engines was a major step forward. Better still, this came with some technical assistance from McLaren and soon the team's form improved, as shown by Giancarlo Fisichella racing to second place at Spa-Francorchamps in 2009.

Since then, a handful of drivers have shone for Force India, most notably Paul di Resta and Adrian Sutil, but then more recently Nico Hulkenberg and Sergio Perez, with the latter kept on his toes through last season by Esteban Ocon.

That this medium-sized team from Silverstone continues to weather both the vagaries of ownership and having to make do with a relatively meagre budget speaks volumes for the calibre and loyalty of its staff. They simply get on with the job in

hand, which is how all racing teams should operate. That Force India has outscored once mighty McLaren for the past three seasons, and by a considerable margin last year, is a massive accolade for all concerned. Sure, the team doesn't build road-going supercars like McLaren, but it's a racing team that does what it says on the tin: it goes racing.

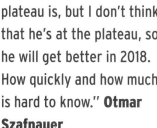

"I don't know how steep Esteban's learning curve will be and where his plateau is, but I don't think that he's at the plateau, so he will get better in 2018. How quickly and how much is hard to know." **Otmar Szafnauer**

Giancarlo Fisichella gave the team its most recent thrill when he came second at Spa in 2009.

Sergio drove extremely well through 2017 but, as happens in all sport, there can always be someone younger and quicker to usurp you. In Sergio's case, this was his team-mate Esteban Ocon, so he will have to fight to regain his reputation.

Sergio is one of those rare drivers who has got markedly better since reaching F1. In truth, his record of winning championships on the way up is sketchy and certainly didn't suggest that he would go on to become a driver who would come within a whisker of winning a grand prix.

Sergio certainly started young, travelling to race in the United States in 2004 at the age of 14, contesting the Skip Barber Dodge series. A far bigger leap followed in 2005 when he raced in the Formula BMW ADAC series in Germany. Having finished sixth in his second campaign, Sergio then tried more power in A1GP before heading to British F3. This tried-and-tested training ground was learnt in his first year when he won the National class before taking a tilt for overall honours in 2008. He fell short in that, but Sergio collected four wins for T-Sport as he ranked fourth.

Stepping up to GP2 for 2009, Sergio started off in the close-season by contesting the Asian series and took a couple of wins. Things were always going to be tougher in the main FIA GP2

Sergio drove beautifully last year, but knows he has a serious challenge from within.

series and his first campaign yielded two podiums but few other results. In 2010, racing for the Barwa team, he raced to five wins but had to settle for being runner-up behind Pastor Maldonado.

Still, with money from Mexican telecoms company Telmex, he found his way into F1 in 2011, signing for Sauber, a team he had tested for in 2010. Impressively, he challenged Fernando Alonso's Ferrari for victory in Malaysia in 2012, but had a spin when he tried to get past, and had to settle for second place. This helped him to rank 10th and then he moved to McLaren for 2013. However, this didn't turn into a dream year as neither he nor team-mate Jenson Button made it to the podium.

Then began Sergio's time at Force India and his best result in his four years to date has been seventh overall with two podium finishes in 2016.

THE CHALLENGE FROM WITHIN

Having outscored his Force India team-mate Nico Hulkenberg in 2016, Sergio's reputation was strong going into last year, and he collected a fourth place in Spain then a fastest lap in Monaco, but less so by the end. The reason for this is that Hulkenberg moved to Renault and was replaced by Esteban Ocon, a promising driver who'd made his F1 debut in the second half of the 2016 season. This should have been a season in which intra-team pressure was reduced, but the reverse proved to be the case as Ocon learnt his craft and then, in the second half of the year, began to challenge him. There were clashes, most notably at the Belgian GP, when Sergio really became rattled by the young French driver's pace. How they get on in 2018 will be interesting, as it appears that Sergio won't be focused as much on trying to pick off drivers from the more competitive teams as he will try to win the battle from within. Being put in the shade at his home race in Mexico City will have been a particular disappointment.

TRACK NOTES

Nationality:	MEXICAN
Born:	26 JANUARY 1990, GUADALAJARA, MEXICO
Website:	www.sergioperezf1.com
Teams:	SAUBER 2011-12, McLAREN 2013, FORCE INDIA 2014-18

CAREER RECORD

First Grand Prix:	2011 BAHRAIN GP
Grand Prix starts:	134
Grand Prix wins:	0 (best result: 2nd, 2012 Malaysian GP)
Poles:	0
Fastest laps:	4
Points:	467
Honours:	2010 GP2 RUNNER-UP, 2007 BRITISH FORMULA THREE NATIONAL CLASS CHAMPION

ESTEBAN OCON

Esteban's first full season marked him out as a feisty racer who wasn't afraid of his more experienced team-mate Sergio Perez, and now this is the year in which he must put down further markers if he is to be promoted to a top team.

Esteban is a driver who put his hand up early to be noticed. He'd done well in kart racing and finished his second year of car racing in the European Formula Renault Championship ranked third overall, as Pierre Gasly won the crown.

However, it is what Esteban did when he advanced to the European Formula Three Championship in 2014 that made people sit up and pay attention, as he was suddenly the class of the field, making his victories for Prema Powerteam look very easy indeed, which is extremely rare at this level. In fact, Esteban took an impressive tally of nine wins from 33 starts by the end of the year and was a clear champion ahead of Tom Blomqvist, with the less experienced Max Verstappen third.

The Lotus F1 team, which races these days as Renault, certainly liked what it saw and signed Esteban on to its books, keeping an eye on him as he joined to contest the F1-supporting GP3 Championship in 2015. Esteban responded well as he was almost never off the podium and made it two titles in two years.

However, without a wealthy family

Esteban got better and better through his first full F1 season. What will 2018 bring?

behind him, Esteban didn't have enough of a budget to advance to GP2, so he was snapped up by Mercedes to race in DTM.

This unplanned move to touring cars wasn't from the motor racing book

of single-seater career advancement, although it did at least seem to offer him a solid career.

However, just after Esteban had claimed a top-10 finish at Zandvoort, he was given a route back into F1 when Manor racer Rio Haryanto's budget expired midway through the 2016 season and, as the team used Mercedes engines, the German manufacturer placed him there.

Despite never having contested GP2, the penultimate rung in the single-seater ladder, and a lack of in-season testing, Esteban was soon matching the team's other driver, Pascal Wehrlein, peaking with a 12th place finish in the season's penultimate round in Brazil, and this was enough for Force India to sign him for 2017.

BATTLING AGAINST PEREZ

Esteban had a clear measuring stick in Sergio Perez when he arrived at Force India after a half-season learning about F1 with tailend team Manor. The 20-year-old French racer duly spent much of the year tussling with the Mexican veteran, much to the team's worry at times when they came close to taking each other out, most notably on a couple of occasions at the Belgian GP, but finally proved himself to be the quicker of the pair before the season was through. Finishing fifth in the Mexican GP turned out to be the highlight of Esteban's season as he started the race from sixth on the grid and ran as high as third place in the early stages of the race before he was overtaken inevitably by the more competitive Ferraris. What Esteban showed through the season was that he was not only getting quicker with almost every round but also seemed to be gaining in composure. Perhaps demonstrating the ruthless characteristic possessed by most champions, he also appeared to expect to succeed rather than simply wish for it. Remember Ayrton Senna?

TRACK NOTES

Nationality:	FRENCH
Born:	17 SEPTEMBER 1996, EVREUX, FRANCE
Website:	www.esteban-ocon.com
Teams:	MANOR 2016, FORCE INDIA 2017-18

CAREER RECORD	
First Grand Prix:	2016 BELGIAN GP
Grand Prix starts:	29
Grand Prix wins:	0 (best result: 5th, 2017 Spanish GP, 2017 Mexican GP)
Poles:	0
Fastest laps:	0
Points:	87
Honours:	2015 GP3 CHAMPION, 2014 FIA EUROPEAN FORMULA THREE CHAMPION

The teams pride themselves on their levels of preparation and their garage floors really are clean enough to eat off.

WILLIAMS

Williams, this once lauded team of teams, can still only dream of its triumphs of the 1980s and 1990s, as its form remains far from those heights. Technical chief Paddy Lowe will be hoping for a better crack of the whip in his second year in charge.

It was a season of learning for Lance Stroll, but he got the Canadian flags waving at his home grand prix when he raced to his first points.

Almost everyone who likes Formula 1 wants Ferrari to be at the sharp end of the field, because that somehow feels right, how things are meant to be for F1's one team that has been present in every year of the World Championship since it began in 1950. In a similar vein, McLaren and Williams should be up there fighting over victories too, but they haven't been for a while and they are having to think hard how to reinvent themselves.

It seems wrong to think of Williams, the third most successful team in F1 history, as a former great, but just one victory achieved over the past 13 seasons lays that bare, as that's a huge reduction from the rate at which Williams gathered victories in its years of dominance in the 1980s and 1990s.

This famously patriotic team has been built in the image of two very British men: Sir Frank Williams and Patrick Head. Williams set the ball rolling when he realised that he wasn't the quickest of the

quick as an F3 racer and, frankly, didn't have the money to continue. So he ran cars in F2 and F3 for others from 1968. Just one year later, Frank Williams Racing Cars had advanced to F1 with Piers Courage and they did well, as Courage twice finished second. In 1970, though, disaster struck when he crashed in the Dutch GP and was killed.

THE POWER AND THE GLORY

PADDY LOWE
Paddy wasn't destined for motor racing after graduating from Cambridge as he went to work for Metal Box. However, he joined Williams in 1987 to head up its electronics division and it was his work on its active suspension that marked him out. Picked by McLaren in 1993 to be its head of R&D, he became chief engineer then engineering director then, from 2011, its technical director. Mercedes employed him as technical director from 2013 to 2016, before Williams lured him back to run its technical programme.

A SEASON WITHOUT A TOP-LINE DRIVER
The last-minute loss of Valtteri Bottas to Mercedes definitely wasn't a positive event for Williams as the team lost its lead driver and had to call back Felipe Massa to fulfil the roll as well as being mentor to teenage signing Lance Stroll. It was always going to be a year of transition as Paddy Lowe started to impose his ideas, but the team's lack of successful development through the season made life ever harder, with Stroll never getting close to repeating his surprise third place in Baku.

2017 DRIVERS & RESULTS

Driver	Nationality	Races	Wins	Pts	Pos
Paul di Resta	British	1	0	0	N/A
Felipe Massa	Brazilian	19	0	43	11th
Lance Stroll	Canadian	20	0	40	12th

FOR THE RECORD

Country of origin:	England
Team base:	Grove, England
Telephone:	(44) 01235 777700
Website:	www.williamsf1.com
Active in Formula One:	From 1972
Grands Prix contested:	741
Wins:	114
Pole positions:	128
Fastest laps:	133

THE TEAM

Team principal:	Sir Frank Williams
Co-founder:	Patrick Head
Deputy team principal:	Claire Williams
Chief executive officer:	Mike O'Driscoll
Chief technical officer:	Paddy Lowe
Head of performance engineering:	
	Rob Smedley
Chief designer:	Ed Wood
Head of aerodynamics:	Kirk de Beer
Chief engineer:	Jakob Andreasen
Team manager:	David Redding
Test driver:	Robert Kubica
Chassis:	FW40
Engine:	Mercedes V8
Tyres:	Pirelli

Over the next few years, Frank took whatever deal he could to stay in the game, but it was teaming up with Head to form Williams Grand Prix Engineering in 1977 that was the turning point, with Frank then able to concentrate on running the team and chasing much-needed backing, while Patrick handled the technical side.

Their first car, ready for 1978, was raced by Alan Jones and it showed great promise, placing second in the US GP. However, it was the arrival of the FW07 in the second half of 1979 that changed everything as Jones raced to four wins in a five-race streak. In 1980, he won five times to be World Champion. Carlos Reutemann was pipped at the last round in 1981, but the team had done enough for a second constructors' title, then Keke Rosberg came out on top of a peculiar 1982 season when the 16 wins were split between 11 drivers.

At the start of what turned into the second age of Williams from 1986, when the team used turbocharged Honda engines to great effect, there was a huge setback. Frank was involved in a car crash on the way back from testing, broke his back, and has been confined to a wheelchair ever since. This might have stopped others, but it only slowed Frank. He was given cheer by Nigel Mansell's wins that year and was as gutted as his driver when Mansell's FW11 had a tyre blow-out at the final round. Nelson Piquet made no mistake the following year.

The third age, and the time of the greatest glory, came when Williams used Renault V10 engines and cars designed jointly by Head and Adrian Newey. These were the class of the field in 1992 when Mansell and the FW14B were all but unbeatable and could never be caught after winning eight of the first 10 races. Alain Prost replaced him

for 1993 and also took the drivers' title. Then Damon Hill was denied in 1994 but came good in 1996, followed by Jacques Villeneuve in 1997. But that was the last of the team's title honours.

A partnership with BMW in 2001 and 2002 showed promise, but Michael Schumacher and Ferrari had things under control and, since Juan Pablo Montoya's victory in the final race of 2004, the only succour the team has enjoyed was Pastor Maldonado's unexpected and never repeated triumph in Spain in 2012.

Patrick Head and race engineer David Brown check out the action with Nigel Mansell in 1991.

"Everyone wants to get into Q3. We've got Mercedes, Ferrari and Red Bull who aren't going to lose their way, leaving Renault, McLaren, Force India and us fighting for those places as well." **Paddy Lowe**

⬤ LANCE STROLL

At the start of last year, this teenaged rookie couldn't record a race finish, but he came good and even grabbed a surprise third place in Azerbaijan. His second year with Williams will prove just how good he is as he builds on this experience.

It was always likely that Lance might become a racing driver as his father, Lawrence, was not only mad about cars, but had the funds to finance any aspirations that Lance might be developing. Stroll Sr had made his fortune through the fashion industry and not only raced and collected Ferraris but bought his own racing circuit too: Mont Tremblant.

Lance started off racing karts at 10. Local titles followed, and then he gained further experience by competing in Italy. This peaked with fifth place in the 2013 World Championship and he was picked for the Ferrari Driver Academy, much to his Ferrari-mad father's delight.

Lance stepped up to race cars in 2014, at the tender age of 15, kicking off in the Ferrari-backed Florida Winter Series and then dominating the Italian F4 Championship. With the goal of doing as many races as possible, Lance then kicked off his 2015 season by racing in the Toyota Racing Series in New Zealand, gathering four wins and the title.

That set Lance up for a shot at the European F3 Championship and he was definitely fast in 2015, but he was wild too,

Lance developed good race craft through 2017 and will be back to go even better.

as a string of crashes attested. Many saw him as a rich kid who could afford to take risks that others couldn't, as his family would easily be able to cover the cost of any damage, but Lance grew up a little and took a win at the final round to rank fifth as the experienced Felix Rosenqvist landed the title with double his score.

So, a second year in the European F3 Championship with Prema Powerteam was required and Lance delivered in style. Less anxious to prove himself fast as well as rich, he won the opening race at Paul Ricard and never looked back, adding 13 more wins to dominate the series.

Alongside his fantastic F3 season, Lance had become a test driver for Williams and with his pace in 2016 suggesting that he'd be able to bypass GP2, this morphed into a race seat for 2017, where team and family reckoned he would gain far more useful experience under the tutelage of an experienced lead driver: Felipe Massa.

TRACK NOTES

Nationality:	CANADIAN
Born:	29 OCTOBER 1998, MONTREAL, CANADA
Website:	www.lancestroll.com
Teams:	WILLIAMS 2017-18

CAREER RECORD

First Grand Prix:	2017 AUSTRALIAN GP
Grand Prix starts:	20
Grand Prix wins:	0 (best result: 3rd, 2017 Azerbaijan GP)
Poles:	0
Fastest laps:	0
Points:	40
Honours:	2016 FIA EUROPEAN FORMULA THREE CHAMPION, 2015 TOYOTA RACING SERIES CHAMPION, 2014 ITALIAN FORMULA FOUR CHAMPION

LEARNING AS HE GOES

The first three races of Lance's maiden F1 season ended early, which certainly wasn't the plan, especially as he crashed out of two of them. Fortunately, Williams encouraged Lance to exert a little caution. Three race finishes followed and then, if you are going to score your first points anywhere, it shows excellent timing to do so in your home grand prix, which is what Lance did, taking ninth place in Montreal. After those first points, Lance then achieved an out-of-the-blue podium next time out. This was on the streets of Baku at the Azerbaijan GP, and he followed Daniel Ricciardo and Valtteri Bottas home in third place after a race of many incidents. One thing that was clear as Lance improved through the year was that he had progressed more in terms of race management than he had in laying down scintillating qualifying laps. There was an exeception when he produced a stunning performance to start second at a wet Monza, albeit having gained two grid positions when Red Bull's drivers were hit with penalties.

SERGEY SIROTKIN

All the talk last autumn had been about Robert Kubica bouncing back from his terrible injury to resume his F1 career with Williams, but then a combination of Sergey's speed in testing and $15m of Russian sponsorship landed him the ride.

Sergey raced karts for a couple of years from 2008, reaching KF2, before stepping up to car racing midway through the 2010 season, once he had turned 15. The first category that he tried was Italy's junior single-seater series: Formula Abarth. He impressed by scoring points in five of his first six outings.

Back for more in 2011, Sergey made obvious improvements, soon scoring his first wins in both the European and lesser Italian series. Swapping teams from Jenzer Motorsport to Euronova Racing midseason didn't interrupt his form, and Sergey was crowned European champion and Italian runner-up at the end of a successful campaign.

With a father high up in the Russian aviation industry, Sergey enjoyed a good level of backing and this propelled him into a far more powerful single-seater category for 2012. This was Auto GP and he was a winner by the second round. Clear progress through the season led to a final ranking of third overall. Euronova also ran him in the Italian F3 series, and he ranked fifth in that in what might have been a

Sergey spent last year kicking his heels and will be really fired up for his F1 debut.

confusing season as the F3 car is a far less powerful and more technical category.

At season's end, Sergey tried Formula Renault 3.5 and elected to race in that class in 2013, ranking ninth for the ISR team as

Kevin Magnussen and Stoffel Vandoorne fought over the title. Although it had been mooted that his healthy budget might buy him his F1 break with Sauber for 2014, it was a diet of Formula Renault 3.5 again, this time with Fortec. Sergey became a winner, fittingly, on home ground at Moscow Raceway. However, a run of non-finishes left him only fifth at year's end.

Sergey did get some F1 seat time in 2014, though, running in various practice sessions from the Russian GP onwards. However, after failing to land a ride for 2015, he raced instead in GP2 and really impressed. Sergey not only won at Silverstone but also ranked third overall. He finished third overall again in 2016, but this didn't open the doors to F1, even though he was signed as a reserve driver by Renault.

TRACK NOTES

Nationality:	RUSSIAN
Born:	27 AUGUST 1995, MOSCOW, RUSSIA
Website:	tba
Team:	WILLIAMS 2018

CAREER RECORD

First Grand Prix:	2018 AUSTRALIAN GP
Grand Prix starts:	0
Grand Prix wins:	0
Poles:	0
Fastest laps:	0
Points:	0
Honours:	2011 EUROPEAN FORMULA ABARTH CHAMPION & ITALIAN FORMULA ABARTH RUNNER-UP

WAITING ON THE SIDELINES

Sergey spent the 2017 season as Renault F1's reserve driver, but no race opportunities arose, leaving him as something of a spare part now that the World Championship has only one in-season test. Trying something completely different, at the behest of Russian-owned SMP Racing, Sergey made his sports-prototype racing debut. At the Le Mans 24 Hours, no less. He shared a LMP2 class Dallara with fellow Russians Mikhail Aleshin and Viktor Shaytar, but they hit trouble and finished 16th in class, 33rd overall. There was one single-seater race outing, albeit in FIA F2, when he stood in for ART Grand Prix in the round supporting the Azerbaijan GP, and really shone by finishing fourth in one of the two races. Sergey was given a couple of days of F1 testing by Williams after the season-concluding Abu Dhabi GP and impressed the team with speed that outdid Robert Kubica's best laps. This, and of course the sponsorship money he could bring, swung the balance in his favour and so ensured that Russia retained a place on the F1 grid following Daniil Kvyat's loss of his ride.

RENAULT

Nico Hulkenberg remains the team's torch-bearer, an undoubted talent who the team know will deliver as and when they can provide him with a car that is both fast and reliable. In Carlos Sainz Jr, he has a rapid new team-mate to keep him on his toes.

Nico Hulkenberg led Renault's charge through 2017, but time and again he was sidelined by mechanical failures that need to be eliminated for 2018.

The Renault team is on the way back up, the way back to becoming a consistent scorer of points, and this speaks volumes for its loyal personnel who have stuck with the team through its assorted changes of ownership across the years.

The team's history dates all the way back to the late 1970s when car transport mogul Ted Toleman started a team in his name in F2. This was so good in 1980, thanks to a brilliant chassis from designer Rory Byrne and great engines from Hart, that Brian Henton and Derek Warwick finished first and second in the points table.

There could only be one step from there: F1. This followed in 1981, but the first Toleman F1 car lacked development and it took until its fourth season, 1984, for the team to find its stride when Ayrton Senna joined it for his first year of F1 and came within an ace of winning in Monaco.

In 1986, the team returned but with a new identity, as knitwear manufacturer Benetton bought its naming rights. The personnel remained the same, with Byrne still penning the cars, but the motivation was different as BMW turbo power put them right on to the pace, with Gerhard Berger outdoing team-mate Teo Fabi's two poles by winning in Mexico.

Benetton would remain the team name until 2001 and it made a major

THE POWER AND THE GLORY

ALAN PERMANE
The team's sporting director is an English engineer with a lengthy history in F1, amazingly having been with this same team through its various name changes since 1986. Alan worked as an electrical engineer when the team raced as Benetton, then as a race engineer through the team's first incarnation as Renault from 2002 to 2006. Since then, Alan has been the team's chief engineer before accepting his current role, with its responsibility of keeping the show on the road, when the team raced as Lotus.

FINDING ITS FEET AGAIN TAKES TIME
Renault's V6 simply wasn't as powerful as rival power units from Mercedes and Ferrari. As a consequence, 2017 was a constant dilemma as to how much they should push for more power at the possible cost of reliability. When the engine was strong enough to go the distance, Nico Hulkenberg would score. Jolyon Palmer seemed to be cursed with bad luck. Then his replacement Carlos Sainz Jr showed good speed in the late-season races, but there were too many retirements.

2017 DRIVERS & RESULTS

Driver	Nationality	Races	Wins	Pts	Pos
Nico Hulkenberg	German	20	0	43	10th
Jolyon Palmer	British	16	0	8	17th
Carlos Sainz Jr	Spanish	4	0	54	9th

signing in 1991 when it snapped up Michael Schumacher after he'd had just one F1 outing with Jordan. This proved to be inspired, as the rookie was clearly a phenomenal talent. Together with Ross Brawn working alongside Byrne, Schumacher starting winning at the end of 1992 before clinching the 1994 drivers' title after a less than sporting clash with Damon Hill in the season finale. He added a second title in 1995 when Benetton swapped from Ford to Renault engines, also helping the team to its first constructors' title.

The loss of Schumacher, Brawn and Byrne to Ferrari was a huge blow and it was only after Renault became the team name in 2002, along with increased financial help from the French manufacturer, that the team moved forward again.

Although the money was French, the team remained based at Enstone in Oxfordshire and kept on using its crew and, certainly had none of the personnel who had been involved when Renault ran its own F1 team from 1977 to 1985.

In 2003, Fernando Alonso joined from Minardi and was a winner before the year was out. Although he didn't win again in 2004, it all came right in 2005 and the Spaniard raced to the first of two consecutive F1 titles, ably supported by Giancarlo Fisichella. They pipped McLaren and then, in 2006, Ferrari.

The loss of Alonso to McLaren in 2007 hit the team hard, but it got the Spanish ace back for 2008, although other teams had advanced more and Renault was no longer capable of running at the front. Indeed, it has remained that way ever since, and this as much as anything else led to another name change for 2012. This is confusing for F1 fans, as Team Lotus had folded in 1994 and the name was taken on when Tony Fernandes launched a new team in 2010. He was then outlawed from using it so, from 2012, the team that had once raced against Lotus, Toleman, had its third change of name... to Lotus.

Money continued to be sparse and wins unheard of, but then Renault upped its stake in the team and so it was rebadged again, back to Renault for a second time in 2016. This fresh hit of money meant that the team could invest again in ongoing development, and the fruits of this, after years of falling away from the pace through the course of a season, were clear for all to see.

"We are still handicapped by whether we can allow ourselves to create performance at the expense of reliability, which is what I believe that we need to do in order to catch up in qualifying." **Cyril Abiteboul**

Fernando Alonso raced to the first of his two consecutive F1 driver titles with Renault in 2005.

NICO HULKENBERG

If Renault can continue to improve its act and put its many mechanical failures behind it, then the Nico of old will be able to use his undoubted speed to complete the job, something that was denied him again and again last year.

The one constant in Nico's career is that he has always been at the front of the field. That has been masked since he reached F1, as he's seldom had the most competitive machinery, but it was crystal clear all the way through the junior ranks.

The tall German was both German junior and senior kart champion before advancing to car racing. This is where some drivers stumble, but Nico simply kept on winning, scoring eight victories to take the Formula BMW ADAC title after a season-long battle with Sebastien Buemi.

Stepping up to F3 proved more difficult, but only because Nico's limited budget forced him to accept a ride with a team running a Ligier rather than the usual Dallara chassis. Then came a career-changer: he tested for A1GP Team Germany and shone. This gave him an off-season championship to learn about more powerful single-seaters and he was the star.

He then spent two seasons in the prestigious European F3 championship, advancing from third in 2007, when Romain Grosjean was champion, to win seven rounds

Nico was hit with endless failures in 2017 and deserves better to achieve his potential.

in 2008. What really cemented his reputation was winning the GP2 crown in his rookie season, with his five wins for ART Grand Prix leaving him well clear of Vitaly Petrov.

Williams promoted Nico from its test team to its race team for 2010 and he took a surprise pole position in Brazil. However, he was dropped in 2011 to make way for the well-heeled Pastor Maldonado. Back with a race seat for 2012, Nico raced for Force India and showed the sort of pace to attract attention from the top teams, but he has since raced only for Sauber, Force India again and, since 2017, Renault, which is a shame, as he's clearly one of the best.

While he waits for F1 highlights, Nico took a week out in 2016 and won the Le Mans 24 Hours for Porsche.

TRACK NOTES

Nationality:	GERMAN
Born:	19 AUGUST 1987, EMMERICH, GERMANY
Website:	www.nicohulkenberg.net
Teams:	WILLIAMS 2010, FORCE INDIA 2012
	& 2014-16, RENAULT 2017-18

CAREER RECORD

First Grand Prix:	2010 BAHRAIN GP
Grand Prix starts:	137
Grand Prix wins:	0 (best result: 4th, 2012
Belgian GP, 2013 Korean GP, 2016 Belgian GP)	
Poles:	1
Fastest laps:	2
Points:	405

Honours: 2015 LE MANS 24 HOURS WINNER, 2009 GP2 CHAMPION, 2008 EUROPEAN F3 CHMPION, 2007 F3 MASTERS WINNER, 2006/07 A1GP CHAMPION, 2005 GERMAN FORMULA BMW ADAC CHAMPION, 2003 GERMAN KART CHAMPION, 2002 JUNIOR KART CHAMPION

SPEED WITH FRUSTRATION

Moving from Force India to Renault for 2017 was Nico's way of linking himself to a manufacturer, his way of trying to improve his chances of getting to the front of an F1 grid. The team was in a poor state, but its reversion to the Renault name, after four years racing as Lotus, suggested that better times might return as Renault invested in the team. As the season advanced and the fruits of this investment started to be seen, Nico was seen ever closer to the front of the grid. Sixth place seemed to be the best that he could achieve as Mercedes, Ferrari and Red Bull led the way, and he managed this three times, in Spain, Britain and Belgium. Had there not been so many mechanical failures, he would have matched his F1 career-best ranking of ninth overall – achieved in 2014 with Sauber and 2016 with Force India – but all too often there would be good speed followed by disappointment. Carlos Sainz Jr took over team-mate Jolyon Palmer's seat towards the end of the season and immediately provided Nico with a stern test, which is just what the team needs if it wants to move up the rankings and boost its prize money.

CARLOS SAINZ JR

This talented Spaniard must have been wondering whether he was ever going to be promoted from Scuderia Toro Rosso and now he has, albeit not with Red Bull Racing but Renault, for whom he showed well in a few outings late last year.

From the late 1980s to early 1990s, the name Carlos Sainz was synonymous with rallying, with the Spaniard becoming World Rally Champion in both 1990 and 1992 for Toyota, his red and white Celica the class of the field whether on snow, gravel or tarmac.

What a lot of people forget is that he had also raced in Formula Ford earlier in his career, and it was to car racing that Carlos Jr turned when he was old enough after a strong career as a child kart racer that peaked with victory in the Monaco Kart Cup in 2009 when he was 14.

Impatient to move on, Carlos Jr started racing cars in 2010 and he finished the year fourth in the European Formula BMW series. Stepping up to Formula Renault in 2011, Carlos Jr had already attracted Red Bull backing and he ended the season as runner-up to Robin Frijns in the European championship while winning the lesser Northern European title.

Strong form in F3 in 2012, when he ranked fifth in the European Championship, prepared Carlos Jr for advancing to GP3, but he was roundly beaten by future team-mate Daniil Kvyat, although he showed better

Carlos showed well with Toro Rosso and gave Hulkenberg a push in the late-season races.

form in a few outings in more powerful Formula Renault 3.5 before deciding to do a full season in the latter in 2014. Carlos Jr's reward was seven wins and the title, and this set him up to graduate to F1.

Signed by Scuderia Toro Rosso for 2015, he settled in well and collected a seventh place finish in the United States GP.

In 2016, Carlos Jr finished sixth three times and that helped him to score twice as many points as Kvyat did for Red Bull Racing. It kept his as the name in the ascendancy, although rising star Max Verstappen was the one who was chosen to replace Kvyat at Red Bull Racing, rather than Carlos Jr. This may have made Carlos Jr wonder whether his time had passed and that he would be dropped from the Red Bull scholarship scheme and from F1 as soon as the next hotshot came along.

TRACK NOTES

Nationality:	SPANISH
Born:	1 SEPTEMBER 1994, MADRID, SPAIN
Website:	www.carlossainzjr.com
Teams:	TORO ROSSO 2015-17, RENAULT 2017-18

CAREER RECORD

First Grand Prix:	2015 AUSTRALIAN GP
Grand Prix starts:	60
Grand Prix wins:	0 (best result: 4th, 2017 Singapore GP)
Poles:	0
Fastest laps:	0
Points:	118
Honours:	2014 FORMULA RENAULT 3.5 CHAMPION, 2011 EUROPEAN FORMULA RENAULT RUNNER-UP & NORTHERN EUROPEAN FORMULA RENAULT CHAMPION, 2009 MONACO KART CUP WINNER, 2008 ASIA/PACIFIC JUNIOR KART CHAMPION, 2006 MADRID CADET KART CHAMPION

A CHANGE IS AS GOOD AS A REST

Midway through his third year with Scuderia Toro Rosso, Carlos could have been forgiven for thinking that his hopes of being promoted to Red Bull Racing were dwindling and that he might end up on the Red Bull scholarship dump, especially when Max Verstappen signed a long-term contract. However, with Jolyon Palmer having a torrid time at Renault, a chink of light appeared. Then it happened, and Carlos leapt at a late-season transfer to the team from Enstone to fill the seat vacated by Palmer, starting at the United States GP. He immediately impressed by matching the highly rated Nico Hulkenberg. This was the best yardstick that Carlos has been compared to in his F1 career and, in many ways, proved that he is ready for promotion to Red Bull Racing in future when Daniel Ricciardo may decide to move on. For Red Bull Racing, too, it was a chance to see how Carlos would fare in a team that is usually a step up from Toro Rosso, a team closer to RBR's own pace. That he adapted to it swiftly and well, finishing seventh, was a feather in his cap.

SCUDERIA TORO ROSSO

A swap to Honda engines for 2018 might not seem like a step forward after Honda's poor form across the past three years, but it's part of a deal that might give parent team Red Bull Racing an engine partner option for the years ahead.

Last year was something of a driver merry-go-round at Scuderia Toro Rosso, as Daniil Kvyat made way for first Pierre Gasly then Brendon Hartley.

This is a team that had never come out on top, all the way through its days as Minardi, when it was F1's underdog, to being bought by Red Bull energy drink creator Dietrich Mateschitz so that his Red Bull Racing outfit could have its own junior team to bring on younger drivers it might want to use. By transforming Minardi into Scuderia Toro Rosso, he morphed the little team from Faenza into a puppet, albeit dampening this blow by giving it a budget way bigger than it had ever had before. The results alone have justified the deal, but the identity of perpetually struggling Minardi appealed more to anyone who roots for the underdog.

Coming from a family steeped in the motor trade, as his grandfather had been a Fiat dealer and his father a racing driver, Giancarlo Minardi followed their lead. He started by running a team in Formula Italia in 1972 and 1973 before stepping up to F2 in 1974, renaming his team as Scuderia Everest in deference to a sponsor. In addition to this, as part of his policy of

bringing along up-and-coming Italian racers, he signed a three-year deal from 1976 to run a Ferrari in non-championship F1 races. Sadly, his cousin, also Giancarlo,

crashed on the warm-up lap at the Race of Champions before placing 10th at the International Trophy at Silverstone and the programme was axed. He did use Ferrari

THE POWER AND THE GLORY

GRAHAM WATSON
This first love of Scuderia Toro Rosso's team manager was rallying, both as a driver and as a co-driver. This led to him leaving New Zealand for Europe in 1989 to work as a mechanic for the Ford works team. He then crossed the great divide to car racing in 1994 when he joined Paul Stewart Racing before stepping up to F1 with Benetton in 1996. A spell at BAR followed from 2001, helping the team to the constructors' title in 2009 when it changed to Brawn. After working as team manager at Caterham, he joined Toro Rosso in 2014.

SOME FLASHES OF SPEED FROM RED BULL'S JUNIORS
Any driver facing their third year with Toro Rosso must wonder what more they need to do to gain promotion. This was certainly what Carlos Sainz Jr must have thought, but he raced to sixth in Monaco and an excellent fourth in Singapore. Daniil Kvyat couldn't hit such heights and, along with Sainz's departure for Renault, it opened the door for two replacements. However, the team was hit by engine failures as it fought with engine supplier Renault to end 2017 sixth.

2017 DRIVERS & RESULTS

Driver	Nationality	Races	Wins	Pts	Pos
Pierre Gasly	French	5	0	0	21st
Brendon Hartley	New Zealander	4	0	0	23rd
Daniil Kvyat	Russian	15	0	5	19th
Carlos Sainz Jr	Spanish	16	0	54	9th

FOR THE RECORD

Country of origin:	Italy
Team base:	Faenza, Italy
Telephone:	(39) 546 696111
Website:	www.scuderiatororosso.com
Active in Formula One:	As Minardi
1985-2005, Toro Rosso 2006 onwards	
Grands Prix contested:	567
Wins:	1
Pole positions:	1
Fastest laps:	1

THE TEAM

Team owner:	Dietrich Mateschitz
Team principal:	Franz Tost
Racing director:	John Booth
Technical director:	James Key
Deputy technical director:	
	Ben Waterhouse
Chief designers:	Paolo Marabini &
	Mark Tatham
Head of aerodynamics:	tba
Head of vehicle performance:	
	Jody Egginton
Team manager:	Graham Watson
Technical co-ordinator:	Sandro Parrini
Chief engineer:	Marco Matassa
Test driver:	tba
Chassis:	Toro Rosso STR13
Engine:	Honda V6
Tyres:	Pirelli

engines, though, in F2, but the results weren't great and his team's fortunes only improved after he started running his own chassis from 1980, designed by Giacomo Caliri. In 1981, Michele Alboreto won for Minardi at Misano and the cars shone in the hands of Alessandro Nannini and Giancarlo's nephew Pierluigi through until they quit F2 at the end of 1984.

Minardi stepped up to F1 in 1985 and so Caliri designed a chassis for that, but this, and the next few years, were hampered by the team using Motori Moderni engines.

Minardi kept the next generation of Italians coming, though, giving F1 breaks to Nannini, Giancarlo Fisichella and Jarno Trulli. He also unearthed Fernando Alonso.

However, money was always tight and the number of personnel way down on their rivals. Yet, the team enjoyed a day of days in 1990 when Martini made the most of Pirelli qualifiers to line up on the front row for the US GP, but then slid back in the race.

Minardi had to agree to various alliances to keep going, like joining forces with BMS Scuderia Italia in 1994, which yielded some top-six finishes. Gabriele Rumi then invested in the team and a top-up was needed from Paul Stoddart to keep it going into 2001, with Mark Webber's surprise fifth place in Australia in 2002 a huge fillip. There was only so long that this underdog could keep going, though, and Mateschitz's Red Bull money led to a change of livery and a huge change to the health of its bank balance as the team was reinvented as Scuderia Toro Rosso for 2006.

Vitantonio Liuzzi and Scott Speed were its drivers in 2006 and finished 10th five times, but failed to score as points went down only to eighth place back then. With a young Sebastian Vettel joining late in 2007 and racing to fourth place at Shanghai, with Liuzzi sixth, fortunes were improving. When Vettel qualified on pole position and then won the 2008 Italian GP

the team had managed to outdo even Red Bull Racing.

However, Toro Rosso continues to be a team that exists to give Red Bull Racing a chance to see what young drivers can do in an F1 environment, and the team's top graduates to the senior team remain Vettel, Daniel Ricciardo and Max Verstappen.

"Our partnership with Honda is very exciting, like a release really. It's a huge challenge, and it's also a huge responsibility to that company as well. It's nice to have it as a partner rather than a supplier." **James Key**

It's all smiles for Mateschitz, Vettel, Tost and Marko at Monza in 2008 after the team's only win.

Last year was a strange one for this 21-year-old Frenchman, as he was sent to race in Japanese Super Formula to gain experience, shone in that and then, with a shot at the title, was given his chance to race in F1 instead.

Pierre had the now standard childhood in karting, rising up through the French ranks before hitting the international scene in 2009 when he was 13. After finishing as runner-up in his second attempt at the European KF3 Champion, Pierre was clearly ready for his progression into car racing.

His first year in cars, in 2011, was in the French F4 Championship and he was soon winning races, going on to rank third.

Formula Renault was next, and Pierre became a podium finisher, but never a winner. Back again in 2013, Pierre really blossomed and won the European title with three wins for Tech 1 Racing. Esteban Ocon was third.

What happened next was the making of Pierre's career, as he was signed up to become a Red Bull Junior driver and used the financial boost to advance to Formula Renault 3.5. Handling the extra horsepower proved to be no problem as Pierre did everything but win. His haul of podium finishes, though, was enough to leave him as the series' runner-up to the more experienced Carlos Sainz Jr, who was then promoted to F1 by Red Bull.

For 2015, Pierre moved on to GP2 and showed good pace and reached the podium

Pierre spent most of 2017 racing in Japan, but benefited from five late-season F1 outings.

several times for DAMS, but F1's traditional feeder formula proved to be a two-year programme, and his move to Prema Racing worked wonders, as Pierre became a race winner and then the 2016 champion.

Over the winter, Pierre tried something completely different, contesting a round of the Formula E Championship. These electric-powered single-seaters take a good deal of adapting to, but he grabbed a hugely impressive fourth place on the temporary street circuit used in New York.

With F1 testing experience already, Pierre might have hoped that Scuderia Toro Rosso would find an opening for him for 2017, but instead he was sent to the Japanese finishing school, Super Formula, to race in a category with long races in power single-seaters. This forced Pierre to learn not only a whole range of new circuits but also how to handle tyre degradation, two things that ought to stand him in good stead in F1.

TRACK NOTES

Nationality:	FRENCH
Born:	7 FEBRUARY 1996, ROUEN, FRANCE
Website:	www.pierregasly.com
Teams:	TORO ROSSO 2017-18

CAREER RECORD	
First Grand Prix:	2017 MALAYSIAN GP
Grand Prix starts:	5
Grand Prix wins:	0
(best result: 12th, 2017 Brazilian GP)	
Poles:	0
Fastest laps:	0
Points:	0
Honours:	2017 JAPANESE SUPER FORMULA RUNNER-UP, 2016 GP2 CHAMPION, 2014 FORMULA RENAULT 3.5 RUNNER-UP, 2013 EUROPEAN FORMULA RENAULT CHAMPION, 2010 EUROPEAN KF3 KART RUNNER-UP

40

PIERRE RISES IN THE EAST

Japan's top single-seater category, Super Formula, is probably second only to F1 as Indycar racing is out on its own limb. So, Helmut Marko, chief of the Red Bull driver scholarship programme, decided to send the 2016 GP2 champion east to gain racing experience in preparation for a possible move to F1. Pierre duly proved his credentials with Honda-owned Team Mugen, to become a winner by the fifth round. Another win and then a second place put him just half a point behind Hiroaki Ishiura going into the final round at Suzuka. However, there was a complication as Pierre had been summoned by Scuderia Toro Rosso to make his debut at the Malaysian GP, taking over Daniil Kvyat's car and doing so well that a decision was going to have to be taken about whether he'd contest the US GP or the Super Formula finale. The latter won out, but was rained off, leaving him as runner-up. By year's end, though, Pierre had contested five grands prix and shown good form.

BRENDON HARTLEY

Brendon can hardly believe his luck. His single-seater career had come to an end when he was 22, but he landed a works ride with Porsche in the World Endurance and, last year, took a sudden swerve into F1 with Toro Rosso.

Brendon's father Bryan raced in the late 1990s. However, his focus soon swung the way of the karting careers of his sons, Nelson and Brendon. Both progressed to car racing, but it soon became clear that Nelson was the fleeter of the pair.

Pitched into Formula Ford in his native New Zealand at just 13, Brendon used Nelson's hand-me-down car to incredible effect to win their Formula Ford Festival. Runner-up across the full Formula Ford Championship, Brendon stepped up to the Toyota Racing Series in 2005 and third place in that encouraged the family to pack him off to Europe to race in Formula Renault.

Brendon will admit now that this was a massive culture shock. However, he won the European Formula Renault title at the second attempt, by which time he had become part of the Red Bull Young Driver programme. A year in British F3 with Carlin followed, but the title went to team-mate Jaime Alguersuari, albeit with future F1 rivals Sergio Perez and Marcus Ericsson ranking behind him.

Then came three years of racing in Formula Renault 3.5 and Brendon collected at least one podium result in each season,

Brendon had no time to prepare when he was given his shock move from sportscars.

but never ranked higher than seventh. Worse than the lack of wins was the fact that he lost Red Bull backing after the 2010 season.

There was a lifeline thrown to him when Ocean Racing Technology drafted him in for some GP2 races in 2012, but Brendon was soon replaced by a driver with money and it appeared that his single-seater days were behind him and he headed to sportscar racing with Murphy Prototypes in the LMP2 class.

A win in the final round of the 2013 European Le Mans Series at Paul Ricard impressed someone at Porsche as he then joined its works squad for its return to sports-prototype racing. They advanced together, with wins starting to flow in 2015 as he, Timo Bernhard and Mark Webber raced to the title.

Last year's promotion to F1, coming out of the blue, really was a case of dreams coming true.

A TALE OF THE UNEXPECTED

Sport can be peppered with highs and lows. For Brendon, though, 2017 will take some beating. The high was presumed to be his fightback victory at Le Mans, the Porsche 919 Hybrid he shared with Earl Bamber and Timo Bernhard coming back from an hour on the sidelines. There were two more wins, at the Nurburgring and Mexico City. Between these, however, came the bombshell that Porsche was quitting the World Endurance Championship. Suddenly, Brendon's future looked uncertain. Tidying up his second WEC by year's end, after another win at the Circuit of the Americas, was a consolation of sorts. By then, though, something had arrived from out of the blue, when Scuderia Toro Rosso's dissatisfaction with Daniil Kvyat and Carlos Sainz Jr's departure to Renault left an opening. So, six years after stepping away from single-seaters, Brendon was an F1 driver... His four outings, after no testing whatsoever, offered a chance to show his ability to adapt and, although he was hit with mechanical failures, Brendon did enough to keep the seat for 2018.

TRACK NOTES

Nationality:	NEW ZEALANDER
Born:	10 NOVEMBER 1989,
	PALMERSTON NORTH, NEW ZEALAND
Website:	www.brendonhartley.co.nz
Teams:	TORO ROSSO 2017-18

CAREER RECORD

First Grand Prix:	2017 UNITED STATES GP
Grand Prix starts:	4
Grand Prix wins:	0
(best result: 13th, 2017 United States GP)	
Poles:	0
Fastest laps:	0
Points:	0
Honours:	2017 WORLD ENDURANCE CHAMPION,
	LE MANS 24 HOURS WINNER & DUBAI 24 HOURS
	WINNER, 2015 WORLD ENDURANCE CHAMPION, 2007
	EUROPEAN FORMULA RENAULT CHAMPION, 2003
	NEW ZEALAND FORMULA FORD FESTIVAL WINNER

Parc fermé is a secure area where the cars are parked after qualifying and the race, with no work allowed to be performed on them until they are released back to their teams.

HAAS F1

This American team refuses to be knocked off course. People expected it to struggle when it made its F1 debut in 2016, but it starred and survived. There was more of the same last year and every expectation that it will do the same in 2018.

Romain Grosjean is remaining for a third year with Haas F1 and will be hoping that the team's level of competitiveness doesn't fall away again.

At the start of the 2010 World Championship, F1 had four new teams getting ready to bolster the grids after being selected from a cast of many hopefuls. They were Lotus F1 Racing (a team with no connection to the original Lotus F1 team), Virgin (soon to become known as Manor), Campos Meta (soon to be renamed as HRT) and Team US F1. The last named failed at the 11th hour and never came to fruition, but the rest would race on. However, none thrived either in 2010 or across the seasons that followed, and all have since faded into oblivion. This makes the showing from the Haas F1 team across its first two seasons all the more impressive, as it is no stranger to scoring points and has very much made a home for itself in the midfield.

This is no small achievement and there were several occasions last year in which it had both of its cars reach the finish in point-scoring positions, which really kicks the sand back in the face of the majority of the F1 establishment who said that the

team was primed only to disappoint. The reason that they said that was that team owner Gene Haas wanted to run it from a headquarters in the USA, something

that had never worked before. Received knowledge suggested that this would be too American, too out of touch with F1's particular ways, too far from F1's European

THE POWER AND THE GLORY

ROB TAYLOR

The team's technical director began his involvement with motor racing by working for John Barnard's British Ferrari design office, then for Arrows. He rose to become the Jaguar F1 team's chief designer and stayed on as the team had a change of identity in 2005 to become Red Bull Racing, designing its first F1 car. With Adrian Newey being brought in to RBR, Rob later joined McLaren before crossing over to Haas F1 when it started recruiting in 2015 ahead of its debut the following year, being signed up to head its design team.

STARTING TO EXPECT TO COLLECT POINTS

Having ended its inaugural season ranked eighth – ahead of Renault, Sauber and soon-to-be-defunct Manor – Haas F1 hoped for better in 2017. Indeed, it enjoyed a three-way battle for sixth place, but the form that enabled Romain Grosjean to finish sixth in the Austrian GP had deserted it. In Grosjean and Kevin Magnussen, the team had two feisty drivers, the Dane having a few scraps in the late-season grands prix when chasing the minor points-paying positions.

2017 DRIVERS & RESULTS

Driver	Nationality	Races	Wins	Pts	Pos
Romain Grosjean	French	20	0	28	13th
Kevin Magnussen	Danish	20	0	19	14th

FOR THE RECORD

Country of origin:	USA
Team bases:	Kannapolis, NC, USA
	& Banbury, England
Telephone:	(1) 704 652 4227
Website:	www.haasf1team.com
Active in Formula One:	From 2016
Grands Prix contested:	41
Wins:	0
Pole positions:	0
Fastest laps:	0

THE TEAM

Team owner:	Gene Haas
Team principal:	Gunther Steiner
Chief operating officer:	Joe Custer
Technical director:	Rob Taylor
Vice-president of technology:	Matt Borland
Team manager:	Dave O'Neill
Chief aerodynamicist:	Ben Agathangelou
Group leader aerodynamicist:	
	Christian Cattaneo
Head of logistics:	Peter Crolla
Chief engineer:	Ayao Komatsu
Test driver:	tba
Chassis:	Haas VF-18
Engine:	Ferrari V6
Tyres:	Pirelli

heartland and so simply not cutting-edge enough, however well-equipped it was. After all, the only American-owned teams that have won rounds of the World Championship – Eagle, Penske and Shadow – have been run from Europe.

Basing itself both alongside the Stewart-Haas NASCAR Cup team at Kannapolis in North Carolina as well as at an operational base at Banbury in England was the reason that this has worked, as having a foothold in Europe has helped with the logistics, something that would have been a problem had the team operated only out of the USA. Having its satellite base means that the team can also benefit from being closer to the majority of its suppliers, while the brains trust under technical director Rob Taylor and chief aerodynamicist Ben Agathangelou operates out of the United States in the close-season, designing and building the car there.

Another pair of factors that enabled the team's American base not to be a

handicap was the fact that former Jaguar F1 technical chief Gunther Steiner was employed from the outset and gave the team a European way of thinking. Clearly, he and the design crew from Dallara that was employed to produce the team's first F1 chassis got it right, for Romain Grosjean raced to a points finish first time out in the opening round in Melbourne in 2016. That he backed up this sixth place with a fifth place next time out, at Sakhir, was extraordinary. This was clearly rather more than simply a NASCAR team owner coming to play against the Europeans. It was a team that had taken the time to consider the options and filled the gaps accordingly.

That first season resulted in Haas F1 ranking eighth overall at season's end, beating not only struggling Sauber and Manor, but Renault too.

Often, a team new to F1 finds its second season more difficult than its first, as it has spent too much of its maiden season fighting just to keep up rather than

designing its car for the follow-up year. Haas F1 managed not to fall into the trap and its 2017 campaign brought more points, peaking with Grosjean's sixth place in the Austrian GP, with number two driver Kevin Magnussen also showing well and getting into the points. This is more than the team's 2016 number two driver Esteban Gutierrez ever managed, which is why Haas F1 was to repeat their eighth rank overall in 2017.

"It seemed harder last year. There are no laggards in this business, so in order to get ahead of your competitors you've just got to be good, and that's hard."
Gene Haas

It appears to be smiles all round for Haas's Romain Grosjean, Kevin Magnussen and Gene Haas.

ROMAIN GROSJEAN

Frustration reared its head last year as Haas F1 found its second year in F1 tougher than its first. This is typical of new teams, but it appeared sometimes to get to Romain and he must try harder to keep that emotion in check in 2018.

Romain has always been one of those drivers who appear to know instinctively how to challenge for titles. Being French also helped, as he was soon signed by Renault for its driver development programme after he won the French Formula Renault title in 2005, at a time when French F1 drivers were rare. If he kept winning, he knew that this could take him all the way to the top.

When Romain was crowned European F3 Champion ahead of Sebastien Buemi and Nico Hulkenberg in 2007, it was expected that Renault would take him to F1. This just left the GP2 title to be won. He warmed up by winning the Asian GP2 title, but ranked only fourth in the main FIA GP2 series, so he came back to try again 2009.

Things were going well when Romain's season took an unexpected turn as Nelson Piquet Jr was dropped by Renault's F1 team for his role in fixing the outcome of the 2008 Singapore GP in favour of his team-mate Fernando Alonso, and Romain was called up to replace him.

He didn't do enough to keep his seat for 2010, though, and so had to make do

Romain scored a fine sixth in Austria but will want to be in the points more often.

with a ride in the lesser Auto GP category for 2010, which he won, then had a third shot at the GP2 crown in 2011. With much relief, he dominated and so earned his F1 return for 2012 when the Renault team of

old, now racing as Lotus, took him back.

Perhaps desperate not to let his second tilt at F1 escape him, Romain tried too hard and was wild as well as fast, winning few friends as he had a run of collisions. A second place and two thirds, though, helped Romain finish eighth.

The 2013 season was better still as he ranked seventh, but then 2014 was tougher.

Moving to the all-new Haas F1 team in 2016 was a risk, but he was straight into the points and scored as many times as the car would allow.

TRACK NOTES

Nationality:	FRENCH
Born:	17 APRIL 1986, GENEVA, SWITZERLAND
Website:	www.romaingrosjean.com
Teams:	RENAULT 2009, LOTUS 2012-15,
	HAAS F1 2016-18

CAREER RECORD	
First Grand Prix:	2009 EUROPEAN GP
Grand Prix starts:	124
Grand Prix wins:	0 (best result: 2nd,
	2012 Canadian GP, 2013 United States GP)
Poles:	0
Fastest laps:	1
Points:	344
Honours:	2012 RACE OF CHAMPIONS
	CHAMPION, 2011 GP2 CHAMPION, 2010
	AUTO GT CHAMPION, 2008 & 2011 GP2
	ASIA CHAMPION, 2007 FORMULA THREE
	EUROSERIES CHAMPION, 2005 FRENCH
	FORMULA RENAULT CHAMPION, 2003 SWISS
	FORMULA RENAULT 1600 CHAMPION

PEAKING WITH A SIXTH PLACE

Following Haas F1's surprisingly good form in its maiden year in F1 in 2016, it was always likely that 2017 would prove harder, especially with a new set of technical rules to work to. There were flashes of form, most notably with Romain's fine sixth-place finish in the Austrian GP. However, when the team's form dropped away and points became a desire rather than an expectation, Romain knew that team owner Gene Haas is not someone to back away from a challenge and so a fix was always being worked on. The principal aim was to improve the Ferrari-powered cars' performance in qualifying, as their poor form left both drivers with more to do in the races than they would have liked. In the second half of the season, as other teams advanced, the Haas VF-17s seemed to use their tyres more heavily than others, leaving the drivers struggling in the races. Perhaps as a sign that he is no longer a hot-headed F1 tyro, though, Romain took over from Jenson Button last year as one of the directors of the Grand Prix Drivers' Association.

KEVIN MAGNUSSEN

Kevin showed real drive and aggression in 2017 after swapping Renault for Haas F1 and he did well to match the speed of team-mate Romain Grosjean, improving through the course of the season. The challenge between them is re-set for 2018.

Kevin has a wise head guiding his career as his F1 racing father Jan knows how taking a few wrong turns can direct a promising career into the sidelines.

Whether Kevin has the out-and-out speed that his father displayed as he forged his way through F3 and on to F1 is a moot point, but he is determined not to lose career momentum and has demonstrated thus far considerably more application to the job than his father ever did.

Jan was busy winning 14 of the 18 races in the British F3 Championship when Kevin came on the scene and it came as no surprise that he raced karts.

Kevin won the Danish Formula Ford Championship at just 15. Then, having showed good speed in 2009 in Formula Renault, he ranked third in German F3 in 2010 for the Motopark Academy Team. As expected, the British F3 Championship was tougher and even though he took seven wins, he was pipped to the 2011 title by his Carlin team-mate Felipe Nasr.

The next step was up to the more powerful Formula Renault 3.5 category and Kevin won that for DAMS at his second

If the car is competitive, Kevin will be sure to score more points in his second year with Haas.

attempt, beating Stoffel Vandoorne, and so McLaren offered him its second seat for 2014 after Sergio Perez left.

People wondered how he'd fare in the team for which his father had driven

fleetingly in 1995, and Kevin amazed everyone by finishing in second place on his debut in Australia. However, that was a flash in the pan and Jenson Button outscored him easily.

With a deal being done to run Honda engines in 2015, the team attracted Fernando Alonso back and Kevin agreed to be demoted to test driver. This was a risky moment for his career as little testing was done, but Renault gave him a race seat for 2016. He then faced another crossroads when Renault wouldn't offer more than a one-year deal, so he moved to Haas F1. Only time will tell if that was the right choice.

TRACK NOTES

Nationality:	DANISH
Born:	5 OCTOBER 1992, ROSKILDE, DENMARK
Website:	www.kevinmagnussen.com
Teams:	McLAREN 2014, RENAULT 2016, HAAS F1 2017–18

CAREER RECORD	
First Grand Prix:	2014 AUSTRALIAN GP
Grand Prix starts:	60
Grand Prix wins:	0 (best result: 2nd, 2014 Australian GP)
Poles:	0
Fastest laps:	0
Points:	81
Honours:	2013 FORMULA RENAULT 3.5 CHAMPION, 2011 BRITISH FORMULA THREE RUNNER-UP, 2009 FORMULA RENAULT NORTHERN EUROPE RUNNER-UP, 2008 DANISH FORMULA FORD CHAMPION

PUSHING HARD TO SUCCEED

Racing for Haas F1 in 2017 was Kevin's third team in three seasons, with 2015 spent on the sidelines after losing his ride at McLaren. So, Kevin had plenty to adjust to and plenty to prove as he settled in to the American team. Getting into the points by finishing eighth second time out, in China, was a help and he would have been pleased that at this point in the season his new team was outscoring his old one: Renault. However, these two teams were to remain incredibly close all year, often through Renault's inability to get its cars to the end of races. Seventh place in Azerbaijan offered a fillip. Kevin's drive to achieve and self-belief was made clear when he responded testily after the Hungarian GP to a comment from Nico Hulkenberg that he'd shoved the German's Renault onto the grass. He is clearly not an individual who will let himself be pushed around and produced some forceful moves in his attempts to get his Haas into the points, including a brilliant passing manoeuvre on Felipe Massa's Williams at Turn 2 in the Japanese GP.

McLAREN

After three uncompetitive years with Honda engines, there's new motivation from Renault for 2018, something that was essential to prevent Fernando Alonso from walking out on this once great team as it tries to put its name back up in lights.

Fernando Alonso had a year of few highlights, apart from this sixth place run in Hungary, but is sure to do better with Renault engines in 2018.

The resumption of a tie-in with Honda had been a deal that gave the team great hope after it parted company with Mercedes at the end of the 2014 World Championship. That it had worked before in considerable style as the McLaren/Honda partnership dominated, to the extent that its stellar driver line-up of Ayrton Senna and Alain Prost won all but one of the 16 grands prix in 1988, proved to be no guarantee that it would work again, and it didn't. It really didn't.

Having finished ahead only of Sauber last year, McLaren will be doing its utmost to rediscover its cutting edge and will be seeking to begin its fightback with Renault V6 engines in 2018.

To understand the team, F1 fans would be really well served to take the time to watch the film released last year about Bruce McLaren, the personable and talented Kiwi racer who created it in his own image in the mid-1960s. What he formed was a band of brothers who all seemed to do everything, seemingly

crafting the car with their bare hands. At times, it's hard to reconcile that carefree bunch with the many hundreds who toil away, often never leaving the team's glass and steel HQ outside Woking, but McLaren isn't alone in having grown like topsy.

Led by this inspirational New Zealander who gave the team his name, who could not

THE POWER AND THE GLORY

JONATHAN NEALE
Electronic warfare systems for submarines isn't the obvious route into F1, but it was Jonathan's first step before joining BAE Systems. From there, he took an MBA and went on to run the Hawk Fast Jet programme. However, in 2001, Jonathan joined McLaren Racing to look after its manufacturing processes and logistics. Promoted to managing director in 2004, he took on the engineering departments before becoming chief operating officer in 2014 to manage the team through the debacle of its engine deal with Honda.

PROGRESSING DESPITE WEAK HONDA ENGINE.
Sometimes it was hard to watch McLaren last year, with not just promising Stoffel Vandoorne but two-time World Champion Fernando Alonso going out into battle almost in vain. Held back by its Honda engines that were not only weak but unreliable, their season was punctuated by retirements. In qualifying, there was progress, but the drivers' application was too often for nought in the races. There were flashes of speed from both, but only for the minor points positions.

2017 DRIVERS & RESULTS

Driver	Nationality	Races	Wins	Pts	Pos
Fernando Alonso	Spanish	19	0	17	15th
Jenson Button	British	1	0	0	N/A
Stoffel Vandoorne	Belgian	20	0	13	16th

FOR THE RECORD

Country of origin:	England
Team base:	Woking England
Telephone:	(44) 01483 261900
Website:	www.mclaren.com
Active in Formula One:	From 1966
Grands Prix contested:	822
Wins:	181
Pole positions:	154
Fastest laps:	154

THE TEAM

Executive director:	Zak Brown
Chief operating officer:	Jonathan Neale
Racing director:	Eric Boullier
Director of design & development:	
	Neil Oatley
Technical director:	Tim Goss
Operations director:	Simon Roberts
Director of engineering:	Matt Morris
Chief engineer:	Peter Prodromou
Chief aerodynamicist:	Marianne Hinson
Team manager:	Paul James
Test driver:	Lando Norris
Chassis:	McLaren MP4-33
Engine:	Renault V6
Tyres:	Pirelli

only win grands prix but was blessed with engineering skills aplenty and the ability to coax the best out of his band of expats, the team started small, but was incredibly dynamic. McLaren also built sportscars in order to win the prizes in the CanAm series that paid for the development of its F1 cars.

The first F1 win came in the 1968 Belgian GP and two more were added by team-mate Denny Hulme before the year was out. Then, after Hulme won once in 1969 as the pair continued to clean up in CanAm, disaster struck in 1970 when Bruce was killed when testing at Goodwood.

With his trusted lieutenants taking over the team, it fought on and, blessed by the availability of the Ford Cosworth DFV engine that left it at no disadvantage in the horsepower stakes, the team settled into being a regular frontrunner. Emerson Fittipaldi gave it its first drivers' title in 1974 and James Hunt its second two years later.

Then, having failed to get to grips with ground effects technology, it fell away and didn't recover until Ron Dennis had taken over at the helm from Teddy Mayer. Extra investment followed and brilliant design work by John Barnard that gave the team the first carbonfibre F1 monocoque enabled first Niki Lauda in 1984 and then Prost in 1985 and 1986 to lift the title.

The arrival of Honda power extended the team's advantage and Senna landed the title in 1988, 1990 and 1991, with Prost being crowned in 1989 as the team collected four constructors' titles on the trot.

As Williams in particular hit rich form, and a lot of McLaren's focus swung to the development of its road car division, McLaren had to wait until 1998 for its next title, after becoming dominant with Mercedes engines, with Mika Hakkinen making it two in a row in 1999. Then came another wait, and a near championship miss in 2003 with Kimi Raikkonen; it took until 2008 for another drivers' title, this time for Lewis Hamilton.

Nothing remains the same forever, and he never repeated that as Brawn GP and then Red Bull Racing moved ahead.

Dennis had been succeeded by Martin Whitmarsh, but moved back into control in 2014. However, there has been a changing of the guard as American racer turned sports marketing expert Zak Brown took over last year and he seems to be shaking things up.

"McLaren has always worked to form lasting partnerships with its technical suppliers and we're convinced that we can bring real value to Renault as we work alongside it to develop its power unit into a regular winner."
Zak Brown

McLaren's brains trust of Neil Oatley, Gordon Murray and Ron Dennis with Ayrton Senna in 1988.

FERNANDO ALONSO

Fernando rediscovered his love of racing last year, not in F1 where McLaren was held back by its Honda engines, but in the Indianapolis 500. Now reunited with Renault power, he wants to start enjoying F1 again, at the sharp end of the field.

Some of the drivers who have gone on to become World Champion have taken a while to get into their stride in the junior single-seater formulae, like Damon Hill. Others have learnt their craft as children in kart racing and are already all but the real thing from the moment that they step up to car racing. Fernando is one such.

A karting world champion by the age of 15, he hit car racing like a meteor, not bothering with the bottom two rungs of the ladder and landing his first title in his first year. This was in Formula Open by Nissan and he stepped directly from that into Formula 3000, the level below F1. Competing against drivers with at least two years more experience, he ranked fourth overall and scored the most dominant win of the year, at Spa-Francorchamps.

For 2001, he was snapped up by Minardi and had a solid first season with the F1 underdogs. Fernando thought his best way to move to a better team was to be a test driver in 2002, and this worked, as Renault gave him one of its race seats for 2003. And Fernando raced to victory in Hungary.

By now, no one could ignore his talent and Fernando ended Michael Schumacher's

Fernando is still one of the F1 greats, and everyone wants to see him winning again.

run of five consecutive drivers' titles with Ferrari by coming out on top in 2005, and then again in 2006. A bid to make it a hat-trick by racing for McLaren in 2007 left him one point short in an acrimonious year, so he returned to Renault for two years. A

move to Ferrari in 2010 saw the wins flow again, but he was pipped by Sebastian Vettel in 2012 and that was the last time he had truly competitive machinery.

TRACK NOTES

Nationality:	SPANISH
Born:	29 JULY 1981, OVIEDO, SPAIN
Website:	www.fernandoalonso.com
Teams:	MINARDI 2001, RENAULT 2003-06, McLAREN 2007, RENAULT 2008-09, FERRARI 2010-14, McLAREN 2015-18

CAREER RECORD

First Grand Prix:	2001 AUSTRALIAN GP
Grand Prix starts:	293
Grand Prix wins:	32

2003 Hungarian GP, 2005 Malaysian GP, Bahrain GP, San Marino GP, European GP, French GP, German GP, Chinese GP, 2006 Bahrain GP, Australian GP, Spanish GP, Monaco GP, British GP, Canadian GP, Japanese GP, 2007 Malaysian GP, Monaco GP, European GP, Italian GP, 2008 Singapore GP, Japanese GP, 2010 Australian GP, German GP, Italian GP, Singapore GP, Korean GP, 2011 British GP, 2012 Malaysian GP, European GP, 2013 Chinese GP, Spanish GP

Poles:	22
Fastest laps:	23
Points:	1,849

Honours: 2005 & 2006 F1 WORLD CHAMPION, 2012 & 2013 F1 RUNNER-UP, 1999 FORMULA NISSAN CHAMPION, 1997 ITALIAN & SPANISH KART CHAMPION, 1996 WORLD & SPANISH KART CHAMPION, 1994 & 1995 SPANISH JUNIOR KART CHAMPION

PERSEVERING AGAINST THE ODDS

McLaren had such high hopes for its second spell of being partnered in F1 by Honda. Naturally, it wasn't expected to set the pace in its first year, 2015, not with Mercedes on such a roll, but the speed would surely come. Except it didn't, and although Fernando always gave it his best shot, you could see his frustration at the lack of decent progress. That is why he was kept sweet by enlightened team management from Zak Brown, who allowed him to skip the Monaco GP to try to win the Indy 500. Racing on an oval was new to Fernando, but he made a huge impression and could have won. He is a driver of catholic taste and a crack at the Le Mans 24 Hours could be next to keep him interested, as a season's best of sixth place in F1, in the Hungarian GP, isn't going to excite him forever. For now, though, Fernando continues to give his all, all the time, for which McLaren ought to thank him because that at least offers clear perspective of how competitive or uncompetitive their machinery is.

STOFFEL VANDOORNE

The points may not have been flowing throughout 2017, but Stoffel did a steady job with his midfield Honda-engined McLaren last year, as his only benchmark was team-mate Alonso who also struggled. For 2018, with Renault power, watch out.

Some drivers show promise on their way through the single-seater formulae, with a good race here or there. To win a single-seater title, though, a driver needs to be on it, to be both fast and consistent throughout the course of an entire season. To do this more than once, against the best of your contemporaries, really marks a driver out as something both special and resilient. Stoffel is one such driver.

Stoffel doesn't come from a wealthy background, so he wouldn't have been able to afford to keep plugging away if he hadn't landed the results that built his career momentum. His record shouts of promotion through results or, more to the point, through championship titles.

Stoffel stepped up to race cars in 2010 after finishing as runner-up in the kart world championship. He landed the F4 Eurocup in his first season.

Next stop was Formula Renault and Stoffel ranked third in the Northern European series, then nailed the full European title the following year, his four wins putting him ahead of Daniil Kvyat.

Bypassing Formula 3, Stoffel graduated to the more powerful Formula Renault 3.5

Stoffel was almost under the radar last year, but should be more visible in 2018.

and he was right in the mix against Kevin Magnussen but had to settle on being runner-up as the Dane finished the year in style by winning the final three races.

He had done enough to advance to the final stop before F1: GP2. No one wants to hang around in GP2, but after finishing as runner-up to Jolyon Palmer for ART Grand Prix in 2014, Stoffel elected to come back in 2015 with the same team and did the one thing he had to: he became champion. And he did it emphatically, with seven wins, to end the year with almost double the points of the runner-up.

With no F1 race seat opening up, McLaren placed Stoffel in Super Formula in Japan and Stoffel came on strong to rank fourth, which was enough for him to take over from the retiring Jenson Button for 2017.

TRACK NOTES

Nationality:	BELGIAN
Born:	26 MARCH 1992, KORTRIJK, BELGIUM
Website:	www.stoffelvandoorne.com
Teams:	McLAREN 2016-18

CAREER RECORD

First Grand Prix:	2016 BAHRAIN GP
Grand Prix starts:	20
Grand Prix wins:	0
	(best result: 7th, 2017 Singapore GP & Malaysian GP)
Poles:	0
Fastest laps:	0
Points:	14
Honours:	2015 GP2 CHAMPION, 2014 GP2 RUNNER-UP, 2013 FORMULA RENAULT 3.5 RUNNER-UP, 2012 EUROPEAN FORMULA RENAULT CHAMPION, 2010 F4 EUROCUP CHAMPION, 2009 WORLD KART RUNNER-UP, 2008 BELGIAN KF2 KART CHAMPION

COMING ON WELL WITH A WEAK V6

Whether your car is the fastest in the field or the slowest, the only contestant that any driver can be truly marked against is a team-mate. So, while all involved could tell that the Honda V6 was still short not just of grunt but of reliability too, the fact that the 2015 GP2 champion was scrapping around outside the points didn't reflect badly on him, since his illustrious team-mate Fernando Alonso was too. All that Stoffel could look to do was to try and match the double World Champion. By season's end, he was almost on the Spaniard's pace, and two seventh places in succession, in Singapore and at Sepang, showed that he could bring the car home too. Drivers spend their childhoods dreaming of reaching F1 and a look at this Belgian racer's career record, bedecked with titles, proves that he's good enough to continue at the sport's top level and that he could become a grand prix winner if he finds himself behind the wheel of a competitive car.

SAUBER

Sauber is looking to make a major step forward in 2018, and new boss Frederic Vasseur employed a quarter more staff to help with this push to drag the team off the final row of the grid and on towards point-scoring race finishes.

Marcus Ericsson was unable to break into the points in 2017 and it will continue to be difficult for Sauber's drivers to do so this season.

For years, this Swiss team was run by the man who founded it, Peter Sauber, a man not given to flights of fantasy, simply a driven, no frills, racing first sort of guy. This is no longer the case, with an investment firm now the major shareholder, and one senses that in terms of having an identifiable character this is not a good thing. However, a financial boost was required as the departure of Manor after 2016 meant that the Swiss team was now bottom of the F1 pile and so maintaining the status quo was not really an option.

Peter Sauber spent the 1970s as a racing driver, competing both in hillclimbs in his native Switzerland, where circuit racing has been banned since 1955, and then in sportscars. Indeed, it was by building his own sportscars that Sauber made his name, with one of his C5s winning the 1976 Interserie title. In 1978, a C5 was entered for a full World Sportscar Championship programme and Swiss hotshot Marc Surer impressed in it at Le Mans.

By 1982, Sauber had built its own Group C sports prototype and its results became ever better through the decade, to the point that Mercedes came on board, under

a veil of secrecy, in 1985. Progress was such that Henri Pescarolo and Mike Thackwell won the Nurburgring 1000 in 1986 and the programme blossomed from there, coming

THE POWER AND THE GLORY

FREDERIC VASSEUR
This 49-year-old aeronautical engineer started his own racing team, ASM, and had great success in junior single-seaters, winning the European F3 title from 2004 to 2007, with Lewis Hamilton crowned in 2005 and Romain Grosjean in 2007. Vasseur also set up ART Grand Prix and first Nico Rosberg then Hamilton lifted the GP2 crown. He also set up Spark Racing Technology to provide the chassis for Formula E. But, after Vasseur joined the Renault F1 team, he fell out with Cyril Abiteboul, so leapt at the chance to take over at Sauber.

SCRABBLING AROUND FOR THE ODD POINT
The highlight of Sauber's 2017 campaign was its first hit of points, scored by Pascal Wehrlein for eighth in Baku. However, with all other teams scoring consistently, this didn't raise the team off the foot of the table and uncertainty about which engines it might use this year delayed its choice of drivers. Keeping on with Ferrari at least opens the door for a Ferrari development driver to boost the team, by bringing in a driver for their ability rather than for their budget.

2017 DRIVERS & RESULTS

Driver	Nationality	Races	Wins	Pts	Pos
Marcus Ericsson	Swedish	20	0	0	20th
Antonio Giovanazzi	Italian	2	0	0	22nd
Pascal Wehrlein	German	18	0	5	18th

FOR THE RECORD

Country of origin:	Switzerland
Team base:	Hinwil, Switzerland
Telephone:	(41) 44 937 9000
Website:	www.sauberf1team.com
Active in Formula One:	From 1993
	(as BMW Sauber 2006-10)
Grands Prix contested:	443
Wins:	1
Pole positions:	1
Fastest laps:	5

THE TEAM

Chairman:	Pascal Picci
Team principal:	Frederic Vasseur
Technical director:	Jorg Zander
Chief designer:	Eric Gandelin
Head of aerodynamics:	
	Nicolas Hennel de Beaupreau
Head of engineering:	tba
Head of track engineering:	Xevi Pujolar
Head of aerodynamic development:	
	Mariano Alperin-Bruvera
Head of aerodynamic research:	
	Seamus Mullarkey
Head of vehicle performance:	
	Elliot Dason-Barber
Team manager:	Beat Zehnder
Test driver:	Antonio Giovinazzi
Chassis:	Sauber C37
Engine:	Ferrari V6
Tyres:	Pirelli

good with five wins in 1988 and then victory in both the Le Mans 24 Hours and the World Sports-Prototype Championship in 1989. By now, the cars raced in Mercedes silver and they won the sportscar title again in 1990, beating Jaguar.

Sauber elected to advance to F1 in 1993 and was disappointed when Mercedes chose not to make the move with him. However, things started well when JJ Lehto finished fifth on their first outing and Sauber ranked sixth at year's end. Impressed, Mercedes came on stream as engine partner in 1994 but then moved on to McLaren the following year, leaving Sauber to do a deal with Ford.

Then the team from near Zurich started running Ferrari customer engines from 1997 on, but remained at the tail end of the midfield until an upswing in form in 2001 when it finished fourth, albeit way behind Ferrari, McLaren and Williams, who were first and second in every race and third in 12.

BMW entered into partnership in 2006 and its investment and engines gave the team its best chance, with Sauber finishing 2007 as runner-up to Ferrari and then taking its one and only win in Canada in 2008 when

Robert Kubica led home team-mate Nick Heidfeld and a second good year in a row was completed in third overall.

The end of Sauber's partnership with BMW meant running Ferrari customer engines from 2011 and highlights since then have been rare, save for Sergio Perez chasing Fernando Alonso's Ferrari before settling for second place behind it at Sepang in 2012 which helped the team rank sixth overall. Since then, 10th has been a more regular end-of-year position.

Frederic Vasseur's aim on taking over at the helm of the team after last year's British GP was to boost staff numbers from 320 to around 420, with aerodynamicists in particular demand. That is quite a hike and won't simply be a case of the team's owners releasing the money, as Sauber has always had a problem hiring and retaining staff, largely because its base is far from the heartland of F1 technology that arcs around London, requiring key personnel to transplant their families into a new environment.

There was talk last year of Sauber taking on an engine supply deal with Honda after McLaren jettisoned the Japanese

manufacturer. This would have helped to ease the team's budgetary problems, but the deal never came together, and so Ferrari horses will be harnessed for an eighth year in 2018. The good news is they will be the latest spec, not those from 2017.

"Taking non-listed Ferrari parts would be the fastest way to improve because teams can take a huge step in three months. It's a good way to improve quickly and come back onto the pace and catch the midfield."

Frederic Vasseur

Robert Kubica gave the team its day of days when he led a Sauber one-two in Canada in 2008.

CHARLES LECLERC

With backing from Ferrari, this 20-year-old from Monaco looks set to be one of the most promising drivers to reach F1 in recent years and his rookie year with Sauber could well be a precursor to something even more impressive.

One of three sons born to a father who liked to contest the annual F3 race that supports their home grand prix in Monaco, Charles was always going to try his hand at racing.

That his father, Herve, ran a kart track at Brignoles certainly helped as Charles made it all look rather easy as he rose through the karting ranks, collecting French titles on the way before he stepped up to international championships when he reached the more senior karting categories.

The 2011 season, when he was 13, really helped to cement his reputation, as Charles won the world KF3 title and was signed by Nicolas Todt's ARM management company. With more titles earned, 2013 was Charles's final year in karts and he finished as runner-up to Max Verstappen in the World KZ Championship.

Then came car racing and Charles finished as runner-up in the ALPS regional Formula Renault series. In 2015, he stepped up to the European F3 Championship and immediately made his mark by winning one of the three races at the opening round at Silverstone. Competing for Van Amersfoort Racing, Charles went on to rank fourth at season's end, then rounded out his year with

Charles arrives in F1 with Ferrari backing after being last year's dominant F2 champion.

second place in the Macau street race, but then elected to race in GP3 instead of coming back for a second crack at this prestigious title. The decision was the right one as he raced on a lot of grand prix circuits for the ART Grand Prix squad and won the title.

Probably the most important event of 2016, though, was being signed up as a member of the Ferrari Driver Academy, not just because it allowed him his first taste of an F1 car, in a Ferrari-powered Haas, but for the possibilities that might be provided by the doors that this scheme would open.

Charles kept his career momentum going in F2 last year, winning the title in considerable style, but also running in F1 practice sessions for Sauber. However, while all was shining out on the track through 2017, he had a major setback when his father died.

TRACK NOTES

Nationality:	MONEGASQUE
Born:	16 OCTOBER 1997, MONTE CARLO, MONACO
Website:	www.charles-leclerc.com
Teams:	SAUBER 2018

CAREER RECORD

First Grand Prix:	2018 AUSTRALIAN GP
Grand Prix starts:	0
Grand Prix wins:	0
Poles:	0
Fastest laps:	0
Points:	0
Honours:	2017 FIA F2 CHAMPION, 2016 GP3 CHAMPION, 2015 MACAU F3 RUNNER-UP, 2014 FORMULA RENAULT ALPS RUNNER-UP, 2013 WORLD KZ KART RUNNER-UP, 2012 UNDER 18 WORLD KART CHAMPIONSHIP RUNNER-UP & EURO KF KART RUNNER-UP, 2011 ACADEMY TROPHY KART CHAMPION, 2010 JUNIOR MONACO KART CUP CHAMPION, 2009 FRENCH CADET KART CHAMPION

MAKING IT LOOK VERY EASY

Long known as GP2, but reinvented last year as FIA F2, the final single-seater step before F1 is a tough nut to crack. This is why so many in the sport are excited by Charles, as he made landing the title look easy last year. Arriving with the GP3 title to his name, Charles joined Prema Racing and claimed pole for the opening round at Sakhir. Third in the first race, he won the sprint race the following day and so assumed a lead in the championship that he was never to lose. Rookie champions at this level are rare and, although Charles was pushed hard to the middle of the season by DAMS racer Oliver Rowland, he wasn't just ultra-quick but incredibly consistent. Having added further wins at Barcelona, Baku, the Red Bull Ring, Silverstone and then a dominant one at Spa-Francorchamps – though he was disqualified after too much of the plank under his car had been worn away on the kerbs – Charles was crowned champion after he won at Jerez, with three races still to run.

MARCUS ERICSSON

When Alfa Romeo took a stake in the Sauber team, it was considered likely that Marcus would lose his drive, but he has hung on and his target for 2018 has to be to get back among the points.

Marcus is rare among the twenty F1 drivers in that he doesn't have a string of championship titles to his name. Sergio Perez doesn't either, but he has the benefit of having shone with midfield teams while Marcus has brought up the rear with Sauber. Max Verstappen is also short on car racing titles, but he did his winning in karts before his super rapid ascent to F1.

Identified at the age of nine by racer Fredrik Ekblom as having talent, Marcus spent seven years in karts, gaining speed but not titles. However, with the support of Ekblom and Sweden's only Indianapolis 500 winner, Kenny Brack, he moved up to car racing with their old team: Fortec Motorsport. This was in the last season of Formula BMW and Marcus won the British title.

Advancing to British F3 in 2008, Marcus ranked fifth, one place behind Perez, as Jaime Alguersuari landed the crown. Although he had taken two pole positions, there were no wins and Brack recommended that he race in Japanese F3 in 2009. This was wise advice, as Marcus

Marcus had to sweat before retaining his ride with Sauber for a fourth season.

shone for the top team, TOMS, winning five times to land the title. Added to this, he dropped in for four races in British F3 and won two of those.

This was enough for Marcus to move up to GP2, F1's feeder category that was to be his home for the next four years. There were flashes of speed, such as winning the second race at Valencia, where the driver who placed eighth in the first race starts on pole, and his seventh place finish enabled him to start from the front row on this street circuit. However, there was inconsistency too. This was the theme for the next three seasons, with his 2013 ranking of sixth overall for DAMS being considered enough for his backers to buy him his F1 break with Caterham in 2014, but the team folded.

For 2015, Marcus moved to Sauber and eighth place in a strange Australian GP season-opener was a dream start, and he scored on four more occasions. Life hasn't been as sweet again.

TRACK NOTES

Nationality:	SWEDISH
Born:	2 SEPTEMBER 1990, KUMLA, SWEDEN
Website:	www.marcusericssonracing.com
Teams:	CATERHAM 2014, SAUBER 2015-18

CAREER RECORD

First Grand Prix:	2014 AUSTRALIAN GP
Grand Prix starts:	76
Grand Prix wins:	0
	(best result: 8th, 2015 Australian GP)
Poles:	0
Fastest laps:	0
Points:	9
Honours:	2009 JAPANESE FORMULA 3 CHAMPION, 2007 BRITISH FORMULA BMW CHAMPION

FALLING JUST SHORT OF POINTS

Points mean prizes in many sports. In F1, points mean prize money, which is especially vital for teams that are struggling financially, like Sauber. Furthermore, for a driver, points mean recognition. Fall just short of the points, that's to say by finishing in 11th place or lower, and that recognition is hard to come by, your place in the F1 record books likely to be little more than a footnote. It's safe to say that none of the trio of drivers who raced for Sauber in 2017 felt that they had machinery competitive enough to expect a run into the top 10. Ericsson came home 11th on a couple of occasions, so fell just short, while team-mate Pascal Wehrlein drew the plaudits for finishing eighth in the Spanish GP. Thus the German put his name up in lights, the Swede did not. They were relatively well matched in qualifying, Ericsson losing that seven against 11, but in the races Wehrlein had the edge. Yet, with Swedish backers propping up the team, it was always likely that Ericsson stood a better chance of being kept on.

Daniel Ricciardo looks past the halo mounted atop his Red Bull Racing RB13. Most drivers reckon the obstruction of view is a price worth paying.

TALKING POINT: HALO HEAD PROTECTION

Formula One cars are going to look like never before in 2018. This isn't because of a relaxation of the aerodynamic limitations dictated by the rulebook, but because the FIA, the sport's governing body, has decided to improve driver safety by introducing halo head protection.

The death of British former Formula 1 racer Justin Wilson after he was hit on the head by a nosecone shorn from a rival's car at in an IndyCar race at Pocono Raceway in 2015 was the catalyst for one of the major changes in F1 design in recent decades.

The reaction from the FIA was that F1 cars would be fitted with extra bodywork in the form of a halo from 2018 to ensure that a driver is safer than ever before.

The halo is a raised arch of bodywork, like the thong on a flip-flop, that rises from a bar that sprouts from the bodywork just in front of the cockpit and then splits above the driver's eyeline and descends to mounting points behind their shoulders.

There is no doubting that the halo doesn't improve the look of the car, and many F1 purists were up in arms about it. However, FIA did a great deal of research on the matter during 2016 and has measured it as being able to withstand 15 times the static load of the car.

Clearly, such a strong structure ought to be able to deflect large incoming objects as well as offering extra protection if a car should become inverted.

When looking at the halo, many felt that it would impede a driver's line of sight. However, the results of FIA testing of haloes suggested that driver's vision shouldn't be "substantially affected". Some of the drivers have pointed out, though, that it will hamper their outlook if they are driving up a very steep section of track, like out of Eau Rouge at Spa or the climb to Turn 1 at Circuit of the Americas.

Another couple of systems were assessed. Red Bull Racing tried what was called the aeroscreen and Ferrari tried a windscreen shield, but the latter got the thumbs down from Sebastian Vettel when he tried it in first free practice for the British GP at Silverstone last summer, as its curved shape offered distorted vision when looked through from some angles. It was so disorientating that Vettel came back to the pits after a lap, reporting that it made him feel dizzy. A further problem with the aeroscreen is that it created a lot of backwash that Vettel said forced his helmet forward.

With this in mind, the FIA elected to go ahead with the halo rather than the other concepts and all cars must be fitted with one for 2018, and the halo concept will filter down to the junior single-seater formulae in the years to come.

Almost uniformly, fans said the cars looked terrible when fitted with haloes, but some drivers pointed out that fans didn't have to consider safety and that safety should come before aesthetics. Others, though, were outspoken against them and Jolyon Palmer was of the opinion that a halo wouldn't have prevented the only death in F1 since 1994 – Jules Bianchi's accident at Suzuka in 2014 when he hit a rescue vehicle – and that it wasn't necessary to make the change. Former F1 champion Niki Lauda is also against haloes, saying that the greatest strides in preventing drivers being struck on the head by errant wheels has come from improving wheel tethers.

One limitation of the halo that can't be denied, however, is the fact that a smaller object, such as the spring that bounced up and clattered Felipe Massa in the head in Hungary in 2009, would still be able to enter the area around the driver's head.

One eventual conclusion might be to go to a closed-cockpit F1 car, but would it then be F1 or simply a single-seater sportscar? Or, to take matters further, there has been occasional talk of trying to eliminate the danger of when single-seaters interlock wheels that can lead to one being thrown into the air. By filling the gaps between front and rear wheels with bodywork to mitigate against this would give us ... yes, sportscars. Fortunately, we haven't reached that conclusion yet.

Opposite top left: Fernando Alonso appears contemplative as he sits in his McLaren MCL32 and assesses how much forward

Opposite top right: Looking down on Lewis Hamilton as he sits in the cockpit of last year's Mercedes F1 W08, it's easy to see how

Opposite bottom: FIA race director Charlie Whiting (centre) and Laurent Mekies (left) chair the press conference explaining why F1 cars will be fitted with a halo from 2018

TALKING POINT:
PAUL RICARD RETURNS

The World Championship welcomes the French GP back into the fold in 2018, and this race returns not to Magny-Cours, the circuit it last used in 2008, but to Paul Ricard, last visited in 1990, albeit a version that has been considerably modernised.

Paul Ricard was a manufacturer of pastis. As pastis was France's aperitif of choice through the 1960s, Ricard accrued considerable wealth and used some of this to commission an eponymous circuit.

With its wide-open spaces, the purpose-built circuit was ultra-modern and certainly considered to be appreciably safer than Reims, Rouen-les-Essarts and Clermont-Ferrand, the tracks that had hosted the French GP through the 1960s. Also, being in the south of the country, its weather was expected to be more constant, with the Mistral wind to keep temperatures in check.

Considering that France held the first-ever grand prix, run near Le Mans in 1906, it has seemed wrong that the nation was off the World Championship calendar for the past nine years. That wrong has been righted, along with the return of the German GP, and the World Championship looks all the more cohesive because of it.

Second time around, Paul Ricard looks magnificent. Its approach looks like that of an exclusive country club, the track not visible until rounding a corner by a lake and spotting the face of its iconic and elegant pit building. Along with every centimetre of tarmac, that too has been upgraded. In fact, it has the feel of an upmarket hotel when entered, with VIP dining areas looking out over the large grass area that lies between the pitlane and the pitwall.

The track itself is both the same and different. The same because its layout is as it used to be until 1985 when it was chopped after Brabham racer Elio de Angelis's fatal accident made the owners cut its length to keep speeds in check. But different because what was once a simple and open venue has gone high tech. After Bernie Ecclestone bought it and turned it into a cutting edge testing facility, something that is helped by the generally hot and sunny weather on this high plateau, everything was made new. Its trademark concentric coloured bands out beyond the kerbs aren't there just to make the place look good and excite the photographers, but to slow the cars should they stray, with increasing degrees of friction provided from the asphalt/tungsten mix used in the stripes the further off a driver strays, as they run from the blue bands into the red ones, thus eliminating the need for gravel traps.

Toyota's short-lived F1 team based its test team there, using its own building on the Mistral Straight.

The circuit in its modern form has already accommodated large crowds, coping with 75,000 attending the Boule d'Or motorbike races. For the drivers and VIPs, there's even an airstrip on site that is long enough for private jets to use.

When the circuit was opened for action in 1970, with its first grand prix in 1971, it felt like F1's new face and it provided some great races too, including the 1975 French GP in which Niki Lauda's leading Ferrari was chased and caught by James Hunt in his Hesketh, with Jochen Mass closing in on both in his McLaren. In 1982, there was a dream result for the home fans, with Rene Arnoux, Alain Prost, Didier Pironi and Patrick Tambay filling the top four finishing positions as Renault scooped a one-two on home ground. Eight years later, in 1990, F1's most recent visit to Paul Ricard, Prost went one better and won for Ferrari in a race where the Leyton House team nearly sprang a surprise, with Ivan Capelli rising from seventh place to lead for more than half of the race until, three laps from home, Prost went past when Capelli slowed with a fuel pick-up problem.

French fans will be hoping their race never falls from the World Championship calendar again, and Circuit Paul Ricard has a five-year deal with which to cement its place. Now they've got a race of their own again, home fans will look to Esteban Ocon, and maybe Romain Grosjean, to lead the way for a new generation of French racers.

TURN 2

TALKING POINT:
WILL MAX BE THE SECOND SUCCESS?

The Red Bull driver scholarship has been running since 2001 and financed Sebastian Vettel's ascent to F1 and then to four world titles. Max Verstappen may become its second champion in 2018, but the scheme has cast away more young drivers than it has promoted.

Dietrich Mateschitz made an enormous fortune from being one of the founders of the Red Bull energy drink brand. Keen for a daredevil image, the company used adrenaline sports to build its image. As an F1 fan, it was no surprise that Mateschitz added racing to that list, first by backing Enrique Bernoldi in F3000 in 1999 and later in F1 with the Arrows team. This backing would shift to Sauber and then Mateschitz would acquire Jaguar Racing to create a team of his own in 2005: Red Bull Racing.

For most, that would be a strong enough way to promote your product, but Mateschitz and his longtime ally the ex-F1 racer Helmut Marko already had a scholarship scheme on the go, and they decided that the best way to see if their F1 hopefuls would be good enough for Red Bull Racing would be to try them in F1 first, so took over tailend F1 team Minardi and renamed it Scuderia Toro Rosso for 2006 for that purpose.

The Red Bull Junior Team had started in 2001, lending financial assistance to eight drivers to help them advance. Of these, racing in all formulae from karting to F3000, three made it to F1. They were Patrick Friesacher, Christian Klien and Mateschitz's standout selection: Sebastian Vettel.

Vettel would be part of the scheme for another six years, in the last of which he stepped up to F1 midway through 2007, then soon advanced from Toro Rosso to Red Bull Racing before taking his four F1 titles.

While two of that first batch reached F3000, with Ricardo Mauricio going on to make a career racing stock cars in his native Brazil and Bernhard Auinger doing the occasional GT race, the other three fell away, with Frank Diefenbacher racing for a while in the European Touring Car Championship, Reinhard Kofler peaking in Formula Renault before returning to race GTs in 2017 and Christopher Wassermann stepping up from karts to Formula BMW before quitting.

The following years followed a similar pattern, with successes and failures. For a while, the scheme was weighted in favour of Austrian drivers, as Mateschitz and Marko wanted to find a young compatriot to continue the line of Austrian racing greats that produced Jochen Rindt, Niki Lauda (whose son Mathias was a Red Bull Junior Team member in 2003 and 2004) and Gerhard Berger.

In the early years there also had been a spread of American drivers, mainly because a concurrent driver scholarship had fired them across the Atlantic to race in Europe between 2003 and 2005. However, Scott Speed was the only one to make it to F1. There was another time when it seemed

that Red Bull selected alphabetically, starting with A, like in 2006 when it fielded Sergei Afanasiev, Filipe Albuquerque, Mikhail Aleshin, Jaime Alguersuari, Michael Ammermuller and Nathan Antunes...

However, the Red Bull Junior Team then focused on promoting the best young talent, and it has propelled 13 drivers to F1 with its two teams and three other drivers have gone on to race in F1 with other teams, but that's from a cast over the decades of 73 hopefuls.

Thus far, Vettel, Daniel Ricciardo and Max Verstappen have gone on to become grand prix winners. But, looking ahead, it's hard to predict which of the recent juniors might follow them. Ironically, it could even be a driver who was rejected after 2009.

While many found that their careers went into freefall when they lost their backing, and some spoke out, others chose to simply thank Marko for the ride. Staying on good terms clearly worked for Brendon Hartley, as although he'd been dropped after four years of Red Bull support in junior single-seaters, he was invited back into the fold towards the end of the 2017 F1 season after becoming a Le Mans winner and starring for Porsche on the World Endurance scene when Marko decided that Kvyat wasn't performing for Toro Rosso. And he grasped the opportunity with both hands.

Opposite top left: Jean-Eric Vergne and Daniel Ricciardo were Scuderia Toro Rosso team-mates in 2012 and 2013. **Opposite top right:** The Australian (right) made the grade – winning GPs with Red Bull Racing – but Vergne did not

Opposite middle: Ricciardo (with champagne in front of him) celebrates his victory in the 2014 Canadian GP – first World Championship win – flanked by members of the Red Bull Racing team in the team garage

Opposite bottom: Max Verstappen leads the field through the first sequence of corners at last year's Mexican GP, as Lewis Hamilton and Sebastian Vettel jockey for position behind him, just before their collision

KNOW THE TRACKS 2018

Not only will F1 fans be treated to one extra round this year, as the World Championship is extended to 21 grands prix, but two of the traditional F1-hosting nations are back in the mix. These are France and Germany, with their races lined up to happen at Paul Ricard and Hockenheim, while the Malaysian GP has been dropped from the roster after a 19-year run.

It seems an extremely long time ago now that the World Championship ran to a 16-race format for year after year, even decade after decade. In fact, the last time that that once regular number was the standard was back in 2003, when Michael Schumacher was part way through his five-year title streak for Ferrari. Since then, as the drivers and most especially the families of the team personnel involved will tell you, the number has kept on going up, the season ending ever later as a result of the extra grands prix. Now, like last year, it stretches for fully two thirds of the year, for eighth months.

The first time that the World Championship hit 21 grands prix in a season was in 2016 and the number goes back up to 21 again in the year ahead, but unusually not with the increase being achieved by the introduction of an all-new circuit.

Having the French GP back again is a particularly welcome move. After all, the first-ever grand prix was held when the French GP ran on a circuit of public roads near Le Mans back in 1906. French involvement in F1 was once huge, especially in the 1980s when as many as a fifth of the drivers were French. This changed when tobacco advertising was banned in sport and so the budgets that had put them there were outlawed, leading to a situation recently when there were no French F1 drivers at all. Fortunately, this has changed now with Romain Grosjean, Esteban Ocon and Pierre Gasly all showing their skills in the sport's top level.

French teams, too, have fallen by the wayside, with the loss of Ligier the most keenly felt, but there is no sign of a revival there. The new home of the French GP is an old home of the French GP, the Paul Ricard circuit, but in greatly modernised form.

Germany's spell on the F1 sidelines lasted only one year, way shorter than France's nine-year hiatus, but new F1 owners Liberty Media know that the country that not only produced the Schumacher brothers, Sebastian Vettel and Nico Rosberg but is home to some of the world's leading automotive manufacturers, really needs a race on home soil. As in 2016, this will be held at Hockenheim, with no planned alternation with the Nurburgring circuit in the new deal.

The French and German GPs will slot into the calendar on 24 June and 22 July as the eighth and 11th rounds respectively. The French GP will start a run that F1 fans might love, but the teams won't, as it will be a tripleheader, that's to say the first race in a sequence that runs across three consecutive weekends as it is followed by grands prix at the Red Bull Ring and Silverstone (pictured) over the next two weekends. There will also be five doubleheader combinations in 2018.

The remainder of the calendar is pretty much the same as it was last year, with the exception of the loss of the Malaysian GP changing the run towards the end of the campaign, this falling by the wayside due to dwindling race attendance at Sepang meaning that the race organisers didn't think that the grand prix hosting fee was tenable any longer, which is such a shame after former President Mahatir Mohamad was such a staunch supporter of F1 back when Malaysia was a country imbued with positive hope and energy. Now the nation appears indifferent to F1, something not helped by no Malaysian driver rising up through the single-seater ranks to race in F1 since its one and only driver at this level, Alex Yoong, did so in 2001, just a couple of years after Malaysia landed its grand prix deal.

There is a minor tweak to the front end of the season, when the traditional opening round at the Albert Park Circuit in Melbourne is followed by the Bahrain GP rather than the Chinese GP, as they swap their 2017 order in a doubleheader of grands prix on consecutive weekends. A more comprehensive repositioning of events comes with the fourth round which will this time be the Azerbaijan GP on the streets of Baku rather than the Russian GP as it had been in 2017, with Russia's race in Sochi taking the slot that had been occupied by Malaysia's race at Sepang.

The run-in to the end of the season, and hopefully to a glorious, title-settling crescendo, is the same as it was last year, with the last five rounds being at Suzuka in Japan, then at the Circuit of the Americas in the USA, at the Autodromo Hermanos Rodriguez in Mexico City, at Interlagos in Brazil before the now traditional season-ender at the Yas Marina Circuit in Abu Dhabi.

MELBOURNE

It is now a long-standing tradition to start the World Championship season in Australia and Melbourne's Albert Park is as good a place as any to kick off the racing action.

Place Melbourne's round of the championship in a mid-season position and you can be sure that its appeal would reduce. By hosting the opening round, though, what is a mediocre track, short of great corners, becomes exciting because we're seeing the reassembling of the troops to bring the close-season to an end.

The weather tends to be good too, but what really makes the event such a popular one is the fact that the three-day programme is packed from dawn to dusk, with an amazing array of support events, all lapped up by a sport-mad crowd.

The Albert Park circuit certainly isn't a Spa-Francorchamps or a Suzuka. It doesn't have the space and topography for that. What it has, though, is a parkland setting and a lap that runs in a clockwise direction around a lake.

The first sector of the lap is point-and-squirt, brake-and-corner in format, with the Turn 1 gravel trap open to visitors at the start of the race and the sharper right at Turn 3 even more of a centre for bent front wings.

Even including the fast kink at Turn 5, it's more of the same until the tighter right at Turn 6 offers something new. For here the track comes out from under the trees and the new open feel is matched by entry to a run of sweeping corners around the far side of the lake. These aren't third gear shuffles but a seventh gear arc. Turns 11 and 12 are tricky, but the speed flows all the way to the heavy braking for Turn 13.

The run to the end of the lap is more like the first part, with short straights and tight corners under the trees. Because of this, much of the overtaking is done in the pits.

INSIDE TRACK
AUSTRALIAN GRAND PRIX

Date:	**25 March**
Circuit name:	**Albert Park**
Circuit length:	**3.295 miles/5.300km**
Number of laps:	**58**
Email:	**enquiries@grandprix.com.au**
Website:	**www.grandprix.com.au**

PREVIOUS WINNERS

2008	**Lewis Hamilton** McLAREN
2009	**Jenson Button** BRAWN
2010	**Jenson Button** McLAREN
2011	**Sebastian Vettel** RED BULL
2012	**Jenson Button** McLAREN
2013	**Kimi Raikkonen** LOTUS
2014	**Nico Rosberg** MERCEDES
2015	**Lewis Hamilton** MERCEDES
2016	**Nico Rosberg** MERCEDES
2017	**Sebastian Vettel** FERRARI

How it started: Australia had a grand prix as long ago as 1928, but the first World Championship round came in 1985, when it was run in Adelaide. Melbourne, considering itself as Australia's sporting city, wrested the deal away, taking over the slot from 1996.

Most memorable race: The 2009 grand prix was extraordinary as it was won by a team that closed at the end of 2008, but was revived at the 11th hour and renamed, as Brawn, even achieving a one-two as Rubens Barrichello followed Jenson Button home.

Do you remember when? Mika Hakkinen was leading for McLaren in 1998 until he misheard a radio message and pitted without the team expecting him. He rejoined behind team-mate David Coulthard, but the Scot let him pass as they had agreed that whichever of them led into Turn 1 would be the one who'd win.

Location: Head a mile or so south from the city centre, and the circuit is located in the middle of municipal Albert Park.

Rising star: There have been a large number of Australians racing in Formula Renault in Europe, but the highest ranked Aussie in single-seaters is 21-year-old Joey Mawson, who spent last year racing in the European F3 Championship after winning the German F4 title in 2016.

66

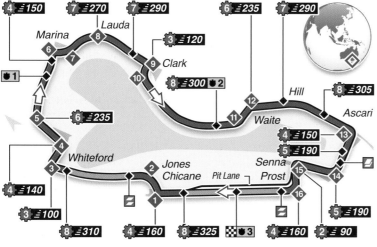

🔧 *Gear*   🏁*111* *Km/h*   ◧ *Timing sector*   ▱ *DRS detection*   ▱ *DRS activation*

2017 POLE TIME: HAMILTON (MERCEDES), 1M22.188S, 144.333MPH/232.282KPH

2017 WINNER'S AVERAGE SPEED: 133.848MPH/215.408KPH

2017 FASTEST LAP: RAIKKONEN (FERRARI), 1M26.538S, 137.077MPH/220.605KPH

LAP RECORD: M SCHUMACHER (FERRARI), 1M24.125S, 141.016MPH/226.944KPH, 2004

SAKHIR

The desire for Arab nations to host a round of the Formula 1 World Championship led to Bahrain getting in ahead of its neighbours and it has hosted a grand prix since 2004.

Having a grand prix in the Middle East made sense to F1's overlords for a number of reasons. First was the desire to improve F1's global spread. Second was that it put a grand prix into a time zone that worked for evening viewing in the key European market. Third was the fact that it placed F1 in a culture that it hadn't tapped into before. Fourth was the fact that there was a national government content to finance building a circuit from scratch and had the money to pay for world-class facilities.

So the Bahrain International Circuit was built on scrubby desert at Sakhir. Playing on this theme, circuit designer Hermann Tilke created an oasis zone around the pits and main straight, with heavily watered grass verges. Once free of Turn 3, though, the track enters its desert zone, with the rocky areas surrounding it having to be sprayed with glue to keep the dust down.

The first few corners use that Tilke trademark of a hairpin at the end of a long straight feeding immediately into a tight second corner, so the consequences of a wide line into the first means a tight one in the second.

The circuit then really opens out from Turn 3, with a long blast to Turn 4 then a great combination of esses on the gently sloping return.

From the Turn 8 hairpin, the track folds itself through a loop behind the paddock before turning left at Turn 11 and entering a climb through the sweep of Turn 12 up to its highest point at Turn 13 before descending the slope to the double-apex final corner.

INSIDE TRACK
BAHRAIN GRAND PRIX

Date:	**8 April**
Circuit name:	**Bahrain International Circuit**
Circuit length:	**3.363 miles/5.412km**
Number of laps:	**57**
Email:	**info@bic.com.bh**
Website:	**www.bahraingp.com.bh**

PREVIOUS WINNERS

2007	**Felipe Massa** FERRARI
2008	**Felipe Massa** FERRARI
2009	**Jenson Button** BRAWN
2010	**Fernando Alonso** FERRARI
2012	**Sebastian Vettel** RED BULL
2013	**Sebastian Vettel** RED BULL
2014	**Lewis Hamilton** MERCEDES
2015	**Lewis Hamilton** MERCEDES
2016	**Nico Rosberg** MERCEDES
2017	**Sebastian Vettel** FERRARI

How it started: Anxious to promote its image on the world stage, Bahrain decided to host a round of the World Championship, to become the first Arab nation to host an F1 grand prix. So the government funded the construction of a circuit and it joined the calendar in 2004.

Most memorable race: The first time that this event became a night race, in 2014, stands out for being different as it felt like a different circuit.

Do you remember when? Toyota, a team that came and went between 2002 and 2009, led the race in 2009. This was a surprise, but its drivers Jarno Trulli and Timo Glock filled the front row after running with negligible fuel load in qualifying. Glock led, then Trulli took over when he pitted. With others pitting later, they were passed by Jenson Button who won for Brawn. Trulli fell to third, Glock to seventh.

Closest finish: This was in 2014 when the Mercedes team was dominant and Lewis Hamilton led team-mate Nico Rosberg home by just 1.085s after the German saved his soft tyres for the final stint and hunted down Hamilton on medium-compound tyres.

Location: The circuit is built on rocky land at Sakhir, which lies to the south of Bahrain's capital city, Manama.

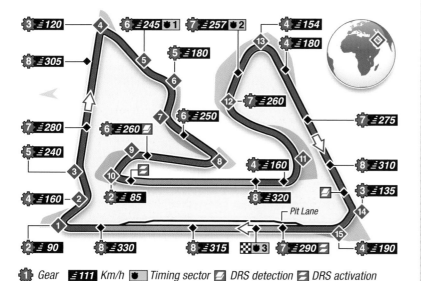

1 *Gear* **111** *Km/h* **■** *Timing sector* *DRS detection* *DRS activation*

2017 POLE TIME: **BOTTAS (MERCEDES)**, 1M28.769S, 136.380MPH/219.482KPH
2017 WINNER'S AVERAGE SPEED: 122.397MPH/196.979KPH

2017 FASTEST LAP: **HAMILTON (MERCEDES)**, 1M32.798S, 130.458MPH/209.952KPH
LAP RECORD: **M SCHUMACHER (FERRARI)**, 1M30.252S, 134.262MPH/216.074KPH, 2004

SHANGHAI

The Shanghai International Circuit offers space aplenty for drivers to really go racing, with a couple of tight corner combinations offering scope to make a move to get by.

INSIDE TRACK
CHINESE GRAND PRIX

Date:	**15 April**
Circuit name:	**Shanghai International Circuit**
Circuit length:	**3.390 miles/5.450km**
Number of laps:	**56**
Email:	**f1@china-sss.com**
Website:	**www.f1china.com.cn**

China opened its doors a crack to the western world several decades ago, with the west eying its population of billions. F1 took until 2004 to have a Chinese GP, with the sponsors eager for exposure in this most massive of markets for their products.

First, of course, they needed a circuit and one was built, with no expense spared, outside the country's most shining and burgeoning metropolis: Shanghai. To say that the land it was built on was unpromising is an understatement, as it was waterlogged. However, by sinking thousands of polystyrene blocks into the marsh, the structures were able to be constructed, with no other F1 grandstand as large and lofty as Shanghai's. In fact, the scale of everything here is vast, the paddock the size of many football pitches.

The circuit is a Hermann Tilke design, with his typically tight opening corner sequence being given a twist as it rises a steep climb then drops sharply back to Turn 3. Turn 1 is one of the most popular passing places. However, Turn 6 runs it close, as there's plenty of run-off area to provide escape options for those who get it wrong.

The drivers can then get stuck into the esses that follow behind the paddock before slowing it down for Turns 9 and 10. A short straight leads to Turn 11, the start of a hockey stick-shaped three-corner sequence onto the extremely long second straight. At its end, in true Tilke fashion, is a hairpin, scene of the most passing moves.

The final corner, Turn 16, looks innocuous, but it frequently bites drivers who run too wide on the exit.

PREVIOUS WINNERS

2008	**Lewis Hamilton** McLAREN
2009	**Sebastian Vettel** RED BULL
2010	**Jenson Button** McLAREN
2011	**Lewis Hamilton** McLAREN
2012	**Nico Rosberg** MERCEDES
2013	**Fernando Alonso** FERRARI
2014	**Lewis Hamilton** MERCEDES
2015	**Lewis Hamilton** MERCEDES
2016	**Nico Rosberg** MERCEDES
2017	**Lewis Hamilton** MERCEDES

How it started: In the years when China kept out the world, the only racing in the region was at the Portuguese protectorate of Macau on China's southern coast. However, the desire to get F1 was strong and the first Chinese GP was in 2004, won by Rubens Barrichello for Ferrari.

Do you remember when? Mercedes quit F1 in 1955 and didn't return as a team in its own right until 2010. Two years later, Nico Rosberg gave the team its first win since the 1955 Italian GP by triumphing at Shanghai in a race that turned into a battle between him and McLaren's Jenson Button. Crucially, Button was brought in for a third pitstop, to give him fresher rubber, but the team fumbled the stop and that was that.

Location: The circuit is to be found around 20 miles to the north of the centre of Shanghai in an area that was open countryside when it was built, but is not so any longer.

Rising star: The most promising young Chinese racer is 18-year-old Guan Yu Zhou who competed in the European F3 series last year and gathered three third places. Next up is Yifei Ye, a 17-year-old who impressed by taking several podium finishes in the European Formula Renault series.

68

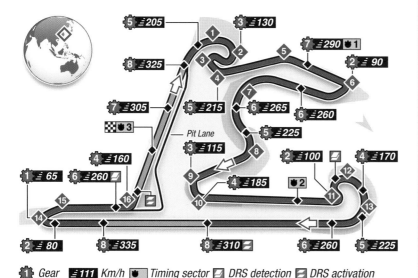

🟦 *Gear* ⬛111 *Km/h* ⬛ *Timing sector* ▱ *DRS detection* ▱ *DRS activation*

2017 POLE TIME: **HAMILTON (MERCEDES), 1M31.678S, 133.003MPH/214.049KPH**
2017 WINNER'S AVERAGE SPEED: **116.529MPH/187.535KPH**

2017 FASTEST LAP: **HAMILTON (MERCEDES), 1M35.378S, 127.844MPH/205.745KPH**
LAP RECORD: **M SCHUMACHER (FERRARI), 1M32.238S, 132.202MPH/212.759KPH, 2004**

BAKU

For this the third visit to Azerbaijan, the drivers and teams now know what to expect of a street circuit that is alternately both high-speed and open, then tight and bumpy.

When the World Championship talks of future expansion to pastures new, there's always a list of names bandied about, countries anxious to get in on the action on the one hand and those seeking to get back on board on the other. A street race in New York has long been mentioned. No one, though, was thinking of Azerbaijan, yet this oil-rich nation on the Caspian Sea put down the money and leapt to the front of the queue.

A race in the heart of its capital, Baku, was what it wanted, and it was what it got. The teams were sceptical. After all, this country had no motorsport history, but the decree from the top made it happen. Money no problem, street closures no problem.

What it brought was a circuit like no other, something discernibly different.

From the boulevard on the city's shoreline, the track adopts typical street track format, that's to say straights which lead into 90-degree bends, like Singapore's Marina Bay Circuit. However, what really makes the Baku City Circuit so special is the part around the citadel, where the streets narrow at Turn 8 and the track is right against the city wall as it starts to climb.

From Turn 12, it opens out again as the cars get to blast past some of Baku's finest buildings before dropping away to the left at Turn 15 down past the city's concert hall to a series of open kinks past a park. From there it is on to Baku Boulevard to complete the lap, at speeds of up to 210mph in top gear, past the pits and on to the best passing spot, which is into Turn 1.

INSIDE TRACK
AZERBAIJAN GRAND PRIX

Date:	**29 April**
Circuit name:	**Baku City Circuit**
Circuit length:	**3.753 miles/6.006km**
Number of laps:	**51**
Email:	**info@bakugp.az**
Website:	**www.bakugp.az**

PREVIOUS WINNERS

2016	**Nico Rosberg** MERCEDES
2017	**Daniel Ricciardo** RED BULL

How it started: Azerbaijan was keen to project an international image and so the city held a street race for GT cars in 2013 and 2014 and its ambitions soared, with the government agreeing to fund an F1 race from 2016 on a different and better-equipped street circuit.

Do you remember when? Sebastian Vettel, frustrated by Lewis Hamilton not gunning it at the restart after the second safety car in last year's race, ran into him, then drove alongside the Mercedes driver and sideswiped him for good measure.

Most challenging corner: The run of 90-degree bends have little to choose between them, but the ability to thread a needle helps drivers when they turn left at the foot of the old city wall at Turn 8, with a lack of width making it feel harder still.

Best passing spot: The longest run to a tight corner is usually a circuit's best spot for overtaking and Baku is no different, so the most likely place for a move to be completed is into Turn 1, with drivers having been able to start that charge at Turn 15.

Location: As a city centre circuit, it comes as no surprise that the circuit is laid out in Baku's city centre... The pits complex is located on prestigious Baku Boulevard, with a view through a park to the Caspian Sea.

Rising star: There is still not a young Azerbaijani racer on the international scene, but you can be sure that this oil-rich nation will be funding one to start climbing racing's ladder in the years to come.

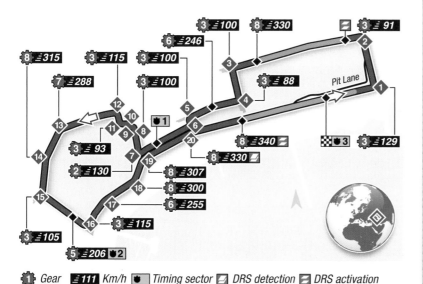

🅖 *Gear*　🔳**111** *Km/h*　🔲 *Timing sector*　🏁 *DRS detection*　🏁 *DRS activation*

2017 POLE TIME: HAMILTON (MERCEDES),
1M40.593S, 133.491MPH/214.834KPH
2017 WINNER'S AVERAGE SPEED:
92.072MPH/148.176KPH

2017 FASTEST LAP: VETTEL (FERRARI),
1M43.441S, 129.816MPH/208.919KPH
LAP RECORD: VETTEL (FERRARI), 1M43.441S,
129.816MPH/208.919KPH, 2017

BARCELONA

The first two corners invariably provide excitement on the opening lap, but the Circuit de Barcelona-Catalunya no longer shows F1 machinery at its most dynamic best.

Until Fernando Alonso came along, Spain had been short on F1 heroes, to put it mildly. Yet the nation has a long history in hosting a grand prix and the Circuit de Barcelona-Catalunya, as it has been renamed, quickly became one of the most visited circuits because it made an ideal testing venue, with its mixture of corners and generally fine weather.

As a circuit for racing, however, it's not what it was, mainly because it lost its trademark swoop in 2007 when a chicane was inserted to interrupt the downhill sweep all the way from Turn 12 to the first corner.

The rest of the lap has remained unchanged, meaning a downhill run to the first corner, which combines with the second to make a right/left combination that some struggle to complete on the

opening lap and have run through the giant gravel bed there. Turn 3 is a rising right that seems to go on forever before drivers find a short straight to an uphill right then a short straight to a sharply dropping left at Turn 5.

One of the hardest corners is Turn 7, a 90-degree left, in which the track veers uphill and immediately kinks right at Turn 8. Turn 9 demands commitment without offering any line of sight until entry has been made over the brow.

The second overtaking place comes at the end of the downhill infield straight, with Turn 10 having plenty of run-off. Turn 11 is a flick on the ascent to Turn 12 before the track flattens out, then falls from Turn 13 down to the chicane before feeding the cars back onto the approach to the final corner.

INSIDE TRACK
SPANISH GRAND PRIX

Date:	**13 May**
Circuit name:	**Circuit de Barcelona-Catalunya**
Circuit length:	**2.892 miles/4.654km**
Number of laps:	**66**
Email:	**info@circuitcat.com**
Website:	**www.circuitcat.com**

PREVIOUS WINNERS

2008	**Kimi Raikkonen** FERRARI
2009	**Jenson Button** BRAWN
2010	**Mark Webber** RED BULL
2011	**Sebastian Vettel** RED BULL
2012	**Pastor Maldonado** WILLIAMS
2013	**Fernando Alonso** FERRARI
2014	**Lewis Hamilton** MERCEDES
2015	**Nico Rosberg** MERCEDES
2016	**Max Verstappen** RED BULL
2017	**Lewis Hamilton** MERCEDES

How it started: Spain has held a round of the World Championship since 1951. That was run in the Pedralbes district of Barcelona and later the city's Montjuich Park held the race, with Jarama, outside Madrid, and Jerez, in the south-west of the country, also having goes. In 1991, though, this new circuit was awarded the race and it has kept it ever since.

Do you remember when? Williams returned from the wilderness in 2012, when the accident-prone Pastor Maldonado came good to not only take a surprise pole position but also go on score his one and only F1 win, and put the team back on a winning track for the first time since Juan Pablo Montoya won the final round of the 2004 series at Interlagos.

Location: The circuit is located in rolling hills at Montmelo some 15 miles north of the centre of Barcelona.

Rising star: After Fernando Alonso and Carlos Sainz Jr, the next best Spanish driver is F2 racer Roberto Merhi but, at 26, he is considered to be too old for F1, so 20-year-old Alex Palou is the next in line after a year spent racing in F3 in Japan before impressing in F2 at the end of the year.

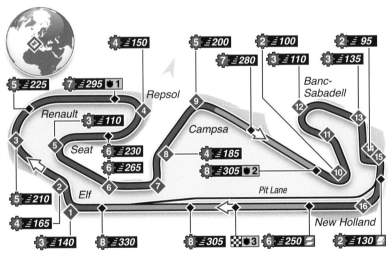

🏁 Gear   **111** Km/h   ⬛ Timing sector   ⬟ DRS detection   ⬟ DRS activation

2017 POLE TIME: **HAMILTON (MERCEDES)**, 1M19.149S, 131.561MPH/211.727KPH
2017 WINNER'S AVERAGE SPEED: 119.338MPH/192.056KPH

2017 FASTEST LAP: **HAMILTON (MERCEDES)**, 1M23.593S, 124.567MPH/200.471KPH
LAP RECORD: **RAIKKONEN (FERRARI)**, 1M21.670S, 127.500MPH/205.192KPH, 2008

MONACO

Some people call this an anachronism, but this charming street circuit on the Riviera offers welcome variety, glamour and a wonderful backdrop that more modern tracks do not.

When sports strive to reinvent themselves continuously, to move to ever larger and more modern stadia, there's a risk that their lifeblood will be thinned. F1 still treasures some old favourites, with its annual return to Monaco providing not just a link to motor racing's earliest days but also to something different.

For those working at the event, there are a myriad inconveniences, with working conditions cramped and only the tiniest of paddocks near the pit garages and the rest of the show over a pedestrian bridge down by the harbourside. Yet, and it's a big yet, F1 needs Monaco more with every passing year. To many, Monaco is F1 and that connection should never be lost.

It remains, though, a circuit hemmed in by buildings, with almost no space to stretch its elbows or indeed for the cars to stretch their legs. The barriers are ever-present, yet the driving challenge that requires precision has been diluted since races were made shorter. In the 1950s, they lasted more than three hours here, with manual gear changes adding to the likelihood of a slip-up, with many a tired driver missing a gear change and sliding into the straw bales, as they were then, and so out of the race.

The lap remains little changed, with Ste Devote still a tight first corner followed by a twisting climb to tricky Massenet, then Casino Square before diving downhill through Mirabeau and the hairpin towards the tunnel. The defining sector is the stretch running alongside the harbourfront, from the chicane, through Tabac and then the flattened chicanes around the piscine and then the tight end to the lap.

INSIDE TRACK
MONACO GRAND PRIX

Date:	**27 May**
Circuit name:	**Circuit de Monaco**
Circuit length:	**2.075 miles/3.339km**
Number of laps:	**78**
Email:	**info@acm.mc**
Website:	**www.acm.mc**

PREVIOUS WINNERS

2008	**Lewis Hamilton** McLAREN
2009	**Jenson Button** BRAWN
2010	**Mark Webber** RED BULL
2011	**Sebastian Vettel** RED BULL
2012	**Mark Webber** RED BULL
2013	**Nico Rosberg** MERCEDES
2014	**Nico Rosberg** MERCEDES
2015	**Nico Rosberg** MERCEDES
2016	**Lewis Hamilton** MERCEDES
2017	**Sebastian Vettel** FERRARI

How it started: Back in 1929, a cigarette manufacturer by the name of Anthony Nogues convinced the Monegasque royal family that the principality needed to have a motor race. Few thought that it would go beyond that first year. How wrong they were as, bar a break from 1938 to 1948, this street race has been a constant in the ever-changing world of motor racing.

Do you remember when? One driver, Derek Daly, found the least successful way to impress a team boss when he got it wrong at the start of the 1980 Monaco GP and clipped the back of Bruno Giacomelli's Alfa Romeo and cartwheeled his Tyrrell over it before hitting Alain Prost's McLaren then flipping again and landing on his team-mate Jean-Pierre Jarier.

Location: The circuit starts down near Monte Carlo's main harbour and climbs the hill behind before returning. It only gained proper pit garages a few years ago.

Rising star: Although many F1 drivers live in Monaco for tax reasons, few true Monegasques have starred as drivers. This is about to change as Ferrari development driver Charles Leclerc looks to be the real deal, cleaning up in last year's FIA F2 series with a round to spare.

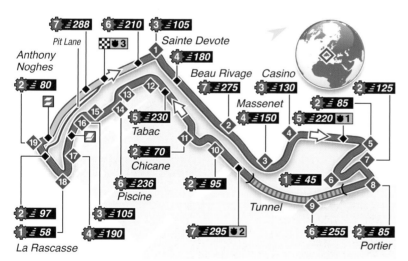

🏁 Gear 📊 Km/h 📹 Timing sector ⚡ DRS detection ⚡ DRS activation

---

2017 POLE TIME: RAIKKONEN (FERRARI),
1M12.178S, 103.420MPH/166.438KPH
2017 WINNER'S AVERAGE SPEED:
92.649MPH/149.105KPH

2017 FASTEST LAP: PEREZ (FORCE INDIA),
1M14.820S, 99.768MPH/160.561KPH
LAP RECORD: M SCHUMACHER (FERRARI),
1M14.439S, 100.369MPH/161.528KPH, 2004

Monaco's street circuit is a place like no other. There's little space for overtaking, but every turn has an identifiable backdrop. This is Lewis Hamilton feeding his Mercedes through the Grand Hotel hairpin.

MONTREAL

Most grand prix circuits are situated in the countryside, but Montreal is a short hop from downtown and its metropolitan flavour makes it one of the tracks the F1 teams love the most.

Until Jacques Villeneuve won the 1997 F1 title, Canada's F1 glory was encapsulated in one driver: Jacques' father Gilles Villeneuve. Never a world champion, but a six-time grand prix winner and an inspiration for his sheer pace and derring-do, he had fans the world over. Yet, Canada has had a grand prix since before his time, starting in 1967, and it continues to be an extremely popular race on F1's world tour.

Visited in early summer, rain isn't unheard of in this part of Quebec, but the sun generally shines and all involved love visiting Montreal, which is a fun and vibrant city.

The circuit on the Ile Notre-Dame feels wide open but is anything but, as it's hemmed in by the rowing lake used in the 1976 Olympic Games on one side and the river on the other, leaving it with a long, thin shape and little space to play with.

There's a slight flick to the right before the first corner, a scene of frequent contact on the opening lap as drivers jockey for position and, if not there, then at Virage Senna which is only 50 metres further on. The track then enters a run with trees lining its course all the way through the twists and turns from Turn 3 to Turn 8, with passing all but impossible, before it emerges back into a feeling of space and a more open blast to L'Epingle, the hairpin at the furthest point from the pits. Plenty of passing manoeuvres are attempted here.

It's then simply a flat-out charge alongside the rowing lake back to the pits, with the cars hitting almost 200mph before culminating in a right/left chicane.

INSIDE TRACK
CANADIAN GRAND PRIX

Date:	10 June
Circuit name:	Circuit Gilles Villeneuve
Circuit length:	2.710 miles/4.361km
Number of laps:	70
Email:	info@circuitgillesvilleneuve.ca
Website:	www.circuitgillesvilleneuve.ca

PREVIOUS WINNERS

2007	**Lewis Hamilton** McLAREN
2008	**Robert Kubica** BMW SAUBER
2010	**Lewis Hamilton** McLAREN
2011	**Jenson Button** McLAREN
2012	**Lewis Hamilton** McLAREN
2013	**Sebastian Vettel** RED BULL
2014	**Daniel Ricciardo** RED BULL
2015	**Lewis Hamilton** MERCEDES
2016	**Lewis Hamilton** MERCEDES
2017	**Lewis Hamilton** MERCEDES

How it started: The Canadian GP had been held at Mosport Park in Ontario and Mont Tremblant in Quebec before the city of Montreal stuck its hand up to have a race on its own patch as Canada became caught up in F1 fever thanks to Gilles Villeneuve, with its first grand prix being held in 1978, which Villeneuve fittingly won in his Ferrari.

Do you remember when? The BMW Sauber team took its one and only win here in 2008, in fact claiming a one-two through Robert Kubica and Nick Heidfeld. Early leader Lewis Hamilton hit the rear of Kimi Raikkonen's stationary Ferrari when attempting to leave the pits during a safety car intervention, and took both out of the running for the day to set up the Saubers.

Location: The circuit is reached from downtown Montreal by car across the Pont de la Concorde over the St Lawrence River or via a metroline under it.

Rising star: Canada had waited a long time between the F1 departure of Jacques Villeneuve in 2006 and the arrival of Lance Stroll last year. After 19-year-old Stroll, the next most promising Canadian tyro is 22-year-old Nicholas Latifi who spent 2017 racing in the FIA F2 series, winning one of the two races at Silverstone.

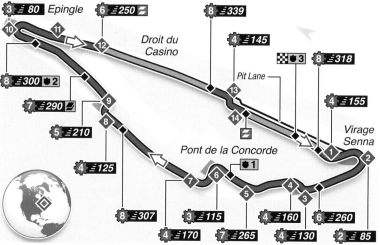

Gear   111 Km/h   Timing sector   DRS detection   DRS activation

2017 POLE TIME: HAMILTON (MERCEDES),
1M11.459S, 131.600MPH/219.700KPH
2017 WINNER'S AVERAGE SPEED:
122.264MPH/196.766KPH

2017 FASTEST LAP: HAMILTON (MERCEDES),
1M14.551S, 130.853MPH/210.588KPH
LAP RECORD: BARRICHELLO (FERRARI),
1M13.622S, 132.511MPH/213.256KPH, 2004

PAUL RICARD

Few circuits get a second shot at the big time, but a massively revamped Paul Ricard is ready to welcome F1 this summer for the first time since 1990 for the return of the French GP.

Blue stripes are what hit you most when you visit Paul Ricard. Added when it was brought back to life as a test venue, these stripes lie beyond the red-and-white kerbs in concentric bands, before they become red beyond that. They serve as a warning for drivers who stray too far, with increased abrasiveness the further from the track a car travels.

From its opening in 1970, Paul Ricard was known for being open, very fast and flowing, with the Signes curve at the top end of the Mistral Straight its most fearsome bend. This all changed after Elio de Angelis inverted his Brabham when testing there in 1986 and died of his injuries, and it was chopped from 3.6 miles to 2.3 to keep speeds down.

After the French GP moved to Magny-Cours in 1991, the circuit dwindled but was reinvented after Bernie Ecclestone bought it in 1999 and turned it into a high-tech test facility, bringing it back to an impressive length, and given a nature similar to the original, with a gentle descent through the "S" de la Verrerie then a chicane to the lowest point at Sainte Baume.

Then comes the old back section, a flat-out ascent. However, there are many track layouts and F1 will use the one with a chicane midway along the 1.12-mile Mistral Straight, to keep speeds in check. Indeed, it's calculated that the cars will hit 213mph before the chicane and then hit that same speed again on the approach to Signes.

From Signes, Le Beausset provides a chance to overtake on the way into what is a long, long right before some sweeping turns and then the sharp final corner.

INSIDE TRACK
FRENCH GRAND PRIX

Date:	**24 June**
Circuit name:	**Circuit Paul Ricard**
Circuit length:	**3.630 miles/5.842km**
Number of laps:	**tba**
Email:	**circuit@circuitpaulricard.com**
Website:	**www.circuitpaulricard.com**

PREVIOUS WINNERS

1978	**Mario Andretti** LOTUS
1980	**Alan Jones** WILLIAMS
1982	**Rene Arnoux** RENAULT
1983	**Alain Prost** RENAULT
1985	**Nelson Piquet** BRABHAM
1986	**Nigel Mansell** WILLIAMS
1987	**Nigel Mansell** WILLIAMS
1988	**Alain Prost** McLAREN
1989	**Alain Prost** McLAREN
1990	**Alain Prost** FERRARI

How it started: Purpose-built circuits were few and far between until this became one of a new crop in 1970, with safety standards way in advance of its rivals and modern pit buildings too. The whole project was financed by drinks manufacturer Paul Ricard, whose pastis was considered almost a national drink.

Second incarnation: Bernie Ecclestone bought Paul Ricard in 1999 and it was redeveloped as a high-tech test circuit, reopening in 2002, with competitive racing returning in 2009. It is still popular as a test circuit, helped by its mild climate and superior facilities.

Most memorable race: If only for the dramatic accident of the start, the 1989 French GP stands out, with Mauricio Gugelmin's March doing aerobatics at the start and ripping the rear wing off Nigel Mansell's Ferrari. Alain Prost then won as he pleased on a weekend when he announced he was to leave McLaren.

Location: The circuit sits on largely flat land on a plateau uphill from France's Riviera, some 20 miles to the north-west of Toulon and 35 miles east of Marseille.

Rising star: France has been looking for a new star for a long time. It had one in Jules Bianchi until his crash at Suzuka, and now has Esteban Ocon and Pierre Gasly in F1, with F2 racer Norman Nato the next in line.

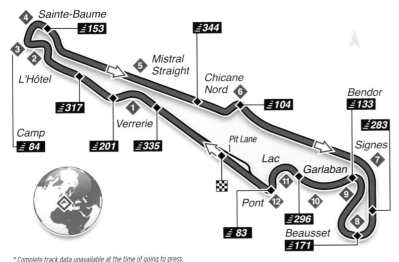

* Complete track data unavailable at the time of going to press.

🏎 *Gear* ⏱*111* *Km/h* ◉ *Timing sector* ▱ *DRS detection* ▱ *DRS activation*

1990 POLE TIME: MANSELL (FERRARI), 1M04.402S, 131.530MPH/211.677KPH	**1990 FASTEST LAP:** MANSELL (FERRARI), 1M08.012S, 125.410MPH/201.828KPH, 1990
1990 WINNER'S AVERAGE SPEED: 121.626MPH/195.738KPH	**LAP RECORD:** MANSELL (FERRARI), 1M08.012S, 125.410MPH/201.828KPH, 1990

RED BULL RING

Some of the world's best circuits benefit from having some rolling land to add to the challenge. The Red Bull Ring certainly has plenty of slopes but remains short on places to pass.

There can be no doubt that the Red Bull Ring offers something different. Approached along a wide valley, the entry road presents the back of a stunning grandstand framed by one thing: a mountain. The grandstand towering over the start/finish straight is at the lowest point of the course and the track is draped across the meadows and runs through wooded sections above that. This is the antithesis of Silverstone.

Anyone who tries to walk up to the first turn, now known as OMV-Kurve, will have burning calf muscles, as the climb is steep. Once there, it flattens out, allowing space for the rescue vehicles to retrieve the cars that almost inevitably clash there…

Then comes the most wonderful sweep up the hillside to the second best place to try a passing move: the Remus Kurve. Like Turn 1, it's steep on the way in, then flattens out. But it's tighter, and ambition has been many a driver's downfall here. Running along the face of the slope, the track drops through the Rauch Kurve, a possible passing place as much on exit as entry.

From here, the track is sinuous in shape as it falls away down the slope to the back of the paddock before kicking up again out of the Wurth Kurve to run through the woods to the trickiest corner of the lap, the Rindt Kurve, where the track drops away into something of a compression at the last corner before firing the cars back on to the start/finish straight.

It's not a demanding circuit, as there are few really fast corners. Walk the perimeter, though, and it's easy to spot a few, albeit these are parts of the track that begat it – the Osterreichring.

INSIDE TRACK
AUSTRIAN GRAND PRIX

Date:	**1 July**
Circuit name:	**Red Bull Ring**
Circuit length:	**2.688 miles/4.326km**
Number of laps:	**71**
Email:	**information@projekt-spielberg.at**
Website:	**www.projekt-spielberg.at**

PREVIOUS WINNERS

1998	**Mika Hakkinen** McLAREN
1999	**Eddie Irvine** FERRARI
2000	**Mika Hakkinen** McLAREN
2001	**David Coulthard** McLAREN
2002	**Michael Schumacher** FERRARI
2003	**Michael Schumacher** FERRARI
2014	**Nico Rosberg** MERCEDES
2015	**Nico Rosberg** MERCEDES
2016	**Lewis Hamilton** MERCEDES
2017	**Valtteri Bottas** MERCEDES

How it started: Austria's first grand prix was held on the old military airfield at Zeltweg in 1963 as a non-championship event. Promoted to championship status, it didn't earn an encore as the track was too rough and bumpy. Instead, the purpose-built Osterreichring, one kilometre away, was used from 1970 until 1987, after which it was thought too fast. Cut back in length to make it slower, the circuit re-emerged as the Red Bull Ring in 1997.

Do you remember when? Ferrari upset everyone in 2002 when it resorted to team orders to force Rubens Barrichello back behind the team's points leader Michael Schumacher, even though this was only the sixth round of 17 and he already had almost double the points of his chief rival.

Location: F1 came to this part of Austria some 45 miles north-west of Graz in the early 1960s simply because there was an airfield, Zeltweg. The Red Bull Ring is on a sloping site just above the valley floor on the north side.

Rising star: The land that produced Jochen Rindt, Niki Lauda and Gerhard Berger needs another F1 driver of its own to cheer. The best placed to achieve this is World Series Formula V8 3.5 racer Rene Binder, but he's 26 and has been at this level since 2012.

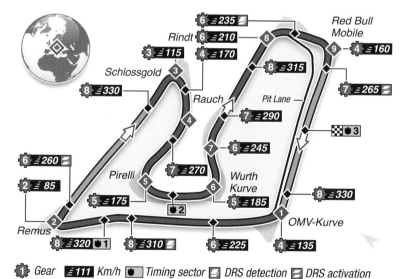

🔧 *Gear* 　🔳 *111 Km/h* 　⏱ *Timing sector* 　 *DRS detection* 　 *DRS activation*

2017 POLE TIME: BOTTAS (MERCEDES), 1M04.251S, 150.333MPH/241.938KPH
2017 WINNER'S AVERAGE SPEED: 139.657MPH/224.757KPH

2017 FASTEST LAP: HAMILTON (MERCEDES), 1M07.411S, 143.286MPH/230.597KPH
LAP RECORD: HAMILTON (MERCEDES), 1M07.411S, 143.286MPH/230.597KPH, 2017

SILVERSTONE

This is the circuit that hosted the inaugural round of the first World Championship back in 1950, and the essence of the fast, open circuit raced on then is still present today.

Many circuits that were created in the late 1940s and early 1950s had the same raw ingredient: a disused World War Two airfield. Silverstone remains the greatest of these and has done so by constant evolution, changing its layout over the years, but not its nature. In comparison to modern, built-from-scratch circuits, it might have shortcomings in some of its facilities, but it has two things that trump those: character and history.

Since the circuit was given a new pit and paddock complex at what was once its far end, between Club and Abbey, the track has a different feel, but its orientation is largely the same, bar the different starting point.

What is now the opening sector is kicked off with a seventh gear flick, Abbey, then slows right down at Village,

a great place to try a passing move. Once through the loop, it's then flat-out down the Wellington Straight, to Brooklands, another place to try a pass.

After rounding double-apex Luffield, it's a blast past the old pits to seventh gear Copse. If this tests a driver's bravery, then the sweepers through Maggotts and Becketts stretch them further. This is the best viewing point in qualifying, where the drivers' commitment is phenomenal, and their cars show why F1 remains the sport's pinnacle, as they turn in at 185mph and jink left, right, left, right in a flash.

Onto the Hangar Straight, the drivers can relax before diving through Stowe into the dip at Vale before dropping down to second gear as they turn left to finish the lap with a flourish through the long, long right at Club.

INSIDE TRACK
BRITISH GRAND PRIX

Date:	8 July
Circuit name:	Silverstone
Circuit length:	3.659 miles/5.900km
Number of laps:	52
Email:	sales@silverstone-circuit.co.uk
Website:	www.silverstone-circuit.co.uk

PREVIOUS WINNERS

2008	**Lewis Hamilton** McLAREN
2009	**Sebastian Vettel** RED BULL
2010	**Mark Webber** RED BULL
2011	**Fernando Alonso** FERRARI
2012	**Mark Webber** RED BULL
2013	**Nico Rosberg** MERCEDES
2014	**Lewis Hamilton** MERCEDES
2015	**Lewis Hamilton** MERCEDES
2016	**Lewis Hamilton** MERCEDES
2017	**Lewis Hamilton** MERCEDES

How it started: There were only two years from its conversion from airfield to race circuit to the opening race of the first-ever World Championship in 1950. Twenty-two cars turned up and it was the Alfa Romeo show as its four works entries filled the first four places on the grid and were the first three home, with Giuseppe Farina victorious.

Do you remember when? There was a tumultuous end to the 1975 British GP when there was a heavy downpour at what was then the far end of the circuit, at Stowe, and car after car aquaplaned off, with McLaren's Emerson Fittipaldi declared winner on countback as he had been in the pits changing to wet weather tyres when all but four other drivers had slid off. With results being declared a lap back, second place went to Carlos Pace, whose Brabham was in the catch fencing.

Location: Centrally located in England rather than near any major cities, Silverstone is near Towcester in Northamptonshire.

Rising star: British drivers are doing extremely well in the junior international formulae, with Oliver Rowland ending 2017 in third place in F2, Lando Norris landing the European F3 title and George Russell being crowned champion in GP3.

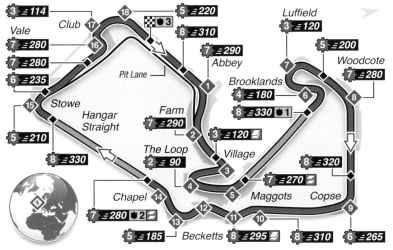

Club · Vale · 18 · Luffield · Abbey · Pit Lane · Woodcote · Brooklands · Stowe · Hangar Straight · Farm · The Loop · Village · Chapel · Maggotts · Copse · Becketts

🏁 **Gear**   **111** Km/h   ⏱ Timing sector   DRS detection   DRS activation

---

2017 POLE TIME: HAMILTON (MERCEDES),
1M26.600S, 152.168MPH/244.891KPH
2017 WINNER'S AVERAGE SPEED:
137.448MPH/221.201KPH

2017 FASTEST LAP: HAMILTON (MERCEDES),
1M30.621S, 145.416MPH/234.025KPH
LAP RECORD: HAMILTON (MERCEDES),
1M30.621S, 145.416MPH/234.025KPH, 2017

HOCKENHEIM

Sense has returned to the World Championship with France and Germany being restored to the calendar. This means that Hockenheim, with its grandstand-lined stadium section, is back.

It's crystal clear that time stands still for no F1 team, with developments needed for every race to stay in the hunt. Circuits have to move on too and while it's great to have Hockenheim back on the calendar, it now has the feel of a circuit from a previous decade.

When it hosted a grand prix for the first time, in 1970, the Hockenheimring was seen as ultra-modern, especially compared to the rival Nurburgring. When F1 made the move across to Hockenheim fulltime in 1977, it was still thought of as such, even though it was a lap of two halves, with the cars leaving the stadium section to disappear onto a loop through the forest.

However, its nature changed forever when the forest loop was lopped off in 2002. Instead of following the sixth-gear first corner with a flat-out blast along arcing straights between the trees, interrupted only by three chicanes, the track turns sharp right at the Bernie Ecclestone hairpin. Then comes the Parabolika, a long, curving run at up to 190mph towards the hairpin at Spitzkehre. This is a definite passing place, with plenty of run-off for those who got it wrong.

The track then doubles back towards the stadium section again, via Turns 8 to 11, before the cars burst back in front of the fans through Mobil 1 Kurve and then snake through Sachskurve and back across to the grandstands for the double right at Sudkurve.

The crowds have dwindled since Michael Schumacher was in his pomp, but the noise emitting from the grandstands, with air horns being sounded, is still a great advertisement for F1.

INSIDE TRACK
GERMAN GRAND PRIX

Date:	22 July
Circuit name:	Hockenheimring
Circuit length:	2.842 miles/4.574km
Number of laps:	67
Email:	info@hockenheimring.de
Website:	www.hockenheimring.de

PREVIOUS WINNERS

2002	**Michael Schumacher** FERRARI
2003	**Juan Pablo Montoya** WILLIAMS
2004	**Michael Schumacher** FERRARI
2005	**Fernando Alonso** RENAULT
2006	**Michael Schumacher** FERRARI
2008	**Lewis Hamilton** McLAREN
2010	**Fernando Alonso** FERRARI
2012	**Fernando Alonso** FERRARI
2014	**Nico Rosberg** MERCEDES
2016	**Lewis Hamilton** MERCEDES

How it started: Built by Mercedes in 1932 as a circuit for testing its road cars, the circuit was 4.779 miles in length. The southern end was chopped in 1965 to make space for a motorway, with a twisting stadium section at the foot of giant grandstands added to keep the lap length up. Then it rose to international prominence with its first grand prix in 1970.

Do you remember when? One of the most dramatic and frightening moments in Hockenheim history occurred in 1994 when Jos Verstappen's Benetton was engulfed in flame when a refueling hose remained open after being pulled back from the nozzle. He was quickly out of the car, but he and five mechanics needed treatment for burns.

Location: The circuit nestles in a forested area on the outskirts of Hockenheim, with Heidelberg the closest major town, 15 miles to the north. Frankfurt is the closest city, some 40 miles further to the north.

Rising star: F1's waiting room, F2, had no German racers in line to become the next Sebastian Vettel. One formula below that, however, there was 20-year-old Maximilian Gunther, who won five races in last year's European Formula 3 Championship and finished third overall.

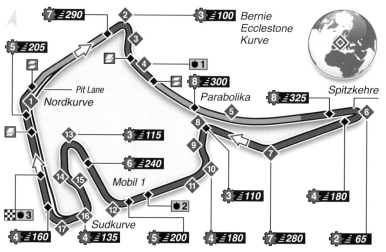

Bernie Ecclestone Kurve

Parabolika

Spitzkehre

Pit Lane
Nordkurve

Mobil 1

Sudkurve

Gear | ◖111 Km/h | Timing sector | DRS detection | DRS activation

2016 POLE TIME: **ROSBERG (MERCEDES)**, 1M14.363S, 137.591MPH/221.432KPH
2016 WINNER'S AVERAGE SPEED: **125.918MPH/202.646KPH**

2016 FASTEST LAP: **RICCIARDO (RED BULL)**, 1M18.442S, 130.437MPH/209.918KPH
LAP RECORD: **RAIKKONEN (McLAREN)**, 1M14.917S, 136.567MPH/219.784KPH, 2004

HUNGARORING

Soaring summer temperatures and a queue of cars seem to be two definite features of any grand prix at the Hungaroring, as overtaking is still very difficult at this scenic circuit.

Nobody really saw the Hungarian GP approaching before it was added to the World Championship roster in 1986. After all, the country was still communist, but a deal was done by that arch dealmaker Bernie Ecclestone. If the teams were sceptical, a crowd of 200,000 amazed them and, since then, the Hungaroring has been a firm fixture.

This F1 badge of approval doesn't make it a great circuit, though, for its twisting nature makes the racing close but overtaking rare. This is a shame, as minor tweaking could open the lap out.

The rolling setting provides great viewing from the grandstands on either side of the valley it occupies. Those sitting above sloping Turn 1 are guaranteed action, as this is the most likely spot for an overtaking move to be attempted, whether a driver opts for the wide-in, tight-out exit or the reverse.

Dropping through the left at Turn 2 and the dip after Turn 3, drivers are met with the fast flick through Turn 4, with a relatively poor line of sight before they turn in. From Turn 5, the track flattens out and winds its way through twists all the way to Turn 10, with precious little scope for passing.

The track then drops from Turn 11 for its return leg before drivers have to slow for Turn 12, a corner that was tightened in 2003.

The last two corners are both uphill, and for drivers the key is being able to get the power down as early as possible for Turn 14, as getting close to a rival's tail here is essential if they want to make a passing bid into Turn 1.

INSIDE TRACK
HUNGARIAN GRAND PRIX

Date:	**29 July**
Circuit name:	**Hungaroring**
Circuit length:	**2.722 miles/4.381km**
Number of laps:	**70**
Email:	**office@hungaroring.hu**
Website:	**www.hungaroring.hu**

PREVIOUS WINNERS

2008	**Heikki Kovalainen** McLAREN
2009	**Lewis Hamilton** McLAREN
2010	**Mark Webber** RED BULL
2011	**Jenson Button** McLAREN
2012	**Lewis Hamilton** McLAREN
2013	**Lewis Hamilton** MERCEDES
2014	**Daniel Ricciardo** RED BULL
2015	**Sebastian Vettel** FERRARI
2016	**Lewis Hamilton** MERCEDES
2017	**Sebastian Vettel** FERRARI

How it started: Opened in 1986, when Hungary was still behind the Iron Curtain, it was a rarity as a world-class racing circuit in a communist country, but it has been in increasing use ever since, especially since the liberalisation of Eastern Europe with the end of the Cold War in 1991.

Do you remember when? One of the greatest surprises in F1 history very nearly happened here in 1997. Reigning World Champion Damon Hill had been dropped by Williams and had to make do with a less competitive Arrows. However, despite having a best result of sixth before the Hungarian GP, he qualified third and led until hydraulic problems slowed his car, letting old team-mate Jacques Villeneuve past halfway around the final lap.

Location: Set on a hillside just outside the village of Mogyorod, the circuit is a dozen miles to the north-east of the capital Budapest.

Rising star: A Hungarian driver, Ferenc Szisz, won the first-ever grand prix, in France in 1906. None of his compatriots have come even close since. Indeed, only Zsolt Baumgartner has reached F1. Last year, there wasn't even one young Hungarian shining in single-seaters, and the most popular Hungarian racer was Norbert Kiss, a frontrunner on the European truck racing scene.

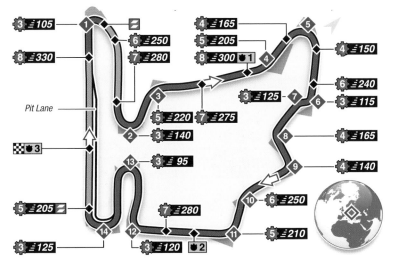

🅖 Gear   **111** Km/h   ⏱ Timing sector   DRS detection   DRS activation

2017 POLE TIME: VETTEL (FERRARI),
1M16.276S, 128.481MPH/206.770KPH
2017 WINNER'S AVERAGE SPEED:
114.572MPH/184.386KPH

2017 FASTEST LAP: ALONSO (McLAREN),
1M20.182S, 122.222MPH/196.697KPH
LAP RECORD: M SCHUMACHER (FERRARI),
1M19.071S, 123.828MPH/199.282KPH, 2004

SPA-FRANCORCHAMPS

This stunning Belgian circuit is old school in the best way possible. Its fastest stretches have long since been lopped off, but the nature of the place remains clear to see.

If you want to build a great circuit, you need gradient changes. Tick, as Spa-Francorchamps has plenty of that. A beautiful backdrop is good too. Tick, as the circuit runs through the Ardennes forest, and long shots of the track show it running between the trees and occasionally popping into clearings around its 4.352-mile lap. Throw in a handful of great, challenging corners and then you have a track worthy of F1. And long may it remain so.

The lap starts with a short uphill sprint to La Source, with this right-hand hairpin a possible passing place but with the risk of race-affecting wing damage.

Then it's steeply downhill past the old pits to the circuit's trademark corner – Eau Rouge. Left at the bottom of the slope turns instantly to a right then a left at the crest. Long considered as a corner that only the brave took without coming off the throttle, the downforce gained by cars in recent years mean that everyone does that now, in seventh gear ...

The track keeps on climbing to Les Combes where, through a right/left twitch, the cars then start descending again, first through the tightish right at Rivage then on through wonderful Pouhon, a left that goes on and on.

The Fagnes sweepers are relatively tame, before the lap reaches its lowest point at Curve Paul Frere where it rejoins the original 9.236-mile circuit on what was its return leg from the neighbouring valley for a really high-speed ascent back towards the pits. Blanchimont is taken at 185mph in sixth gear before the Bus Stop chicane slows everything down.

INSIDE TRACK
BELGIAN GRAND PRIX

Date:	26 August
Circuit name:	Spa-Francorchamps
Circuit length:	4.352 miles/7.004km
Number of laps:	44
Email:	secretariat@spa-francorchamps.be
Website:	www.spa-francorchamps.be

PREVIOUS WINNERS

2008	**Felipe Massa** FERRARI
2009	**Kimi Raikkonen** FERRARI
2010	**Lewis Hamilton** McLAREN
2011	**Sebastian Vettel** RED BULL
2012	**Jenson Button** McLAREN
2013	**Sebastian Vettel** RED BULL
2014	**Daniel Ricciardo** RED BULL
2015	**Lewis Hamilton** MERCEDES
2016	**Nico Rosberg** MERCEDES
2017	**Lewis Hamilton** MERCEDES

How it started: The circuit was created in 1924 out of a triangular combination of public roads, even with a chicane between some houses on the Masta straight in the neighbouring valley as the lap ran through forests and fields.

Do you remember when? One of the most dramatic moments in Spa-Francorchamps's F1 history occurred on the exit of La Source on the opening lap in 1998 when David Coulthard's McLaren was tipped sideways and car after car clattered into each other, leaving four out of the running. Later, in heavy rain and spray, Coulthard was told to move aside to let Michael Schumacher lap him. He did so but, as he slowed to let him by, Schumacher hit him, ripping a wheel off his Ferrari.

Location: Spa is the most popular resort town in the hilly Ardennes region in the east of Belgium and the circuit is some five miles south-east of there, just outside the village of Francorchamps.

Rising star: The land that produced Jacky Ickx and Thierry Boutsen has long sought a talent to follow in their wheeltracks and 19-year-old Max Defourny looks best-placed to do so, having been a frontrunner in the European Formula Renault series in 2017 and even made his F3 debut.

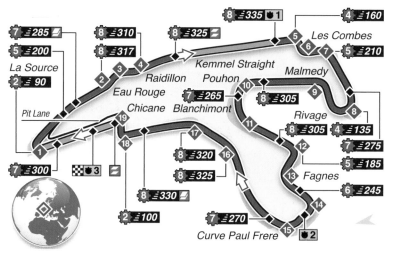

Gear | *111 Km/h* | *Timing sector* | *DRS detection* | *DRS activation*

2017 POLE TIME: **HAMILTON (MERCEDES),** 1M42.553S, 152.774MPH/245.867KPH
2017 WINNER'S AVERAGE SPEED: **135.572MPH/218.183KPH**

2017 FASTEST LAP: **VETTEL (FERRARI),** 1M46.577S, 147.006MPH/236.583KPH
LAP RECORD: **VETTEL (FERRARI), 1M46.577S,** 147.006MPH/236.583KPH, 2017

MONZA

While F1 races come and go, as long as there's a World Championship, there should always be an Italian GP and it should always be at the historic Monza circuit.

People who think that they know Monza from watching races here on the television are in for a real treat when they visit the place, as lurking in the infield is a key part of its past: a massive and now sadly decaying banked corner. This was one end of the banked oval that could be used on its own or combined with what is pretty much the current track to form a 6.214-mile lap that must have been pretty terrifying when it opened in 1922. F1 last used the banking in 1960 when Phil Hill, fittingly, won for Ferrari.

The lap begins with a sprint to the first chicane, a right/left called Variante del Rettifilo, where what seems a wide track on approach is soon whittled down to only a narrow racing line.

Arcing right through Curva Biassono, the next challenge is the left/right chicane at Variante della Roggia. Like the first chicane, this is a definite passing place, but also a crashing place.

The Lesmos are a pair of rights that lead onto the blast under part of the old banking before arriving up a slight climb into the third chicane, Ascari. This is more open than the other two, and it's followed by a decently long straight down to the final corner, the Curva Parabolica, approached at 210mph, and requiring great balance to inspire the confidence to carry as much speed as possible through there to help a driver line up a possible passing manoeuvre on the long, wide run down to the first chicane.

One thing that always strikes a chord is the thought of what the circuit must have been like until 1971, when its flow wasn't broken by those three chicanes...

INSIDE TRACK
ITALIAN GRAND PRIX

Date:	**2 September**
Circuit name:	**Autodromo Nazionale Monza**
Circuit length:	**3.600 miles/5.793km**
Number of laps:	**53**
Email:	**infoautodromo@monzanet.it**
Website:	**www.monzanet.it**

PREVIOUS WINNERS

2008	**Sebastian Vettel** TORO ROSSO
2009	**Rubens Barrichello** BRAWN
2010	**Fernando Alonso** FERRARI
2011	**Sebastian Vettel** RED BULL
2012	**Lewis Hamilton** McLAREN
2013	**Sebastian Vettel** RED BULL
2014	**Lewis Hamilton** MERCEDES
2015	**Lewis Hamilton** MERCEDES
2016	**Nico Rosberg** MERCEDES
2017	**Lewis Hamilton** MERCEDES

How it started: One of the most remarkable facts about Monza is that the circuit was built in just 100 days, back in 1922. The next most remarkable thing is how little the layout has changed across almost a century since then.

Do you remember when? It rained almost throughout the 2008 Italian GP. Qualifying was wet and Sebastian Vettel shone by taking pole for Scuderia Toro Rosso. It was wet again the following day, but the then 21-year-old German wasn't expected to repeat this form in the race, yet he did and this minor team celebrated hard when he led all but a few laps during the pitstop sequence to take both its first win and his own. Closest challenger, Lewis Hamilton, was thwarted when extreme wets were fitted in midrace and the rain eased.

Location: The town of Monza is roughly 10 miles to the north-east of Milan, with the circuit to be found in a walled royal park within its northern outskirts.

Rising star: Italy has two young talents who became F2 race winners last year, with 23-year-old Luca Ghiotto and 21-year-old Antonio Fuoco both moving to the front of the pack at the end of the season after Raffaele Marciello moved across to race GTs instead.

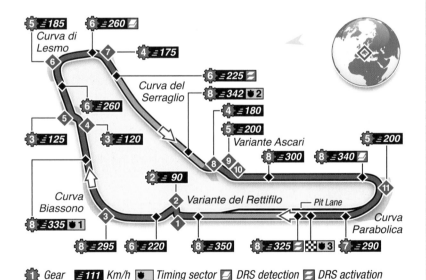

🔧 *Gear*   ▰▰▰ *111 Km/h*   ▣ *Timing sector*   ▱ *DRS detection*   ▰ *DRS activation*

2017 POLE TIME: **HAMILTON (MERCEDES), 1M35.554S, 135.615MPH/218.251KPH**
2017 WINNER'S AVERAGE SPEED: **151.382MPH/243.626KPH**

2017 FASTEST LAP: **RICCIARDO (RED BULL), 1M23.361S, 155.451MPH/250.174KPH**
LAP RECORD: **M SCHUMACHER (FERRARI), 1M21.046S, 159.909MPH/257.349KPH, 2004**

MARINA BAY

If F1 had to create a street circuit that would look great for a night race, then Singapore would be that place, with its neon-lit backdrop bringing something very different to the mix.

Taking F1 to the people has long been something that the sponsors have sought. Of course, they appreciate the sport's diehard enthusiasts, but their messages reach far more people if cars with their brand names are seen by people right on their doorstep.

Add to this the fact that Singapore is an important market and that its race can be run at night to enable a manageable viewing time for F1's key European fanbase and its appeal is clear.

Like almost all street circuits, it is made up predominantly of 90-degree turns. However, it also offers several straights worthy of the name plus a number of corners of interest.

The key corner, especially on the opening lap, is the first one, where the track sweeps left then right before doubling back at the Turn 3 hairpin. There's plenty of space for drivers to make moves, although not all work.

The run along Raffles Boulevard from Turn 5 is long enough to use the DRS and try a move into the left-hand turn at its end, second-gear Memorial Corner. Variety comes in the open parkland from Turn 8 to Turn 12 as the track goes around the home of the Singapore Cricket Club and past Raffles Hotel.

The stretch of track across the white metal Anderson Bridge is spectacular, then a sharp left offers another straight along the wide bridge carrying the Nicoll Highway. Also different from the norm is the run under the grandstand between Turns 18 and 19, with the Singapore Flier ferris wheel inside the last corner offering amazing viewing from above.

82

INSIDE TRACK
SINGAPORE GRAND PRIX

Date:	**16 September**
Circuit name:	**Marina Bay Circuit**
Circuit length:	**3.152 miles/5.073km**
Number of laps:	**61**
Email:	**info@singaporegp.sg**
Website:	**www.singaporegp.sg**

PREVIOUS WINNERS

2008	**Fernando Alonso** RENAULT
2009	**Lewis Hamilton** McLAREN
2010	**Fernando Alonso** FERRARI
2011	**Sebastian Vettel** RED BULL
2012	**Sebastian Vettel** RED BULL
2013	**Sebastian Vettel** RED BULL
2014	**Lewis Hamilton** MERCEDES
2015	**Sebastian Vettel** FERRARI
2016	**Nico Rosberg** MERCEDES
2017	**Lewis Hamilton** MERCEDES

How it started: Dreamed of for years, the Marina Bay Circuit was ready for racing towards the end of 2008, going from idea to reality in short order thanks to support from government circles helping to cut through the red tape that engulfs so many putative street racing venues.

Do you remember when? Many a Singapore GP has been interrupted by a post-incident period with the field being led around by a safety car, which is very much par for the course on an any circuit lined with concrete walls. However, the safety car that was called for in 2015 was for a most unusual reason: a spectator had wandered into the circuit. This would be unsafe on any occasion, but was doubly so as the race is run after nightfall and its arrival hampered Daniel Ricciardo's charge after leader Sebastian Vettel.

Location: The Marina Bay circuit is right downtown, with its pit and paddock area in what was unused land off Republic Boulevard by the Benjamin Sheares Bridge.

Rising star: Singaporean drivers are relatively rare on the international motor racing scene, with only 18-year-old Pavan Ravishankar out seeking single-seater glory in the BRDC British F3 series, while Danial Frost contested the South-East Asia F4 series.

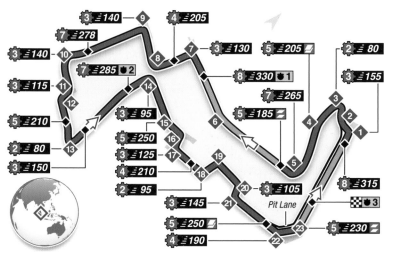

Gear | *111 Km/h* | *Timing sector* | *DRS detection* | *DRS activation*

2017 POLE TIME: **VETTEL (FERRARI)**, **1M39.941S, 113.880MPH/183.272KPH**
2017 WINNER'S AVERAGE SPEED: **88.719MPH/142.780KPH**

2017 FASTEST LAP: **HAMILTON (MERCEDES)**, **1M45.008S, 107.897MPH/173.643KPH**
LAP RECORD: **HAMILTON (MERCEDES)**, **1M45.008S, 107.897MPH/173.643KPH, 2017**

SOCHI

Having been run in spring last year, Russia's grand prix has reverted to a summer date for F1's fifth visit to the Sochi circuit in President Putin's favourite resort on the Black Sea shoreline.

The World Championship had long sought a Russian GP, with attention turning from Moscow, after many failed bids from various proposed venues in and around the capital city, to St Petersburg. When this too appeared to be going nowhere, President Putin entered the mix and landed Russia a date on the F1 calendar, with a race for Sochi.

This was a good way to have both a global event on home soil as well as a further use of the investment he had authorised for this summer and winter resort to host the Winter Olympic Games in 2014 by using some of the infrastructure. Also, as it's a year-round resort, there were hotels aplenty.

The Sochi Autodrom is unusual in having a fast, open first corner rather than a tight one as so many other circuits

do. It's a kink really and the cars can hit almost 200mph before having to brake for Turn 2. There is plenty of space there too, with generous track width. Then comes the most unusual feature, a 180-degree left-hand curve around a garden in front of the Fisht Olympic Stadium – a football World Cup venue in 2018 – before the track begins a series of largely 90-degree turns.

However, the run from Turn 10 to Turn 12 offers something different, a chance for the cars to be let loose after this run of third and fourth-gear bends and get up some speed, up to 190mph.

The lap slows down considerably through the next four corners, before opening out a little more as it runs through the last two corners around the back of the paddock to complete the lap.

INSIDE TRACK
RUSSIAN GRAND PRIX

Date:	30 September
Circuit name:	Sochi Autodrom
Circuit length:	3.634 miles/5.848km
Number of laps:	53
Email:	info@sochiautodrom.ru
Website:	www.sochiautodrom.ru

PREVIOUS WINNERS
2014	Lewis Hamilton	MERCEDES
2015	Lewis Hamilton	MERCEDES
2016	Nico Rosberg	MERCEDES
2017	Valtteri Bottas	MERCEDES

How it started: There was considerable building work required to convert the area around some of the key buildings from when Sochi hosted the Winter Olympic Games at the start of 2014 so that the venue was ready to receive the F1 teams just seven months later.

Do you remember when? On F1's second visit, in 2015, Romain Grosjean provided spectacle in a way that he wouldn't have planned, crashing his Lotus when he perhaps got too close to the rear wing of Jenson Button's McLaren and lost downforce midway through Turn 3 and clattered into the barriers, breaking his seat ...

Location: Built in the grounds of the headquarters of the Winter Olympic Games in what is now a giant theme park, the Sochi Autodrom is in the south-eastern suburb of Sochi in the Krasnodar Krai region on Russia's Black Sea riviera.

Trickiest corner: Although the stretch of track from Turn 2 to Turn 4 is testing as it keeps turning left, perhaps the trickiest corner is Turn 10. It is such a key one, as it feeds onto the second longest flat-out section of the lap. It's a 90-degree left-hander, and getting the power down as soon as possible is key.

Rising star: Russia has a huge crop of young drivers charging through the junior single-seater ranks, with 23-year-old Artem Markelov winning four F2 races last year and Sergey Sirotkin getting F1 testing experience with Renault, while Matevos Isaakyan and Egor Orudzhev have shone in World Series Formula V8 3.5.

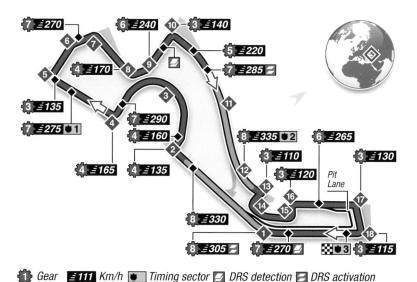

🔧 *Gear* ⛐*111 Km/h* 🏴 *Timing sector* 🏁 *DRS detection* 🏁 *DRS activation*

2017 POLE TIME: **VETTEL (FERRARI)**, 1M33.194S, 140.369MPH/225.902KPH
2017 WINNER'S AVERAGE SPEED: 128.536MPH/206.859KPH

2017 FASTEST LAP: **RAIKKONEN (FERRARI)**, 1M36.844S, 135.078MPH/217.388KPH
LAP RECORD: **RAIKKONEN (FERRARI)**, 1M36.844S, 135.078MPH/217.388KPH, 2017

● SUZUKA

Sometimes it can feel that there are two Suzukas: one bathed in autumnal sunshine, the other awash from heavy rain. Either way, it remains one of the great tracks.

Suzuka only landed a round of the World Championship in 1987, but it feels as though it has been part of the show for longer than that.

The key to why it is one of the most revered circuits used in F1 is that its 3.6-mile lap scarcely contains a single simple corner as it winds its way around its hillside setting.

The downhill run to the first corner sets the scene, with its sixth-gear entry requiring no little bravery. The track that turns back up the hill and the "S"-Curves are an epic test of speed and precision. By Turn 8, Dunlop Curve, the slope has flattened out and the run to and through the first of the Degner curves is relatively straightforward, providing drivers are confident in their car's balance. However, Degner 2 is much narrower and requires a clean entry if they want to try and pass a rival into the hairpin that follows after the track passes, unusually, under its return leg.

Turn 12 seems to never stop turning right, but it finally does so when it flattens out and turns left over the brow. There's a compression as the track runs through the tighter Spoon Curve and then a long run all the way to the final sequence of corners, with once feared 130R now taken flat out in top gear.

The entry to what follows, the chicane known as the Casio Triangle, is a passing place, but it has also proved more than occasionally to be a colliding place, so care is needed.

From there, the track starts dipping again to start its descent down the main straight.

INSIDE TRACK
JAPANESE GRAND PRIX

Date:	**7 October**
Circuit name:	**Suzuka Circuit**
Circuit length:	**3.608 miles/5.806km**
Number of laps:	**53**
Email:	**info@suzukacircuit.co.jp**
Website:	**www.suzukacircuit.co.jp**

PREVIOUS WINNERS

2006	**Fernando Alonso** RENAULT
2009	**Sebastian Vettel** RED BULL
2010	**Sebastian Vettel** RED BULL
2011	**Jenson Button** McLAREN
2012	**Sebastian Vettel** RED BULL
2013	**Sebastian Vettel** RED BULL
2014	**Lewis Hamilton** MERCEDES
2015	**Lewis Hamilton** MERCEDES
2016	**Nico Rosberg** MERCEDES
2017	**Lewis Hamilton** MERCEDES

How it started: Built by Honda as a test facility, the Suzuka Circuit opened its doors in 1962 and ran rounds of the increasingly well-contested Japanese single-seater, sportscar and touring car series until it was promoted to the World Championship a quarter of a century later.

Do you remember when? Suzuka has held so many dramatic races, often because it was the final round. However, Kimi Raikkonen's astonishing move to wrest the lead from Renault's Giancarlo Fisichella as they went onto the final lap in 2005 stands out. The Finn was 5.4s down with eight laps to go and got his McLaren closer and closer until Fisichella was a little too cautious at the chicane on the penultimate lap and this let Raikkonen get close enough to use his tow past the pits and finish the job.

Location: The Suzuka circuit is located above the small town of the same name some 30 miles south-west of the city of Nagoya on the south coast of Japan's main island, Honshu.

Rising stars: Nobuharu Matsushita looks to be the most promising driver to come out of Japan for a few years, the 24-year-old taking two wins in F2 last year, while Nirei Fukuzumi was winning races in GP3.

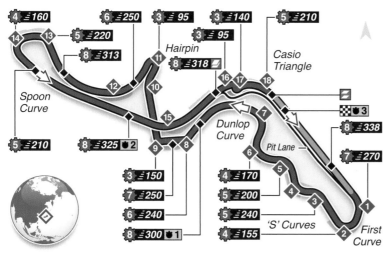

Spoon Curve

Hairpin

Casio Triangle

Dunlop Curve

Pit Lane

'S' Curves

First Curve

1 Gear   **111** Km/h   ● Timing sector   DRS detection   DRS activation

2017 POLE TIME: **HAMILTON (MERCEDES),**
1M27.319S, 148.763MPH/239.411KPH
2017 WINNER'S AVERAGE SPEED:
130.978MPH/210.789KPH

2017 FASTEST LAP: **BOTTAS (MERCEDES),**
1M33.144S, 139.460MPH/224.439KPH
LAP RECORD: **RAIKKONEN (McLAREN),**
1M31.540S, 141.904MPH/228.373KPH, 2005

CIRCUIT OF THE AMERICAS

The United States GP has finally settled down after decades of crossing the country to try new venues and, in this characterful circuit outside Austin, appears to have found a worthy home.

Having jumped from circuit to circuit, the United States GP knew that its latest home needed to have good ingredients: a decent budget and a hilly plot of land outside the popular Texan city of Austin.

These were combined by circuit architect Hermann Tilke who was asked to create a circuit that borrowed some of the best corners from circuits around the world. The result, the Circuit of the Americas, was a good one and it became an instant hit with drivers.

The lap begins with a steep climb to the first corner, rather like at the Red Bull Ring. From this right-hander, the circuit starts its anti-clockwise course, diving immediately into a precipitous drop to Turn 2, before the track runs through a sequence of esses from Turn 3 to Turn 9 – like the Becketts complex at Silverstone or Suzuka's "S"-Curves – where balance is everything.

Designed to be broken into sections, the lap then straightens out for the run through a left kink to the hairpin at Turn 11 before entering its longest straight down to Turn 12, with cars topping 190mph before having to brake heavily for the second-gear left. This is perhaps the best passing place of the lap.

The third section of the lap is tighter, with three slowish corners before a more open 180-degree turn beneath the iconic observation tower. The lap is completed by a slightly downhill Turn 19 and then a tighter final corner onto the foot of the start/finish straight. Naturally, a good exit from here is essential for any driver hoping to make a passing manoeuvre at its far end.

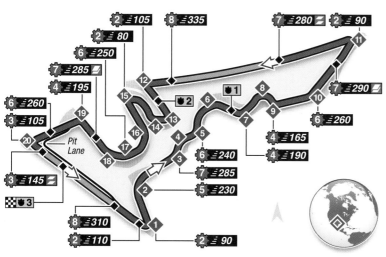

🏎 *Gear* ▰▰▰ **111** *Km/h* 🔲 *Timing sector* ▱ *DRS detection* ▰ *DRS activation*

2017 POLE TIME: **HAMILTON (MERCEDES),**
1M33.108S, 132.450MPH/213.158KPH
2017 WINNER'S AVERAGE SPEED:
122.515MPH/197.169KPH

2017 FASTEST LAP: **VETTEL (FERRARI),**
1M37.766S, 126.140MPH/203.003KPH
LAP RECORD: **VETTEL (FERRARI), 1M37.766S,**
126.140MPH/203.003KPH, 2012

INSIDE TRACK
UNITED STATES GRAND PRIX

Date:	**21 October**
Circuit name:	**Circuit of The Americas**
Circuit length:	**3.400 miles/5.472km**
Number of laps:	**56**
Email:	**info@circuitoftheamericas.com**
Website:	**www.circuitoftheamericas.com**

PREVIOUS WINNERS

2012	**Lewis Hamilton** McLAREN
2013	**Sebastian Vettel** RED BULL
2014	**Lewis Hamilton** MERCEDES
2015	**Lewis Hamilton** MERCEDES
2016	**Lewis Hamilton** MERCEDES
2017	**Lewis Hamilton** MERCEDES

How it started: The United States' seemingly perennial quest to find a venue that would draw large crowds to its grand prix completed its ninth move when it arrived in Austin in 2013. And, money issues aside, it's so far, so good.

Do you remember when? Lewis Hamilton arrived with the points lead in 2015 but his Mercedes team-mate Nico Rosberg claimed pole position. Then the German was slow off the mark and this allowed Hamilton to make a move into the first corner on the opening lap. He dived up the inside and forced Rosberg wide. With the Red Bulls getting past as he recovered, the win Rosberg required to deny Hamilton was beyond him.

Most challenging corner: There is no doubt that Turn 1 is a different corner on the opening lap from how it is for the rest of the race, as a pack of cars cresting the brow for this left-hand hairpin is a different proposition from when a driver arrives alone and can pick a wider line on turning.

Location: COTA is around 10 miles outside of Austin but also, importantly, close enough to the USA's southern border to attract Mexican fans to make a visit.

Rising star: Alexander Rossi was meant to be America's next F1 star, but his move to IndyCars included a win at Watkins Glen, so he looks set there. This leaves the way clear for 19-year-old Santino Ferrucci to continue to try to impress in F2, but he has some way to go.

MEXICO CITY

Such has been the welcome in Mexico since F1's return in 2015 that it feels as if F1 had never been away, even though the circuit has changed slightly since it left in the early 1990s.

Mexico City is a giant, sprawling place and it encloses the park that contains the circuit, making it easy to miss. However, once inside the complex, it's clear just how sports-mad this nation is, not only because its infield contains tennis and basketball courts, football pitches and a running track, but also because it now contains a giant baseball stadium.

Opened in 1962, it welcomed the World Championship in 1963, although F1 stayed away after crowds spilled onto the track in 1970. By 1986, with fencing to keep the fans out of harm's way, F1 was back and the nature of the circuit then remains to this day.

The blast to the first corner is both long and wide, as it needs to be for the variety of lines that drivers take into it as they try to overtake or defend their position.

It's part of a three-corner complex, with many a driver running across the grass before rejoining.

After a straight comes the chicane at Turn 4 and Turn 5, then a hairpin at Turn 6. From there, there's a short straight before a run of esses that bring the cars to Turn 12, a sharpish right that feeds the track into the baseball stadium. There, beneath the steeply-banked grandstands, the track folds sharply left, then right, and out onto the old final sweep of the Peraltada and back onto the main straight.

The circuit was renamed the Autodromo Hermanos Rodriguez after the brothers, Ricardo and Pedro, both of whom were the nation's great hopes and reached F1 but died racing, with Ricardo killed here in practice for a non-championship race in 1962.

INSIDE TRACK
MEXICAN GRAND PRIX

Date:	28 October
Circuit name:	Autodromo Hermanos Rodriguez
Circuit length:	2.674 miles/4.303km
Number of laps:	71
Email:	Rosario@cie.com.mx
Website:	www. autodromohermanosrodriguez.com.mx

PREVIOUS WINNERS

1986	**Gerhard Berger** BENETTON
1987	**Nigel Mansell** WILLIAMS
1988	**Alain Prost** McLAREN
1989	**Ayrton Senna** McLAREN
1990	**Alain Prost** FERRARI
1991	**Riccardo Patrese** WILLIAMS
1992	**Nigel Mansell** WILLIAMS
2015	**Nico Rosberg** MERCEDES
2016	**Lewis Hamilton** MERCEDES
2017	**Max Verstappen** RED BULL

How it started: The circuit opened in 1962 and held a non-championship F1 race, won by works Lotus drivers Trevor Taylor and Jim Clark, who had been disqualified for receiving a push start. Clark took over Taylor's car 10 laps into the 60-lap race. Given World Championship status in 1963, Clark won again.

Do you remember when? Lap one of the 2016 Mexican GP was wild. Lewis Hamilton arrived at this penultimate round 26 points behind his Mercedes team-mate Nico Rosberg and was determined to lead from pole. But he locked up into the first corner and skated off the track, while Rosberg was clouted by Max Verstappen's Red Bull. Hamilton went on to win, but second place for Rosberg sent him to the last race with a clear advantage.

Location: The Autodromo Hermanos Rodriguez is in Mexico City's eastern suburbs, at Pino, out beyond its international airport.

Rising star: Who will be the next Mexican F1 driver after Sergio Perez is a question the nation's racing mad fans are asking. Diego Menchaca, 23, looks to be the best tip, but it's hard to judge as he was racing in the less than competitive World Series Formula V8 3.5, and only once made the podium in that.

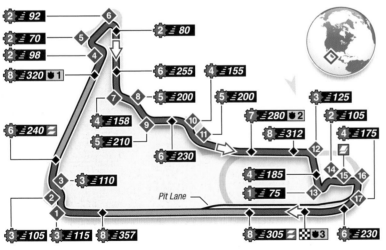

Gear | 111 Km/h | Timing sector | DRS detection | DRS activation

---

2017 POLE TIME: VETTEL (FERRARI), 1M16.488S, 125.872MPH/202.572KPH
2017 WINNER'S AVERAGE SPEED: 118.042MPH/189.970KPH

2017 FASTEST LAP: VETTEL (FERRARI), 1M18.785S, 122.202MPH/196.666KPH
LAP RECORD: VETTEL (FERRARI), 1M28.785S, 122.202MPH/196.666KPH, 2017

Home fans had much to cheer about as local hero Sergio Perez drove his Force India to a very creditable seventh place at the 2017 Mexican Grand Prix.

INTERLAGOS

This longtime home of the Brazilian GP is proof that you don't need shiny new facilities to make a great circuit, as it has the topography to do that and the show is carried by passionate fans.

Many circuits don't name their corners, giving them numbers instead. This lacks character, as proved by the fact that Interlagos's names resonate with F1 fans around the world, from the Senna S to Ferradura to Juncao.

Blessed with a sloping site on the outskirts of Sao Paulo, with the original circuit winding around lakes at the foot of the slope, hence the name Interlagos – translated as "between the lakes".

Cut back to almost half of its original length in 1990, it still uses most of the upper section, dropping out of the Descida do Sol into the Senna S at the compression below. Then, arcing left, the track runs down to Descida do Lago before turning back up the slope. Cresting the hill at Ferradura, it then plunges down again, out of Laranja. There's a great flow all the way

through Pinheirinho, back up to Cotovelo then down again to Mergulho.

Then comes a tighter left, Juncao, at the foot of a long, long, curving climb beneath the foot of the grandstands, almost in a cutting, all the way past the pits. Getting a run to try to pass a rival at the start of the following lap is possible, although it requires bravery, as the exit of the corner can't be seen until the driver is committed at the corner entry.

What makes Interlagos special is not its paddock – the facilities are scrappy and space is limited – but the sheer love of F1 and especially its own F1 drivers, that drives the crowds packing the grandstands into a frenzy of excitement from the moment that the gates open in the morning through until the race is over, or the last Brazilian driver has retired ...

INSIDE TRACK
BRAZILIAN GRAND PRIX

Date:	**11 November**
Circuit name:	**Autodromo Jose Carlos Pace Interlagos**
Circuit length:	**2.667 miles/4.292km**
Number of laps:	**71**
Email:	**info@gpbrazil.com**
Website:	**www.gpbrazil.com**

PREVIOUS WINNERS

2008	**Felipe Massa** FERRARI
2009	**Mark Webber** RED BULL
2010	**Sebastian Vettel** RED BULL
2011	**Mark Webber** RED BULL
2012	**Jenson Button** McLAREN
2013	**Sebastian Vettel** RED BULL
2014	**Nico Rosberg** MERCEDES
2015	**Nico Rosberg** MERCEDES
2016	**Lewis Hamilton** MERCEDES
2017	**Sebastian Vettel** FERRARI

How it started: With an opening date of 1940, Interlagos is one of the oldest circuits visited by the F1 circus, but it didn't make its World Championship debut until 1973 after holding a non-championship race in 1972.

Do you remember when? In a country that has produced multiple F1 World Champions Ayrton Senna, Nelson Piquet and Emerson Fittipaldi, it might take a trawl through the history books to understand why Interlagos is named after another Brazilian ace. This is Carlos Pace who won here in 1975 for Brabham, taking victory when runaway leader Jean-Pierre Jarier's Shadow broke. This was to prove his only F1 win before he died in a light aircraft crash in 1977.

Location: Sao Paulo's spread is enormous, as you might imagine of a city with a population of 12 million and rising. Interlagos is nine miles to the south-west of the city centre, in the Cidade Dutra suburb.

Rising star: There used to be a production line of promising Brazilians trying to emulate compatriot Ayrton Senna. Right now, however, that appears to have stalled and F2 race-winner Sergio Sette Camara is the best bet, but even though his form improved through 2017, the 19-year-old is certainly no Senna.

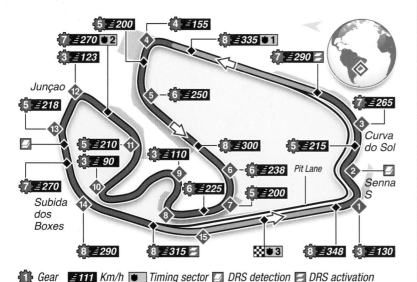

Junçao

Curva do Sol

Pit Lane

Senna S

Subida dos Boxes

🔧 *Gear*   **111** *Km/h*   *Timing sector*   *DRS detection*   *DRS activation*

2017 POLE TIME: BOTTAS (MERCEDES),
1M08.322S, 140.508MPH/226.125KPH
2017 WINNER'S AVERAGE SPEED: 1h31m26.262
124.730MPH/200.733KPH

2017 FASTEST LAP: VERSTAPPEN (RED BULL)
1M11.044S, 135.676MPH/218.349KPH
LAP RECORD: VERSTAPPEN (RED BULL)
1M11.044S, 135.676MPH/218.349KPH, 2017

YAS MARINA

Abu Dhabi's racing circuit is a jewel-like venue with immaculate facilities, but what makes it stand out is the fact that it hosts the season-concluding and hopefully title-deciding race.

When building a circuit in a desert, one factor that clearly needs to be considered is the heat. This is one of the reasons that the Yas Marina circuit holds its race as early evening turns swiftly to night. There are also two more reasons for this. The first is that by holding the race back from a typical afternoon slot, it moves its start time to prime European TV-viewing time. The second is that this circuit looks brilliant when lit up at night, especially the stretch where it dives underneath a hotel and the area around the pits.

The circuit was meant to impress from the moment that the Abu Dhabi government decided to finance it. No money was spared in its design and construction, and Hermann Tilke designed it to contain two long straights into tight corners in order to encourage overtaking.

The lap starts with a hard left before a flowing section down to a chicane at Turns 5 and 6, which is where passing and attempted passing moves are made.

Out of the hairpin at Turn 7, it's then a long, DRS-assisted blast at up to 200mph down to a tight left that feeds straight into a right at the foot of a huge grandstand and so on to an arc that takes the drivers to the second straight. Again, drivers get close to 200mph before having to lose around 140mph for the left/right combination at Turn 11.

The return leg from Turn 14 is a bit more point-and-squirt as the track rounds a marina, dips under the Yas Viceroy Hotel and finally turns sharp right onto the start/finish straight.

INSIDE TRACK
ABU DHABI GRAND PRIX

Date:	**25 November**
Circuit name:	**Yas Marina Circuit**
Circuit length:	**3.451 miles/5.554km**
Number of laps:	**56**
Email:	**customerservice@ yasmarinacircuit.com**
Website:	**www.yasmarinacircuit.com**

PREVIOUS WINNERS

2009	**Sebastian Vettel**	RED BULL
2010	**Sebastian Vettel**	RED BULL
2011	**Lewis Hamilton**	McLAREN
2012	**Kimi Raikkonen**	LOTUS
2013	**Sebastian Vettel**	RED BULL
2014	**Lewis Hamilton**	MERCEDES
2015	**Nico Rosberg**	MERCEDES
2016	**Lewis Hamilton**	MERCEDES
2017	**Valtteri Bottas**	MERCEDES

How it started: Dubai, a neighbouring member of the United Arab Emirates, was cornering international sporting events in the region, so Abu Dhabi built an F1-class circuit as part of a sports complex and landed a round of the 2009 World Championship.

Most memorable race: The 2010 Abu Dhabi GP stands out as it was a four-way title battle. Yet, it wasn't title favourites Fernando Alonso or Mark Webber who took the crown, but Webber's Red Bull Racing team-mate Sebastian Vettel to start a four-year reign.

Do you remember when? In 2016 Lewis Hamilton knew that winning wasn't going to be enough to take the title. What he needed to do was to prevent his Mercedes team-mate Nico Rosberg from finishing second. He tried all he could to back Rosberg into the chasing Sebastian Vettel, but the Ferrari driver just couldn't get by so Nico became champion.

Location: Abu Dhabi has several islands and the circuit is on Yas Island, to the east of the capital, as part of a major sporting complex that also includes the Ferrari World theme park, a drag racing strip and a golf course.

Rising star: Other Arab nations are starting to produce drivers in junior single-seater categories and GT Racing, but Abu Dhabi has yet to bring on one of its own.

🏁 **Gear** ⬛111 **Km/h** ⬛ **Timing sector** 🏴 **DRS detection** 🏴 **DRS activation**

2017 POLE TIME: BOTTAS (MERCEDES), 1m36.231s, 129.102MPH/207.770KPH

2017 WINNER'S AVERAGE SPEED: 120.808MPH/194.422MPH

2017 FASTEST LAP: BOTTAS (MERCEDES), 1M40.650S, 123.436MPH/198.652KPH

LAP RECORD: VETTEL (RED BULL), 1M40.279S, 123.893MPH/199.387KPH, 2009

A Formula 1 pitstop is over almost as fast as an eye can focus. Each and every one of the pitcrew has to do their particular job with accuracy and in perfect harmony with those around them. Practice makes perfect.

SEASON REVIEW 2017

The teams had to learn last year how to make their cars go better when fitted with wider tyres and broader wings. That Ferrari took the opening round meant Mercedes had a challenge on its hands. Then Red Bull Racing came on song, yet Lewis Hamilton rose to the top to bag his fourth title, with the challenge making this all the more satisfying.

Following on from Mercedes' domination of the 2016 World Championship, F1 was ready for an adjustment of the rulebook. Sure, the cars were going to look better as they were allowed wider wings both in front and at the back, but they were also fitted with broader, old-school slick tyres, making them look more purposeful. That was an added bonus, for the crux of the change was the fact that it was a team other than Mercedes that took the honours in the opening race in Australia. Yes, Sebastian Vettel's victory made people believe that the Silver Arrows were going to have a fight on their hands if they wanted to make it four constructors' titles in a row.

When Ferrari, and Vettel in particular, added two more wins and

three second-place finishes in the next five rounds, Mercedes soon realised that, even though Lewis Hamilton triumphed second time out in China and his eleventh-hour team-mate Valtteri Bottas won round four in Russia, it had a fight on its hands.

At this point, Red Bull Racing didn't appear to have the grunt from its engine to pitch into the battle, but even so it took Hamilton (above, at Spa) until the 13th of the season's 20 grands prix to move into the championship lead. This lead change in the points race happened, gallingly for the *tifosi* on their home ground, as Hamilton and Bottas left Vettel to settle for third place at Monza.

As the season entered its final third, Red Bull Racing was third in the rankings, well clear of Force India, but 161 points behind Ferrari,

with just Daniel Ricciardo's win in Azerbaijan to cheer it on. But then Red Bull hit increasingly strong form, with Max Verstappen notably getting right onto the pace. He won at Sepang, but really laid down a marker with a dominant victory in Mexico. This was where Hamilton wrapped up his fourth title, with two rounds remaining, but it proved that Red Bull ought to be right on song in 2018, especially if it can match its new-found pace with reliability, as both drivers had too many retirements last year to mount a serious challenge.

Hamilton really upped Mercedes' game through the season and came out on top, while Bottas added another win, in Austria, but increasingly found himself unable to match his team leader, although he was back on form by season's end.

At Ferrari, it remained the Vettel show, which was just how he liked it, with Kimi Raikkonen content just to turn up, race and gather points. However, perhaps as he was in with a shot at victory, Vettel displayed several errors of judgement, including swerving intentionally into Hamilton behind a safety car in Azerbaijan and then taking out Verstappen and Raikkonen at the start in Singapore, both incidents sullying his reputation.

Verstappen, on the other hand, appeared to become the flavour of the day at Red Bull Racing, including being given a development engine for the United States GP not only ahead of Ricciardo, but without the Australian even being told. Yet, his dominance in Mexico

showed that the Dutchman is surely a World Champion in waiting.

No driver beyond the top three teams was able to win a race, but one driver in particular showed that he might if given more competitive machinery. This was Esteban Ocon, who came on strong to increasingly outpace his team leader Sergio Perez, as Force India cemented its position as the best of the rest.

Williams knew that this was going to be a learning year for teenage rookie Lance Stroll, who took an amazing third in the fractured Azerbaijan GP, but team-mate Felipe Massa disappointed as the team fell away from the pace. Conversely, Scuderia Toro Rosso made strides thanks to Carlos Sainz Jr, most notably with his excellent fourth place in Singapore. In outright pace, Renault was superior, but Nico Hulkenberg was despondent at season's end as result after result was snatched away by mechanical failure. The lack of a strong second driver held the team back, with Jolyon Palmer being dropped.

Haas was part of the midfield pack, as were Toro Rosso and Renault, for whom Romain Grosjean and Kevin Magnussen both pressed hard.

McLaren brought an end to its dreadful relationship with Honda and suffered despite the best efforts of Fernando Alonso and Stoffel Vandoorne. For a team of this calibre to rank ninth out of 10 teams is a travesty. Expect massive progress in 2018.

Sauber brought up the rear, with Pascal Wehrlein's eighth place in Spain a rare highlight.

There was a new look at the opening race of the season. Not just because the cars looked different, but because it wasn't Mercedes at the front, and Lewis Hamilton had to watch as Ferrari's Sebastian Vettel triumphed in a swing in form.

A new season always offers hope of a change, even after a lengthy spell of domination, like Mercedes', especially if there have been changes to the rulebook. So, with wider tyres and more downforce adding up to cars that were markedly faster than before, hope was abundant before the first race of 2017.

Yet practice and qualifying suggested that Mercedes was still in the driving seat as Lewis Hamilton took a clear pole and had new team-mate Valtteri Bottas secure third on the grid. Fortunately, Sebastian Vettel had qualified second fastest for Ferrari, a quarter of a second down on the Mercedes driver's best, with Kimi Raikkonen a distant fourth for Ferrari, while Red Bull wasn't in the mix.

Although Hamilton led away from pole position, Vettel declined to be dropped in his wake, instead staying on his tail all the way to the Mercedes driver's pitstop on lap 17. This certainly wasn't in the Mercedes script, as Hamilton had elected to come in six laps earlier than planned so that he could get off the ultra-soft tyres with which he was struggling to find grip.

Hamilton's next problem was to come out behind Max Verstappen's Red Bull and then find himself unable to pass it as his new tyres lost their edge as he remained contained.

The Dutchman pitted, as did Bottas and Raikkonen, and this promoted Hamilton, but only to second place, as Vettel had matters under control and raced away to win by 10s. Bottas completed the podium on his Mercedes debut, well clear of fellow Finn Raikkonen.

The most disappointed driver in Melbourne, though, was Daniel Ricciardo who had a poor day at his home race. He started 15th because of a gearbox change penalty, then fell to last on the opening lap with a gearbox sensor problem and retired when a power unit failed.

There was a point for F1 debutant Esteban Ocon for finishing 10th for Force India after overcoming Fernando Alonso, who was fighting a losing battle in his poor Honda-engined McLaren.

Lewis Hamilton leads away, but he wasn't able to remain ahead of Sebastian Vettel's Ferrari.

ALBERT PARK ROUND 1
DATE: **26 MARCH 2017**

Laps: **57** • Distance: **187.822 miles/302.271km** • Weather: **Warm & bright**

Pos	Driver	Team	Result	Stops	Qualifying Time	Grid
1	**Sebastian Vettel**	Ferrari	1h24m11.672s	1	1m22.456s	2
2	**Lewis Hamilton**	Mercedes	1h24m21.647s	1	1m22.188s	1
3	**Valtteri Bottas**	Mercedes	1h24m22.922s	1	1m22.481s	3
4	**Kimi Raikkonen**	Ferrari	1h24m34.065s	1	1m23.033s	4
5	**Max Verstappen**	Red Bull	1h24m40.499s	1	1m23.485s	5
6	**Felipe Massa**	Williams	1h25m35.058s	1	1m24.443s	7
7	**Sergio Perez**	Force India	56 laps	1	1m25.081s	10
8	**Carlos Sainz Jr**	Toro Rosso	56 laps	1	1m24.487s	8
9	**Daniil Kvyat**	Toro Rosso	56 laps	2	1m24.512s	9
10	**Esteban Ocon**	Force India	56 laps	1	1m25.568s	13
11	**Nico Hulkenberg**	Renault	56 laps	2	1m25.091s	11
12	**Antonio Giovinazzi**	Sauber	55 laps	1	1m26.419s	16
13	**Stoffel Vandoorne**	McLaren	55 laps	1	1m26.858s	18
R	**Fernando Alonso**	McLaren	50 laps/suspension	1	1m25.425s	12
R	**Kevin Magnussen**	Haas	46 laps/suspension	2	1m26.847s	17
R	**Lance Stroll ***	Williams	40 laps/brakes	2	1m27.143s	20
R	**Daniel Ricciardo ***	Red Bull	25 laps/engine	0	no time	15
R	**Marcus Ericsson**	Sauber	21 laps/engine	0	1m26.465s	14
R	**Jolyon Palmer**	Renault	15 laps/brakes	0	1m28.244s	19
R	**Romain Grosjean**	Haas	13 laps/engine	0	1m24.074s	6

FASTEST LAP: RAIKKONEN, 1M26.538S, 137.077MPH/220.605KPH ON LAP 56 • RACE LEADERS: HAMILTON 1-16, VETTEL 17-22 & 26-57, BOTTAS 23-24, RAIKKONEN 25
* 5-PLACE GRID PENALTY FOR CHANGING GEARBOX

CHINESE GP

Embarrassed by how Ferrari beat it with such ease in Australia, Mercedes regained a modicum of pride when Lewis Hamilton proved himself to be the pick of the pack in Shanghai and, as before, the other teams were left trailing in their wake.

Wet weather limited the teams' practice sessions, perhaps hampering the chances of those teams not yet on the pace to close the gap, and so qualifying was again between Hamilton and Vettel, this time with Valtteri Bottas rising to the task to get right into the mix in the second Mercedes. In the end, Hamilton made it two poles from two and Bottas lost out to Vettel by 0.001s.

The track was wet at the start and Vettel wasn't brilliant off the line, so had to repel Bottas rather than attack Hamilton. Williams' Canadian teenager Lance Stroll then triggered a virtual safety car period by ending his race at Turn 10 on the opening lap after a clash with Sergio Perez and this was the trigger for Vettel to dive in to the pits to swap from intermediate tyres to slicks.

Unfortunately for the German, Antonio Giovinazzi – like Stroll, also making his second F1 start – then crashed at the end of lap 4, caught out by his Sauber team-mate Marcus Ericsson returning to the circuit ahead of him, and this brought out the safety car which then led the cars through the pitlane for a few laps while the debris was cleared. And so Ferrari's early stop was cancelled out, leaving Vettel fifth when proper racing resumed as Hamilton led from Daniel Ricciardo, Kimi Raikkonen and Max Verstappen, up from 16th on the grid after a coil failed in Q1.

It took Vettel until lap 28 of 56 to make his way past the trio chasing Hamilton to reach second, passing Raikkonen into Turn 6 on lap 20, then Ricciardo in a very brave move at Turn 7 on lap 22, before finishing the job by getting by Verstappen at the Turn 14 hairpin, though he was helped when the Dutchman locked up. This all cost time, and Hamilton had a 10s buffer as he controlled the race.

Vettel was far from finished, though, and pressed on, but Hamilton had enough in hand at the end to still be 6s clear at the chequered flag. Verstappen deserved most of the plaudits though for his charge from the back, especially for passing nine cars on lap 1.

SHANGHAI ROUND 2

DATE: **9 APRIL 2017**

Laps: **56** • Distance: **189.559 miles/305.066km** • Weather: **Overcast & cool**

Pos	Driver	Team	Result	Stops	Qualifying Time	Grid
1	**Lewis Hamilton**	Mercedes	1h37m36.158s	2	1m31.678s	1
2	**Sebastian Vettel**	Ferrari	1h37m42.408s	2	1m31.864s	2
3	**Max Verstappen**	Red Bull	1h38m21.350s	2	1m35.433s	16
4	**Daniel Ricciardo**	Red Bull	1h38m22.193s	2	1m33.033s	5
5	**Kimi Raikkonen**	Ferrari	1h38m24.234s	2	1m32.140s	4
6	**Valtteri Bottas**	Mercedes	1h38m24.966s	2	1m31.865s	3
7	**Carlos Sainz Jr**	Toro Rosso	1h38m49.051s	1	1m34.150s	11
8	**Kevin Magnussen**	Haas	55 laps	2	1m34.164s	12
9	**Sergio Perez**	Force India	55 laps	3	1m33.706s	8
10	**Esteban Ocon**	Force India	55 laps	3	1m35.496s	17
11	**Romain Grosjean ***	Haas	55 laps	3	1m35.223s	19
12	**Nico Hulkenberg**	Renault	55 laps	2	1m33.580s	7
13	**Jolyon Palmer ***	Renault	55 laps	1	1m35.279s	20
14	**Felipe Massa**	Williams	55 laps	3	1m33.507s	6
15	**Marcus Ericsson**	Sauber	55 laps	1	1m35.046s	14
R	**Fernando Alonso**	McLaren	33 laps/halfshaft	1	1m34.372s	13
R	**Daniil Kvyat**	Toro Rosso	18 laps/hydraulics	1	1m33.719s	9
R	**Stoffel Vandoorne**	McLaren	17 laps/fuel pressure	1	1m35.023s	15
R	**Antonio Giovinazzi ****	Sauber	3 laps/spun off	1	no time	18
R	**Lance Stroll**	Williams	0 laps/collision	0	1m34.220s	10

FASTEST LAP: **HAMILTON, 1M35.378S, 127.844MPH/205.745KPH ON LAP 44** • RACE LEADERS: **HAMILTON 1-56**
* 5-PLACE GRID PENALTY FOR NOT SLOWING FOR WAVED YELLOW FLAGS; ** 5-PLACE GRID PENALTY FOR CHANGING GEARBOX

Smiles all round as Lewis Hamilton celebrates with Sebastian Vettel and Max Verstappen.

BAHRAIN GP

Ferrari versus Mercedes was becoming the story of the 2017 season and Bahrain's grand prix was no different as the two teams fought again and, somehow, Ferrari turned around a qualifying deficit for Sebastian Vettel to come through to win.

Valtteri Bottas laid down a marker by claiming pole, emphasising how good Mercedes' choice was when it picked a replacement for Nico Rosberg. And he turned the pole into an early-race lead. Lewis Hamilton, however, had reasons to be frustrated as his DRS had failed in final qualifying and then he got out-dragged by Sebastian Vettel to the first corner.

Then, with the two Red Bulls running in this tight quintet, Ferrari thought on its feet and brought Vettel in earlier than his rivals for his first pitstop. It caught the others on the hop, then Max Verstappen crashed when his rear brakes failed. Better still for the Ferrari driver, the safety car was deployed when Carlos Sainz Jr came out of the pits and clattered into Lance Stroll at Turn 1.

This triggered a dive for the pits and a problem for Mercedes, as Hamilton needed to come in on the same lap and elected to back the pack up so that the team would have time to get Bottas's stop done. The trouble was that he slowed his pace too much and this earned him a 5s penalty. Worse still for Mercedes, a faulty wheelgun meant that Bottas's pitstop was a slow one and the same problem also affected Hamilton.

This all worked to Vettel's advantage as not only did this put him into the lead, but also Hamilton emerged from his stop back in fourth place, although he was soon able to pass Ricciardo and then found himself faster than Bottas but stuck behind the Finn.

It took the team a while to decide to ask Bottas to move over, during which time Vettel gained nearly 5s. Although Hamilton cut 4s out of Vettel's lead, he had the pitstop plus the 5s penalty to serve and this left him still second on his return, but now 20s down on Vettel. Charge as he might, cutting 14s out of the deficit, it was race over.

Bottas ended up some way back in third, a couple of seconds ahead of Kimi Raikkonen, with Ricciardo recovering from a spell when his new tyres didn't get to temperature to repass Felipe Massa for fifth.

SAKHIR ROUND 3

DATE: **16 APRIL 2017**

Laps: **57** • Distance: **191.530 miles/308.238km** • Weather: **Warm & dry**

Pos	Driver	Team	Result	Stops	Qualifying Time	Grid
1	Sebastian Vettel	Ferrari	1h33m53.374s	2	1m29.247s	3
2	Lewis Hamilton	Mercedes	1h34m00.034s	2	1m28.792s	2
3	Valtteri Bottas	Mercedes	1h34m13.771s	2	1m28.769s	1
4	Kimi Raikkonen	Ferrari	1h34m15.849s	2	1m29.567s	5
5	Daniel Ricciardo	Red Bull	1h34m32.720s	2	1m29.545s	4
6	Felipe Massa	Williams	1h34m47.700s	2	1m30.074s	8
7	Sergio Perez	Force India	1h34m55.980s	2	1m32.318s	18
8	Romain Grosjean	Haas	1h35m08.239s	2	1m30.763s	9
9	Nico Hulkenberg	Renault	1h35m13.562s	2	1m29.842s	7
10	Esteban Ocon	Force India	1h35m29.085s	2	1m31.684s	14
11	Pascal Wehrlein	Sauber	56 laps	1	1m31.414s	13
12	Daniil Kvyat	Toro Rosso	56 laps	2	1m30.923s	11
13	Jolyon Palmer	Renault	56 laps	2	1m31.074s	10
14	Fernando Alonso	McLaren	54 laps/engine	2	No time	15
R	Marcus Ericsson	Sauber	50 laps/gearbox	1	1m32.543s	19
R	Carlos Sainz Jr	Toro Rosso	12 laps/collision	1	1m32.118s	16
R	Lance Stroll	Williams	12 laps/collision	1	1m31.168s	12
R	Max Verstappen	Red Bull	11 laps/brakes	0	1m29.687s	6
R	Kevin Magnussen	Haas	8 laps/electrics	0	1m32.900s	20
NS	Stoffel Vandoorne	McLaren	Engine	-	1m32.313s	17

FASTEST LAP: **HAMILTON, 1M32.798S, 130.458MPH/209.952KPH ON LAP 46** •
RACE LEADERS: **BOTTAS 1-13, VETTEL 14-33 & 42-57, HAMILTON 34-41**

The Ferrari pit crew welcome their main man home as Sebastian Vettel makes it two wins.

RUSSIAN GP

F1 fans love a first-time winner, so Valtteri Bottas's success in Russia gave the sport a boost as Mercedes' last-minute replacement after Nico Rosberg retired got ahead of Ferrari's front row starters to put his team-mate Lewis Hamilton in the shade.

When Valtteri Bottas was first to the chequered flag for Mercedes after resisting considerable pressure from Sebastian Vettel, there was delight up and down the pitlane as the Finn is such a popular character, a level-headed guy who had finally been given the equipment to do the job and delivered.

He out-qualified team-mate Lewis Hamilton again, but this was only to decide which side of the second row would be his as Ferrari filled the front row after managing to get heat into its Pirelli ultra-soft tyres better than the opposition, with Sebastian Vettel on pole by a fraction from Kimi Raikkonen.

At the start of the grand prix, Bottas got a scorcher and leapt past both Ferraris, passing first Raikkonen and then using Vettel's tow down towards Turn 2 where he dived past. It was an excellent few seconds of racing and transformed the outcome of the race, for no longer was Ferrari in control.

Not all those behind made it around the opening lap, as Jolyon Palmer and Romain Grosjean clashed, but then Bottas began to ease clear of Vettel, until losing some of the hard-earned fractions of a second when they began to lap the tailenders. Bottas made his one pitstop on lap 27, Vettel coming in seven laps later. Then the German had tyres with more life in them and closed in again. Bottas had a scare when he locked up approaching Turn 13 on lap 38 and the flat spots on both front tyres made the last 14 laps of his race incredibly uncomfortable. Vettel closed right in but Bottas displayed the grit that attracted the Williams team to sign him back in 2012 and held on to the finish. The margin was tiny, just 0.617s, but that only made his maiden F1 win all the sweeter.

Hamilton was very much the second best Mercedes racer in Sochi and finished fourth, 36.3s down on his team-mate, and 25s behind Raikkonen. Talk of this being a year in which the title would be a straight fight between Vettel and Hamilton looked to be wrong, as Bottas was clearly Mercedes' main man here.

Valtteri Bottas hoped he'd be a winner with his promotion to Mercedes and did it in round four.

SOCHI ROUND 4

DATE: **30 APRIL 2017**

Laps: **52** • Distance: **188.832 miles/303.897km** • Weather: **Warm & bright**

Pos	Driver	Team	Result	Stops	Qualifying Time	Grid
1	**Valtteri Bottas**	Mercedes	1h28m08.743s	1	1m33.289s	3
2	**Sebastian Vettel**	Ferrari	1h28m09.360s	1	1m33.194s	1
3	**Kimi Raikkonen**	Ferrari	1h28m19.743s	1	1m33.253s	2
4	**Lewis Hamilton**	Mercedes	1h28m45.063s	1	1m33.767s	4
5	**Max Verstappen**	Red Bull	1h29m09.159s	1	1m35.161s	7
6	**Sergio Perez**	Force India	1h29m35.531s	1	1m35.337s	9
7	**Esteban Ocon**	Force India	1h29m43.747s	1	1m35.430s	10
8	**Nico Hulkenberg**	Renault	1h29m44.931s	1	1m35.285s	8
9	**Felipe Massa**	Williams	51 laps	2	1m35.110s	6
10	**Carlos Sainz Jr ***	Toro Rosso	51 laps	1	1m35.948s	14
11	**Lance Stroll**	Williams	51 laps	1	1m35.964s	11
12	**Daniil Kvyat**	Toro Rosso	51 laps	1	1m35.968s	12
13	**Kevin Magnussen**	Haas	51 laps	1	1m36.017s	13
14	**Stoffel Vandoorne ****	McLaren	51 laps	2	1m37.070s	20
15	**Marcus Ericsson**	Sauber	51 laps	2	1m37.507s	18
16	**Pascal Wehrlein**	Sauber	50 laps	2	1m37.332s	17
R	**Daniel Ricciardo**	Red Bull	5 laps/brakes	0	1m34.905s	5
R	**Jolyon Palmer**	Renault	0 laps/collision	0	1m36.462s	16
R	**Romain Grosjean**	Haas	0 laps/collision	0	1m37.620s	19
NS	**Fernando Alonso**	McLaren	Power unit	-	1m36.660s	15

FASTEST LAP: **RAIKKONEN, 1M36.844S, 135.078MPH/217.388KPH ON LAP 49** • RACE LEADERS: **BOTTAS 1-26 & 35-52, VETTEL 27-34**
* 3-PLACE GRID PENALTY FOR CAUSING A COLLISION IN PREVIOUS RACE;
** 15-PLACE GRID PENALTY FOR USING ADDITIONAL POWER UNIT ELEMENTS

SPANISH GP

Pole to victory suggests that Hamilton had it easy in Spain, but that was to play down Ferrari's advantage in qualifying and ignore Lewis's poor start before he was able to fight back once team-mate Bottas had delayed Vettel in his second stint.

Such was Ferrari's speed in qualifying that pole should have belonged to the Italian marque, but Sebastian Vettel made a slip-up at the chicane and failed to beat Hamilton's pole lap.

Come the start, Vettel got the jump on Hamilton to take the lead before they reached the first corner, where Bottas and Kimi Raikkonen collided after the Mercedes driver bounced off the inside kerb. This forced the Ferrari into Max Verstappen's path, causing Raikkonen and the Dutchman to spear across the painted area beyond the kerbs. Both had too much damage to continue. Behind them, Fernando Alonso and Felipe Massa clashed, but both were able to race on.

Vettel duly controlled the race, but he pitted on lap 14 and so Hamilton took over at the front, staying there until he made his first stop seven laps later. Having both started on Pirelli softs, Hamilton didn't copy Vettel in fitting another set, instead opting to run medium compound tyres for the middle stint. It was a gamble, as he would lose ground before hoping to gain it all back again, and more, when Vettel had to swap to mediums for the final stint and Hamilton would run to the finish on softs. Bottas would have a role to play in this, as Mercedes decided that he'd run a really long first stint so that he'd be in the lead when Hamilton came in, thus delaying Vettel on his soft rubber. Such was the pace of the German's Ferrari, though, that he soon drove past.

All these tactics were given a shake when Stoffel Vandoorne crashed his McLaren into Massa at Turn 1 on lap 33, triggering a virtual safety car period. This gave Hamilton the chance to pit earlier than he'd expected to get off the mediums and on to softs, which turned the race in his favour. He still had to pass Vettel, which he managed into Turn 1 on lap 44, then went on to win, with third-placed Daniel Ricciardo 72s further back.

Pascal Wehrlein gave Sauber a rare reason to smile as he scored the Swiss team's first points of the year by finishing eighth.

Lewis smiles as he feels that the balance has swung his way, though Vettel wasn't far behind.

CATALUNYA ROUND 5

DATE: **14 MAY 2017**

Laps: **66** • Distance: **190.825 miles/307.104km** • Weather: **Hot & sunny**

Pos	Driver	Team	Result	Stops	Qualifying Time	Grid
1	**Lewis Hamilton**	Mercedes	1h35m56.497s	2	1m19.149s	1
2	**Sebastian Vettel**	Ferrari	1h35m59.987s	2	1m19.200s	2
3	**Daniel Ricciardo**	Red Bull	1h37m12.317s	2	1m20.175s	6
4	**Sergio Perez**	Force India	65 laps	2	1m21.070s	8
5	**Esteban Ocon**	Force India	65 laps	2	1m21.272s	10
6	**Nico Hulkenberg**	Renault	65 laps	2	1m21.397s	13
7	**Carlos Sainz Jr**	Toro Rosso	65 laps	2	1m21.371s	12
8	**Pascal Wehrlein ***	Sauber	65 laps	1	1m21.803s	15
9	**Daniil Kvyat**	Toro Rosso	65 laps	2	1m22.746s	19
10	**Romain Grosjean**	Haas	65 laps	2	1m21.517s	14
11	**Marcus Ericsson**	Sauber	64 laps	2	1m22.332s	16
12	**Fernando Alonso**	McLaren	64 laps	3	1m21.048s	7
13	**Felipe Massa**	Williams	64 laps	3	1m21.232s	9
14	**Kevin Magnussen**	Haas	64 laps	3	1m21.329s	11
15	**Jolyon Palmer**	Renault	64 laps	3	1m22.401s	17
16	**Lance Stroll**	Williams	64 laps	2	1m22.411s	18
R	**Valtteri Bottas**	Mercedes	38 laps/power unit	1	1m19.373s	3
R	**Stoffel Vandoorne ****	McLaren	32 laps/collision	1	1m22.532s	20
R	**Max Verstappen**	Red Bull	1 lap/collision	0	1m19.706s	5
R	**Kimi Raikkonen**	Ferrari	0 laps/collision	0	1m19.439s	4

FASTEST LAP: **HAMILTON, 1M23.593S, 124.567MPH/200.471KPH ON LAP 64** •
RACE LEADERS: VETTEL 1-13 & 25-43, HAMILTON 14-21 & 44-66, BOTTAS 22-24
* 5-SECOND PENALTY FOR FAILING TO KEEP RIGHT OF PIT ENTRY BOLLARD;
** 10-PLACE GRID PENALTY FOR USING EXTRA POWER UNIT ELEMENTS

Kimi Raikkonen was upset when Ferrari adjusted his tactics during the race to hand this prestigious victory to his Ferrari team-mate Sebastian Vettel, but it gave Vettel a 25-point lead after a weekend in which Lewis Hamilton had to start far down the grid.

It was by the smallest of margins, just 0.043s, but pole position was Kimi Raikkonen's ahead of Sebastian Vettel. For any driver who has just ended a drought that stretched back to the 2008 French GP, it would have been a great feeling. Better still, it was at Monaco, where overtaking is appreciably harder than any other circuit F1 visits.

So, Raikkonen might have fancied adding his first win since the 2013 Australian GP, but the team would decide otherwise...

Ferrari already had an advantage as Lewis Hamilton had stumbled in qualifying. His best lap in Q2 was scuppered when Stoffel Vandoorne crashed. Starting from 12th, with Monaco providing almost no opportunities for passing, Hamilton simply had to bide his time. Meanwhile, the Ferrari duo dominated, with Valtteri Bottas a distant best of the rest.

When Bottas and the Red Bull drivers, who were running fourth and fifth, started to close the gap, Ferrari brought Raikkonen in for his pitstop at mid-distance. He and his engineer protested, but they were overruled while Vettel was allowed to stay out five laps longer. This sent him to the front as his tyres came good again over the extra laps he did in his first stint. When he emerged from his one stop, Vettel was in front and stayed there for Ferrari's first one-two result since 2010. Daniel Ricciardo used a similar tactic to move ahead of team-mate Max Verstappen, and Bottas too, to claim the final place on the podium.

McLaren had a revised line-up, welcoming Jenson Button back for one race while Fernando Alonso tried his hand at contesting the Indianapolis 500. The Spaniard has long sought other challenges and, with McLaren so far from form, reckoned he could afford to skip Monaco. The result was retirement for Button after a collision with Pascal Wehrlein, while Alonso actually led the Indy 500 before retiring when his Honda engine failed, making it not dissimilar to his F1 campaign ...

Hamilton came home in seventh place, leaving him 25 points behind Vettel.

MONTE CARLO ROUND 6

DATE: **28 MAY 2017**

Laps: **78** • Distance: **161.734 miles/260.286km** • Weather: **Bright & hot**

Pos	Driver	Team	Result	Stops	Qualifying Time	Grid
1	Sebastian Vettel	Ferrari	1h44m44.340s	1	1m12.221s	2
2	Kimi Raikkonen	Ferrari	1h44m47.485s	1	1m12.178s	1
3	Daniel Ricciardo	Red Bull	1h44m48.085s	1	1m12.998s	5
4	Valtteri Bottas	Mercedes	1h44m49.857s	1	1m12.223s	3
5	Max Verstappen	Red Bull	1h44m50.539s	2	1m12.496s	4
6	Carlos Sainz Jr	Toro Rosso	1h44m56.378s	1	1m13.162s	6
7	Lewis Hamilton	Mercedes	1h45m00.141s	1	1m14.106s	13
8	Romain Grosjean	Haas	1h45m02.490s	1	1m13.349s	8
9	Felipe Massa	Williams	1h45m03.785s	2	1m20.529s	14
10	Kevin Magnussen	Haas	1h45m05.783s	2	1m13.959s	11
11	Jolyon Palmer	Renault	1h45m07.077s	1	1m14.696s	16
12	Esteban Ocon	Force India	1h45m08.065s	3	1m14.101s	15
13	Sergio Perez !!!	Force India	1h45m33.429s	3	1m13.329s	7
14	Daniil Kvyat	Toro Rosso	71 laps/collision	1	1m13.516s	9
15	Lance Stroll	Williams	71 laps/retired	2	1m14.893s	17
R	Stoffel Vandoorne *	McLaren	66 laps/spun off	1	no time	12
R	Marcus Ericsson **	Sauber	63 laps/spun off	1	1m15.276s	19
R	Jenson Button !	McLaren	57 laps/collision	1	1m13.613s	20
R	Pascal Wehrlein !!	Sauber	57 laps/collision	2	1m15.159s	18
R	Nico Hulkenberg	Renault	15 laps/gearbox	0	1m13.628s	10

FASTEST LAP: **PEREZ, 1M14.820S, 99.768MPH/160.561KPH ON LAP 76** • RACE LEADERS: **RAIKKONEN 1-33, VETTEL 34-78**
* 3-PLACE GRID PENALTY FOR CAUSING A COLLISION IN PREVIOUS RACE; ** 5-PLACE GRID PENALTY FOR CHANGING GEARBOX;
! 15-PLACE GRID PENALTY FOR USING ADDITIONAL POWER UNIT ELEMENTS; !! 5-SECOND PENALTY FOR UNSAFE RELEASE;
!!! 10-SECOND PENALTY FOR CAUSING A COLLISION

Sebastian Vettel flashes over the finish line to extend his championship lead to 25 points.

CANADIAN GP

Lewis Hamilton's disappointment at Monaco was confined to history by a bounce-back performance in Montreal in which he dominated the race, helped by Sebastian Vettel's front wing being damaged at the first corner by Max Verstappen.

There can be no denying that Lewis Hamilton didn't enjoy his visit to Monaco or the negative press which followed after his lacklustre seventh place finish. Yet, as has happened before, Lewis responded in a way that suggests that he sometimes needs to be fired up and truly delivered in the final qualifying session.

Like at Monaco, pole is of extra importance on the Circuit Gilles Villeneuve, and it was clear that there was little between him and Vettel in terms of pace. Both were right on the edge and it was the Ferrari driver who slipped up at Turn 2 on his flier to hand Hamilton pole by 0.3s. They were so far clear of the rest that Vettel was still 0.4s clear of the best of the rest.

At the start, Hamilton got away well, Vettel less so, allowing Valtteri Bottas to attack up the inside. As Vettel looked for space, he then found a flying Max Verstappen on the outside and the Dutchman's left rear wheel hit his front wing endplate, the incident dropping him to fourth and then forcing him to make his one pitstop much earlier than had been planned. It left him 18th and last on rejoining behind Pascal Wehrlein's Sauber and with a lot of overtaking to do.

Hamilton got a further boost on lap 10 when Verstappen's battery failed. This promoted Bottas to second and the race was under control from there.

The main interest through the first 20 laps was Vettel's progress and he attacked to reach seventh by mid-distance. Most drivers were pitting just once and Vettel was still seventh when he re-emerged from his second stop, then set off after Kimi Raikkonen's Ferrari.

He passed the Finn on lap 60 when his team-mate's brake-by-wire system failed, and Vettel did not take long to overtake the Force Indias of Esteban Ocon – on lap 66 – and Sergio Perez two laps later. Had the race been a lap longer, he might have passed Daniel Ricciardo too for a rostrum place.

Yet, after a far more serene run, Hamilton scooped the 25 points for victory to close the gap to series leader Vettel to just 12 points.

MONTREAL ROUND 7

DATE: **11 JUNE 2017**

Laps: **70** • Distance: **189.686 miles/305.270km** • Weather: **Hot & sunny**

Pos	Driver	Team	Result	Stops	Qualifying Time	Grid
1	Lewis Hamilton	Mercedes	1h33m05.154s	1	1m11.459s	1
2	Valtteri Bottas	Mercedes	1h33m24.937s	1	1m12.177s	3
3	Daniel Ricciardo	Red Bull	1h33m40.451s	1	1m12.557s	6
4	Sebastian Vettel	Ferrari	1h33m41.061s	2	1m11.789s	2
5	Sergio Perez	Force India	1h33m45.630s	1	1m13.018s	8
6	Esteban Ocon	Force India	1h33m45.870s	1	1m13.135s	9
7	Kimi Raikkonen	Ferrari	1h34m03.786s	2	1m12.252s	4
8	Nico Hulkenberg	Renault	1h34m05.528s	1	1m13.271s	10
9	Lance Stroll	Williams	69 laps	1	1m14.209s	17
10	Romain Grosjean	Haas	69 laps	1	1m13.839s	14
11	Jolyon Palmer	Renault	69 laps	1	1m14.293s	15
12	Kevin Magnussen !	Haas	69 laps	1	1m14.318s	18
13	Marcus Ericsson	Sauber	69 laps	1	1m14.495s	19
14	Stoffel Vandoorne	McLaren	69 laps	1	1m14.182s	16
15	Pascal Wehrlein *	Sauber	68 laps	2	1m14.810s	20
16	Fernando Alonso	McLaren	66 laps/engine	1	1m13.693s	12
R	Daniil Kvyat !!	Toro Rosso	54 laps/wheelnut	2	1m13.690s	11
R	Max Verstappen	Red Bull	10 laps/battery	0	1m12.403s	5
R	Felipe Massa	Williams	0 laps/accident	0	1m12.858s	7
R	Carlos Sainz Jr	Toro Rosso	0 laps/accident	0	1m13.756s	13

FASTEST LAP: HAMILTON, 1M14.551S, 130.853MPH/210.588KPH ON LAP 64 • RACE LEADER: HAMILTON 1-70
* 5-PLACE GRID PENALTY FOR CHANGING GEARBOX; ! 5-SECOND PENALTY FOR OVERTAKING UNDER VIRTUAL SAFETY CAR;
!! 10-SECOND PENALTY FOR SAFETY CAR INFRINGEMENT

Second after contact with Ferrari's Sebastian Vettel, Max Verstappen retired with battery failure.

In years to come, few fans may recall that Daniel Ricciardo triumphed for Red Bull Racing in Baku, but most will remember the moment when Sebastian Vettel drove his Ferrari into Lewis Hamilton's Mercedes when they circulated behind a safety car.

Petulance isn't an endearing character trait in an infant, so it's safe to say that it's certainly not expected from a multiple World Champion. This is why Sebastian Vettel's move in the Azerbaijan GP was so shocking.

To get to the moment of impact, one needs to go back to the early stages of the race. Hamilton led away from pole and immediately there was trouble as Kimi Raikkonen squeezed Valtteri Bottas at Turn 2 and the Finn's Mercedes hit the inside kerb and then bounced into his compatriot's Ferrari, forcing both to pit.

So, Hamilton led from Vettel and that was how it stayed through two safety car deployments, each allowing Vettel back onto his tail. At the end of the second safety car period, to clear up debris, Hamilton chose not to accelerate out of Turn 15 at the restart and Vettel clipped his tail. These things can happen, but his response was what earned him a 10s penalty, as he immediately jinked to Hamilton's left, drove alongside and then swerved into the Mercedes. It was extraordinary.

All wasn't rosy in the Force India garden either. Indeed, it was already simmering after a team order dispute in Canada and then it got worse as Esteban Ocon tried to dive up the inside of Sergio Perez into Turn 2 as they fought over fourth and collided.

After a red flag stoppage that lasted 23 minutes, Hamilton led away at the restart, but then fell to eighth as he lost time having to pit for a loose headrest to be reaffixed. Vettel wasn't able to benefit, as he had those extra 10s to serve in the pits, and so Daniel Ricciardo found himself in a lead he wasn't to surrender. Surprisingly, after his first lap clash dropped him to last, Bottas came back to finish second. Also, with so many incidents, Williams's maligned teenager Lance Stroll was able to follow up his maiden points score in Canada with his first F1 podium.

Vettel finished a few seconds back and one place ahead of Hamilton, who felt the German's penalty hadn't been sufficient. Few disagreed.

Vettel follows Hamilton behind the safety car before he made a rash move and drove into him.

BAKU ROUND 8

DATE: **25 JUNE 2017**

Laps: **51** • Distance: **190.170 miles/306.049km** • Weather: **Hot & sunny**

Pos	Driver	Team	Result	Stops	Qualifying Time	Grid
1	**Daniel Ricciardo**	Red Bull	2h03m55.573s	3	1m43.414s	10
2	**Valtteri Bottas**	Mercedes	2h03m59.477s	3	1m41.027s	2
3	**Lance Stroll**	Williams	2h03m59.582s	2	1m42.753s	8
4	**Sebastian Vettel**	Ferrari	2h04m01.549s	2	1m41.841s	4
5	**Lewis Hamilton**	Mercedes	2h04m01.761s	2	1m40.953s	1
6	**Esteban Ocon**	Force India	2h04m25.871s	3	1m42.186s	7
7	**Kevin Magnussen**	Haas	2h04m37.326s	2	1m43.796s	12
8	**Carlos Sainz Jr ***	Toro Rosso	2h04m44.973s	2	1m43.347s	15
9	**Fernando Alonso !**	McLaren	2h04m55.124s	2	1m44.334s	19
10	**Pascal Wehrlein**	Sauber	2h05m24.666s	3	1m44.603s	14
11	**Marcus Ericsson**	Sauber	2h05m27.736s	2	1m44.795s	17
12	**Stoffel Vandoorne ****	McLaren	2h05m27.733s	3	1m45.030s	18
13	**Romain Grosjean**	Haas	50 laps	4	1m44.468s	16
14	**Kimi Raikkonen**	Ferrari	46 laps/floor	2	1m41.693s	3
R	**Sergio Perez**	Force India	39 laps/collision	2	1m42.111s	6
R	**Felipe Massa**	Williams	25 laps/suspension	2	1m42.798s	9
R	**Nico Hulkenberg**	Renault	24 laps/accident	2	1m44.267s	13
R	**Max Verstappen**	Red Bull	12 laps/engine	0	1m41.879s	5
R	**Daniil Kvyat**	Toro Rosso	9 laps/electronics	0	1m43.186s	11
R	**Jolyon Palmer**	Renault	7 laps/ignition	0	no time	20

FASTEST LAP: **VETTEL, 1M43.441S, 129.816MPH/208.919KPH ON LAP 47** • RACE LEADERS: HAMILTON 1-30, VETTEL 31-33, RICCIARDO 34-51
* 3-PLACE GRID PENALTY FOR CAUSING A COLLISION IN A PREVIOUS RACE;
** 5-PLACE GRID PENALTY FOR CHANGING GEARBOX PLUS 30-PLACE GRID PENALTY FOR USING EXTRA ADDITIONAL POWER UNIT ELEMENTS;
! 40-PLACE GRID PENALTY FOR USING EXTRA ADDITIONAL POWER UNIT ELEMENTS

Valtteri Bottas's second F1 win looked to be a formality before a late-race tyre problem allowed Sebastian Vettel to close right in, while Lewis Hamilton recovered to fourth position after starting only eighth on the grid, following a gearbox change.

Many of the teams and drivers, but notably Mercedes and Lewis Hamilton, were less than impressed when they arrived at the Red Bull Ring following the news that Sebastian Vettel had escaped a ban for his intentional collision behind the safety car during the Azerbaijan GP and so would be free to attempt to increase his championship lead in Austria.

Hamilton knew that he already had a handicap in that he was going to have to take a five-place grid penalty for a gearbox change, and so he must have been praying that Vettel would slip up in qualifying. As it turned out, Hamilton's team-mate Bottas claimed pole, so that was a relief for Hamilton, but Vettel's Ferrari would start alongside. Even before his grid penalty was added, Hamilton was fast enough only for third, so this dropped him back to eighth on the grid, leaving him with a mountain to climb.

When the lights went green, Bottas absolutely nailed the start and was first up the steep ascent to Turn 1. Vettel slotted in to second place while rival Hamilton gained one place immediately when Max Verstappen's Red Bull suffered a clutch problem and fell back into the pack, only to be hit at the first corner by Daniil Kvyat and eliminated.

Hamilton then passed Sergio Perez for sixth and then Romain Grosjean, at Turn 4 on lap 8, for fifth. His next target was Kimi Raikkonen, but the Finn proved to be a harder nut to crack.

Bottas led all the way to the only planned round of pitstops, with Vettel 8s behind. After their stops, the Ferrari upped its pace and halved the gap. It kept coming down and was given a helping hand when Raikkonen, still to pit, delayed Bottas. However, the advantage still looked big enough to last to the finish but, three laps out, Bottas hit a tyre problem and Vettel closed right in, only to reach the chequered flag 0.658s down.

That said, Vettel could still smile that he had at least outscored Hamilton by six points as the Briton had failed to overtake Daniel Ricciardo in the battle for third place.

A relieved Valtteri Bottas is flanked by Vettel and Hamilton after taking his second 2017 win.

RED BULL RING ROUND 9 — DATE: 9 JULY 2017

Laps: 71 • Distance: **190.420miles/306.452km** • Weather: **Hot & sunny**

Pos	Driver	Team	Result	Stops	Qualifying Time	Grid
1	**Valtteri Bottas**	Mercedes	1h21m48.523s	1	1m04.251s	1
2	**Sebastian Vettel**	Ferrari	1h21m49.181s	1	1m04.293s	2
3	**Daniel Ricciardo**	Red Bull	1h21m54.535s	1	1m04.896s	4
4	**Lewis Hamilton ***	Mercedes	1h21m55.953s	1	1m04.424s	8
5	**Kimi Raikkonen**	Ferrari	1h22m08.893s	1	1m04.779s	3
6	**Romain Grosjean**	Haas	1h23m01.683s	1	1m05.480s	6
7	**Sergio Perez**	Force India	70 laps	1	1m05.605s	7
8	**Esteban Ocon**	Force India	70 laps	1	1m05.674s	9
9	**Felipe Massa**	Williams	70 laps	1	1m06.534s	17
10	**Lance Stroll**	Williams	70 laps	1	1m06.608s	18
11	**Jolyon Palmer**	Renault	70 laps	1	1m06.345s	16
12	**Stoffel Vandoorne**	McLaren	70 laps	1	1m05.741s	13
13	**Nico Hulkenberg**	Renault	70 laps	1	1m05.597s	11
14	**Pascal Wehrlein !**	Sauber	70 laps	1	1m07.011s	20
15	**Marcus Ericsson**	Sauber	69 laps	1	1m06.857s	19
16	**Daniil Kvyat**	Toro Rosso	68 laps	2	1m05.884s	14
R	**Carlos Sainz Jr**	Toro Rosso	44 laps/engine	1	1m05.726s	10
R	**Kevin Magnussen**	Haas	29 laps/hydraulics	0	no time	15
R	**Fernando Alonso**	McLaren	1 lap/collision	0	1m05.602s	12
R	**Max Verstappen**	Red Bull	0 laps/collision	0	1m04.983s	5

FASTEST LAP: HAMILTON, 1M07.411S, 143.286MPH/230.597KPH ON LAP 69 • RACE LEADERS: BOTTAS 1-41 & 44-71, RAIKKONEN 42-43
* 5-PLACE GRID PENALTY FOR CHANGING GEARBOX; ! STARTED FROM PITLANE BECAUSE CAR MODIFIED IN PARC FERME

BRITISH GP

Every now and then, Lewis Hamilton turns on the style and leaves his rivals trailing in his wake. This was one such time, and the fact that he produced such a scintillating drive on home ground at Silverstone made the fourth win of his 2017 campaign all the sweeter.

In the lead-up to the British GP, Lewis Hamilton did himself no favours by being the only F1 driver not to attend an F1 promotional event on the streets of London. So, he was very much on the back foot when he arrived at Silverstone. On top of that, he arrived 20 points down on title rival Sebastian Vettel, so there was a lot to put right.

The first step towards silencing his critics was to secure pole and he did this by a chunky margin of 0.547s ahead of Kimi Raikkonen, with the second Ferrari of Vettel a further fifth of a second back.

As Hamilton had been in Austria, so team-mate Valtteri Bottas was hit with a five-place grid penalty at Silverstone for his Mercedes having a new gearbox, so it was going to be rather difficult for him to play much of a supporting role. However, Mercedes elected that he'd start on Pirelli's soft tyres and see what he could do.

Hamilton led away from Raikkonen, while Vettel tussled with Max Verstappen and lost out before a safety car period was triggered by the Toro Rosso duo of Carlos Sainz Jr and Daniil Kvyat clashing.

Up to the pitstops, Hamilton had everything under control. Ferrari brought Vettel in on lap 18. This worked, as Verstappen had a delay when he came in a lap later and lost third to Vettel. Bottas worked his way up to second place before he pitted on lap 32. Fourth on his return, behind the Ferraris, he was now on supersofts and that gave him the pace to hunt them down. Then both Ferraris suffered flat tyres in the closing laps and while Raikkonen was able to return to finish third, Vettel tumbled down the order and finally finished seventh. Hamilton thus had sliced 19 out of his 20-point deficit.

The other British driver hoping to shine on home ground had a peak in his run of bad luck. This was Jolyon Palmer and his bad season got worse when he was unable to start from 11th on the grid as his Renault suffered a hydraulic problem on the formation lap.

SILVERSTONE ROUND 10

DATE: 16 JULY 2017

Laps: **51** • Distance: **186.602 miles/300.307km** • Weather: **Warm & overcast**

Pos	Driver	Team	Result	Stops	Qualifying Time	Grid
1	**Lewis Hamilton**	Mercedes	1h21m27.430s	1	1m26.600s	1
2	**Valtteri Bottas ***	Mercedes	1h21m41.493s	1	1m27.356s	9
3	**Kimi Raikkonen**	Ferrari	1h22m04.000s	2	1m27.147s	2
4	**Max Verstappen**	Red Bull	1h22m19.555s	2	1m28.130s	4
5	**Daniel Ricciardo !**	Red Bull	1h22m33.385s	1	1m42.966s	19
6	**Nico Hulkenberg**	Renault	1h22m35.539s	1	1m28.856s	5
7	**Sebastian Vettel**	Ferrari	1h23m01.419s	2	1m27.356s	3
8	**Esteban Ocon**	Force India	50 laps	1	1m29.074s	7
9	**Sergio Perez**	Force India	50 laps	1	1m28.902s	6
10	**Felipe Massa**	Williams	50 laps	1	1m31.482s	14
11	**Stoffel Vandoorne**	McLaren	50 laps	1	1m29.418s	8
12	**Kevin Magnussen**	Haas	50 laps	1	1m42.577s	16
13	**Romain Grosjean**	Haas	50 laps	2	1m29.549s	10
14	**Marcus Ericsson**	Sauber	50 laps	1	1m42.633s	18
15	**Daniil Kvyat**	Toro Rosso	50 laps	3	1m30.355s	12
16	**Lance Stroll**	Williams	50 laps	2	1m42.573s	15
17	**Pascal Wehrlein**	Sauber	50 laps	3	1m42.593s	17
R	**Fernando Alonso !!**	McLaren	32 laps/fuel pump	1	1m30.600s	20
R	**Carlos Sainz Jr**	Toro Rosso	0 laps/collision	0	1m31.368s	13
NS	**Jolyon Palmer**	Renault	0 laps/hydraulics	-	1m30.193s	11

FASTEST LAP: **HAMILTON, 1M30.621S, 145.416MPH/234.025KPH ON LAP 48** • RACE LEADER: **HAMILTON 1-51**
* 5-PLACE GRID PENALTY FOR CHANGING GEARBOX; ! 15-PLACE GRID PENALTY FOR CHANGING GEARBOX & USING EXTRA POWER UNIT ELEMENTS; !! 30-PLACE GRID PENALTY FOR USING EXTRA POWER UNIT ELEMENTS

Lewis Hamilton was fastest in the wet in practice, started from pole and won as he pleased.

HUNGARIAN GP

Beaten at Silverstone, Ferrari was back on form at the tighter, twistier Hungaroring, and its one-two result, with Sebastian Vettel beating Kimi Raikkonen, proved to Lewis Hamilton that the 2017 F1 World Championship was still going to require a fight.

The Ferraris powered away at the start of the race, helped by Valtteri Bottas having to settle for third as he was forced to focus on repelling attacks from Max Verstappen rather than trying to advance, with the Red Bull duo having already beaten Hamilton to the first corner.

At Turn 2, though, Verstappen slid into his Red Bull team-mate, putting Daniel Ricciardo into a foul mood and out of the race.

The Hungaroring is famously difficult circuit at which to make passing manoeuvres, so there were no changes in the top five places up to the start of the pitstops. It was at this point, though, that Verstappen lost fourth to Hamilton, when he was held for an extra 10s as a punishment for taking out his team-mate.

This meant that Hamilton was able to advance to fourth, but as he was lapping faster than Bottas, the team let him move up to third so that he could go after the Ferraris. This was on one premise, though, that if he failed, he'd hand the place back to Valtteri. Although Hamilton got close, he realised that the Ferraris had enough pace to repel him and so, with a lap to go, he let Bottas back past. Some thought that this was crazy and that the three-point difference between finishing third and fourth could, in such a closely-fought season, prove to be the difference between winning the F1 title and not.

Ferrari didn't have any similar ideas and stuck to its regular policy of favouring just its number one driver, Vettel, so Raikkonen meekly sat in his wheeltracks for almost the entire race distance.

The Red Bull boys weren't the only team-mates to get too close to each other, as Force India's Sergio Perez and Esteban Ocon also collided, at Turn 1, lap 1. Renault's Nico Hulkenberg wasn't too pleased to be forced off the track by Haas's Kevin Magnussen and a war of words ensued.

F1 welcomed back Paul di Resta who was called up as an 11th-hour stand-in for Felipe Massa at Williams when the Brazilian fell ill. An oil leak forced him out with 10 laps to go.

HUNGARORING ROUND 11

DATE: **30 JULY 2017**

Laps: **70** • Distance: **190.531 miles/306.630km** • Weather: **Hot & sunny**

Pos	Driver	Team	Result	Stops	Qualifying Time	Grid
1	Sebastian Vettel	Ferrari	1h39m46.713s	1	1m16.276s	1
2	Kimi Raikkonen	Ferrari	1h39m47.621s	1	1m16.444s	2
3	Valtteri Bottas	Mercedes	1h39m59.175s	1	1m16.530s	3
4	Lewis Hamilton	Mercedes	1h39m59.598s	1	1m16.707s	4
5	Max Verstappen	Red Bull	1h39m59.989s	1	1m16.797s	5
6	Fernando Alonso	McLaren	1h40m57.936s	1	1m17.549s	7
7	Carlos Sainz Jr	Toro Rosso	69 laps	1	1m18.912s	9
8	Sergio Perez	Force India	69 laps	1	1m18.639s	13
9	Esteban Ocon	Force India	69 laps	1	1m18.495s	11
10	Stoffel Vandoorne	McLaren	69 laps	1	1m17.894s	8
11	Daniil Kvyat *	Toro Rosso	69 laps	1	1m18.538s	16
12	Jolyon Palmer	Renault	69 laps	1	1m18.415s	10
13	Kevin Magnussen !!	Haas	69 laps	1	1m19.095s	15
14	Lance Stroll	Williams	69 laps	1	1m19.102s	17
15	Pascal Wehrlein	Sauber	68 laps	1	1m19.839s	18
16	Marcus Ericsson	Sauber	68 laps	2	1m19.972s	20
R	Nico Hulkenberg !	Renault	67 laps/gearbox	1	1m17.468s	12
R	Paul di Resta	Williams	60 laps/oil leak	1	1m19.868s	19
R	Romain Grosjean	Haas	20 laps/loose wheel	1	1m18.771s	14
R	Daniel Ricciardo	Red Bull	0 laps/accident	0	1m16.818s	6

FASTEST LAP: ALONSO, 1M20.182S, 122.222MPH/196.697KPH ON LAP 69 • RACE LEADERS: VETTEL 1-31 & 43-70, RAIKKONEN 32-33, VERSTAPPEN 34-42
* 3-PLACE GRID PENALTY FOR IMPEDING ANOTHER DRIVER; ! 5-PLACE GRID PENALTY FOR CHANGING GEARBOX;
!! 5-SECOND PENALTY FOR FORCING A DRIVER OFF TRACK

Fernando Alonso not only finished in sixth place, but set the race's fastest lap for McLaren.

BELGIAN GP

Sebastian Vettel both arrived in and departed from Belgium leading the championship table. However, by finishing in second place, admittedly only 2.358s behind Lewis Hamilton, he found that his points advantage had been reduced to a mere seven.

The first step for Lewis Hamilton was to claim pole position, which he managed ahead of Sebastian Vettel by 0.242s, with the added thrill of this putting him equal top with Michael Schumacher for poles secured, at 68.

When this was translated into the lead at the start, as the Mercedes ace was first both into and out of La Source, things had started well. Vettel tucked in behind, but initially was unable to challenge.

Midway through the race, there was a glitch in Hamilton's control when the safety car had to be deployed after Force India drivers Esteban Ocon and Sergio Perez clashed, leaving debris on the track. When it withdrew five laps later, Hamilton was less than impressed, reckoning that it had been put out more to close up the lead battle, and allow Vettel closer to his Mercedes' tail, than for any safety reasons.

This allowed Vettel to advance into his slipstream, meaning Hamilton faced a renewed challenge. In addition, Vettel had Pirelli's supersoft tyres fitted for the final sprint to the finish which gave him a performance advantage over the soft-shod Hamilton. The run to the flag was immensely hard work, but Hamilton hung on to win by more than 2s.

Daniel Ricciardo made it three teams in the top three, crossing the line 10s down, both he and Ferrari number two driver Kimi Raikkonen advancing at the cost of Valtteri Bottas who had to settle for fifth after they blasted past him at the very same time as he stumbled at the race restart.

Max Verstappen might reasonably have expected to take a decent point-scoring placing, but the Dutch charger wasn't around at the finish as he'd retired with his third engine failure of the year, leaving him less than happy.

While Nico Hulkenberg had a sensibly paced run to sixth place for Renault, his team-mate Jolyon Palmer was less contented after Fernando Alonso pushed him wide at Rivage and held him offline so that Carlos Sainz Jr could slide by as well.

The story of 2017 was Lewis Hamilton running ahead of Sebastian Vettel, as he did at Spa.

SPA-FRANCORCHAMPS ROUND 12 DATE: 27 AUGUST 2017

Laps: **44** • Distance: **191.414 miles/308.052km** • Weather: **Warm & bright**

Pos	Driver	Team	Result	Stops	Qualifying Time	Grid
1	**Lewis Hamilton**	Mercedes	1h24m42.820s	2	1m42.553s	1
2	**Sebastian Vettel**	Ferrari	1h24m45.178s	2	1m42.795s	2
3	**Daniel Ricciardo**	Red Bull	1h24m53.611s	2	1m43.863s	6
4	**Kimi Raikkonen**	Ferrari	1h24m57.291s	2	1m43.270s	4
5	**Valtteri Bottas**	Mercedes	1h24m59.276s	2	1m43.094s	3
6	**Nico Hulkenberg**	Renault	1h25m10.907s	2	1m44.982s	7
7	**Romain Grosjean**	Haas	1h25m14.373s	2	1m45.133s	11
8	**Felipe Massa ****	Williams	1h25m19.469s	2	1m45.823s	16
9	**Esteban Ocon**	Force India	1h25m20.974s	3	1m45.369s	9
10	**Carlos Sainz Jr**	Toro Rosso	1h25m22.267s	2	1m45.439s	13
11	**Lance Stroll**	Williams	1h25m31.819s	2	1m46.915s	15
12	**Daniil Kvyat !**	Toro Rosso	1h25m32.760s	2	1m46.028s	19
13	**Jolyon Palmer ***	Renault	1h25m36.059s	2	no time	14
14	**Stoffel Vandoorne !!**	McLaren	1h25m39.898s	2	no time	20
15	**Kevin Magnussen**	Haas	1h25m50.082s	3	1m45.400s	12
16	**Marcus Ericsson ***	Sauber	1h25m52.531s	3	1m47.214s	17
17	**Sergio Perez**	Force India	42 laps/crash damage	3	1m45.244s	8
R	**Fernando Alonso**	McLaren	25 laps/engine	1	1m45.090s	10
R	**Max Verstappen**	Red Bull	7 laps/engine	0	1m43.380s	5
R	**Pascal Wehrlein ***	Sauber	2 laps/suspension	0	1m47.679s	18

FASTEST LAP: **VETTEL, 1M46.577, 147.006MPH/236.583KPH ON LAP 41** • RACE LEADERS: **HAMILTON 1-11 & 15-44, VETTEL 12-14**
* 5-PLACE GRID PENALTY FOR CHANGING GEARBOX; ** 5-PLACE GRID PENALTY FOR FAILING TO SLOW FOR YELLOW FLAGS;
! 20-PLACE GRID PENALTY FOR USING EXTRA POWER UNIT ELEMENTS;
!! 65-PLACE GRID PENALTY FOR CHANGING GEARBOX & USING EXTRA POWER UNIT ELEMENTS

Italian F1 fans have nothing against Lewis Hamilton and more than likely respected his peerless performance at Monza, but they booed him on the podium for he, and team-mate Valtteri Bottas, had restricted their Ferrari ace Vettel to third place.

Look back at the stats for the Italian GP and you will see that Lewis Hamilton qualified on pole and led every lap bar two - when he came in for his one and only pitstop - and Mercedes team-mate Valtteri Bottas took over until he too pitted. Thereafter, Hamilton raced on to a comfortable victory that put him into the championship lead for the first time in 2017 ahead of Sebastian Vettel.

However, because it was such an emphatic triumph, the victory did more than that. It took the wind out of the *tifosi*'s sails as it made their beloved Ferrari look good enough only to be described as the best of the rest. Worse still, the red cars weren't really even in the hunt as the gap between the teams was huge. Vettel finished third, but was 36s adrift by flagfall and that's what really hurt.

Hamilton took the lead at the start and stayed there. The identity of the driver starting alongside him on the front row was a surprise. It was Lance Stroll, who showed impressive form in the wet, and was promoted two places by the Red Bull drivers who'd out-qualified him both being pushed back by grid penalties.

In fact, grid penalties were the predominant topic under discussion at Monza, with nine of the 20 drivers being hit with them. One who suffered from this was Max Verstappen, put back from second to 13th for his Red Bull being fitted with extra power unit elements. This put him into the midfield, where collisions are always at their most likely. In the young Dutchman's case, he clashed with Felipe Massa's Williams as he tried to pass it for seventh, and was delayed by a puncture. Daniel Ricciardo fared best of those punished, forcing his way up from 16th on the grid to fourth and recording the fastest lap too.

Stroll didn't stay second for long as he was demoted in short order by Esteban Ocon, Bottas and then Vettel. The Force India driver also slid back as Bottas came through to tie up second. Vettel also rose to a podium position, running a few places behind team-mate Raikkonen but reaching third by lap 8.

MONZA ROUND 13

DATE: **3 SEPTEMBER 2017**

Laps: **53** • Distance: **190.587 miles/306.720km** • Weather: **Hot & sunny**

Pos	Driver	Team	Result	Stops	Qualifying Time	Grid
1	**Lewis Hamilton**	Mercedes	1h15m32.312s	1	1m35.554s	1
2	**Valtteri Bottas**	Mercedes	1h15m36.783s	1	1m37.833s	4
3	**Sebastian Vettel**	Ferrari	1h16m08.629s	1	1m38.064s	6
4	**Daniel Ricciardo *!!**	Red Bull	1h16m12.647s	1	1m36.841s	16
5	**Kimi Raikkonen**	Ferrari	1h16m32.394s	1	1m37.987s	5
6	**Esteban Ocon**	Force India	1h16m43.840s	1	1m37.719s	3
7	**Lance Stroll**	Williams	1h16m46.468s	1	1m37.032s	2
8	**Felipe Massa**	Williams	1h16m47.146s	1	1m38.251s	7
9	**Sergio Perez ***	Force India	1h16m47.588s	1	1m37.582s	10
10	**Max Verstappen !!**	Red Bull	52 laps	2	1m36.702s	13
11	**Kevin Magnussen**	Haas	52 laps	1	1m40.489s	9
12	**Daniil Kvyat**	Toro Rosso	52 laps	1	1m38.245s	8
13	**Nico Hulkenberg ****	Renault	52 laps	1	1m38.059s	14
14	**Carlos Sainz Jr ****	Toro Rosso	52 laps	1	1m38.526s	15
15	**Romain Grosjean ***	Haas	52 laps	2	1m43.355s	20
16	**Pascal Wehrlein**	Sauber	51 laps	1	1m41.875s	12
17	**Fernando Alonso !!!!**	McLaren	50 laps/gearbox	1	1m38.202s	19
18	**Marcus Ericsson**	Sauber	49 laps/accident	1	1m41.732s	11
R	**Stoffel Vandoorne !!!**	McLaren	33 laps/power unit	0	1m39.157s	18
R	**Jolyon Palmer !**	Renault	29 laps/transmission	1	1m40.646s	17

FASTEST LAP: RICCIARDO, 1M23.361S, 155.451MPH/250.174KPH ON LAP 49 • RACE LEADERS: HAMILTON 1-31 & 34-53, BOTTAS 32-33
* 5-PLACE GRID PENALTY FOR CHANGING GEARBOX; ** 10-PLACE GRID PENALTY FOR USING EXTRA POWER UNIT ELEMENTS;
! 15-PLACE GRID PENALTY FOR USING EXTRA POWER UNIT ELEMENTS; !! 20-PLACE GRID PENALTY FOR USING EXTRA POWER UNIT ELEMENTS;
!!! 25-PLACE GRID PENALTY FOR USING EXTRA POWER UNIT ELEMENTS; !!!! 35-PLACE GRID PENALTY FOR USING EXTRA POWER UNIT ELEMENTS

The Monza podium celebrations are always among the most spectacular of the season.

Never look a gift horse in the mouth is certainly good advice and Lewis Hamilton was delighted to accept a win that was gifted to him when Max Verstappen got squeezed by the Ferraris on the dash to the first corner on the opening lap, putting all three out.

The headlines through practice and qualifying were that Ferrari had done its sums right, while Mercedes hadn't and its cars were off the pace. Indeed, Lewis Hamilton was able to qualify only fifth and felt that his only hope was the arrival of rain.

As it transpired, he was given a helping hand from another quarter. When the lights went green, Kimi Raikkonen made a fantastic getaway from fourth and team-mate Sebastian Vettel a poor one from pole. With Max Verstappen looking to take the lead, Vettel decided to move across on him. However, with Raikkonen alongside him next to the pitwall, there was nowhere to go and the Red Bull racer clipped Raikkonen's Ferrari, which then snapped around and took out Vettel's to make it a disaster for Ferrari as, in a flash, the three were out of the race. Many were astonished that the driver who triggered the incident, Vettel, wasn't punished.

Luckily, most of those behind managed to avoid them, with Hamilton getting around Daniel Ricciardo to take the lead. One who wasn't so lucky, though, was Fernando Alonso who had been relieved to qualify his improving McLaren eighth and made an outstanding start that was to prove his undoing, as he was caught up in the accident, his car sustaining damage as it was pitched into the air by Verstappen just as he moved into third position. He reckoned that he was heading for the podium, even the win. So, seventh place for team-mate Stoffel Vandoorne was good but scant consolation for the team.

With Hamilton duly winning as he pleased, and Ricciardo following him home in second position, the final podium place went to an off-form Valtteri Bottas who was pushed hard by Nico Hulkenberg until the German's Renault failed. Carlos Sainz Jr claimed fourth for Toro Rosso after resisting pressure from Sergio Perez. Not that far behind in sixth was a driver who, while delighted with taking his best F1 finish, knew his seat was under threat: Renault's Jolyon Palmer.

Disaster for Ferrari as Vettel's move takes out himself, team-mate Raikkonen and Verstappen too.

SINGAPORE ROUND 14

DATE: **17 SEPTEMBER 2017**

Laps: **58** • Distance: **182.455 miles/293.633km** • Weather: **Hot & wet**

Pos	Driver	Team	Result	Stops	Qualifying Time	Grid
1	**Lewis Hamilton**	Mercedes	2h03m23.544s	2	1m40.126s	5
2	**Daniel Ricciardo**	Red Bull	2h03m28.051s	2	1m39.840s	3
3	**Valtteri Bottas**	Mercedes	2h03m32.344s	2	1m40.810s	6
4	**Carlos Sainz Jr**	Toro Rosso	2h03m46.366s	2	1m42.056s	10
5	**Sergio Perez**	Force India	2h03m48.903s	3	1m42.246s	12
6	**Jolyon Palmer**	Renault	2h03m50.803s	3	1m42.017s	11
7	**Stoffel Vandoorne**	McLaren	2h03m53.932s	3	1m41.398s	9
8	**Lance Stroll**	Williams	2h04m05.240s	3	1m44.728s	18
9	**Romain Grosjean**	Haas	2h04m06.826s	3	1m43.883s	15
10	**Esteban Ocon**	Force India	2h04m08.339s	4	1m42.760s	14
11	**Felipe Massa**	Williams	2h04m10.080s	5	1m44.014s	17
12	**Pascal Wehrlein**	Sauber	56 laps	5	1m45.059s	19
R	**Kevin Magnussen**	Haas	50 laps/power unit	4	1m43.756s	16
R	**Nico Hulkenberg**	Renault	48 laps/oil leak	4	1m41.013s	7
R	**Marcus Ericsson ***	Sauber	35 laps/spun off	5	1m45.570s	20
R	**Daniil Kvyat**	Toro Rosso	10 laps/spun off	2	1m42.338s	13
R	**Fernando Alonso**	McLaren	8 laps/crash damage	2	1m41.179s	8
R	**Sebastian Vettel**	Ferrari	0 laps/collision	0	1m39.491s	1
R	**Max Verstappen**	Red Bull	0 laps/collision	0	1m39.814s	2
R	**Kimi Raikkonen**	Ferrari	0 laps/collision	0	1m40.069s	4

FASTEST LAP: HAMILTON, 1M45.008S, 107.897MPH/173.643KPH ON LAP 55 • RACE LEADER: HAMILTON 1-58
* 5-PLACE GRID PENALTY FOR CHANGING GEARBOX

MALAYSIAN GP

A theme that emerged through 2017 was that Ferrari had the pace to match Mercedes, but made something of a habit of squandering it. F1's final visit to Sepang was another example of this, so Lewis Hamilton was happy to stretch his advantage.

Lewis Hamilton will have felt good after he qualified fastest at Sepang, as his chief title rival Sebastian Vettel would be starting from the back of the grid and facing a massive challenge to collect a worthwhile haul of points.

Then, as Kimi Raikkonen brought the other Ferrari and parked it alongside his Mercedes on the front row of the grid, Hamilton looked across and noticed a lot of activity as the Finn's car refused to start and its race was run even before it had started.

Hamilton duly led away from pole position, but the Ferrari misfortunes didn't leave him without any challenge as Max Verstappen was on the hunt. In fact, having resisted a move by fast-starting Valtteri Bottas at Turn 2 on the opening lap, he wasn't content just to give chase. By lap 3, he was close enough coming out of the last corner to try a move for the lead into Turn 1. With a good tow, he dived up the inside and Hamilton, sensing that the Red Bull RB13 had more pace so a pass would be inevitable, gave him space rather than suffer damage in a clash. And that, at a meeting in which Mercedes didn't reckon that it had the pace of rivals Ferrari and Red Bull, was that, with Verstappen able to pull clear to notch up his second F1 win with ease.

Hamilton collected the 18 points for finishing second, but Vettel was tigerish and worked his way past Force India's Sergio Perez and then a lacklustre Bottas to finish fourth, and so lost only six points in their title battle. Bizarrely, he and Lance Stroll collided on the slowing-down lap.

Any driver outperforming Fernando Alonso in the same equipment deserves the plaudits and Stoffel Vandoorne gathered those after he came seventh for the second race in a row, while his McLaren team-mate fell back to 12th.

With Malaysia having hosted a grand prix since 1999, but recently fallen out of love with F1, the teams and drivers were generally sad after the race that this was their last chance to visit one of Hermann Tilke's best circuits.

Max Verstappen made the run to his second F1 win look very easy as he picked off Hamilton.

SEPANG ROUND 15

DATE: 1 OCTOBER 2017

Laps: 56 • Distance: 192.878 miles/310.408km • Weather: **Cloudy & hot**

Pos	Driver	Team	Result	Stops	Qualifying Time	Grid
1	**Max Verstappen**	Red Bull	1h30m01.290s	1	1m30.541s	3
2	**Lewis Hamilton**	Mercedes	1h30m14.060s	1	1m30.076s	1
3	**Daniel Ricciardo**	Red Bull	1h30m23.809s	1	1m30.995s	4
4	**Sebastian Vettel ***	Ferrari	1h30m38.652s	1	No time	20
5	**Valtteri Bottas**	Mercedes	1h30m57.311s	1	1m30.758s	5
6	**Sergio Perez**	Force India	1h31m19.920s	1	1m31.658s	9
7	**Stoffel Vandoorne**	McLaren	55 laps	1	1m31.582s	7
8	**Lance Stroll**	Williams	55 laps	1	1m32.307s	13
9	**Felipe Massa**	Williams	55 laps	1	1m32.034s	11
10	**Esteban Ocon**	Force India	55 laps	1	1m31.478s	6
11	**Fernando Alonso**	McLaren	55 laps	1	1m31.704s	10
12	**Kevin Magnussen**	Haas	55 laps	1	1m33.434s	17
13	**Romain Grosjean**	Haasa	55 laps	2	1m33.308s	16
14	**Pierre Gasly**	Toro Rosso	55 laps	1	1m32.558s	15
15	**Jolyon Palmer**	Renault	55 laps	1	1m32.100s	12
16	**Nico Hulkenberg**	Renault	55 laps	2	1m31.607s	8
17	**Pascal Wehrlein**	Sauber	55 laps	1	1m33.483s	18
18	**Marcus Ericsson**	Sauber	54 laps	1	1m33.970s	19
R	**Carlos Sainz Jr**	Toro Rosso	29 laps/electrical	0	1m32.402s	14
NS	**Kimi Raikkonen**	Ferrari	0 laps/power unit	0	1m30.121s	2

FASTEST LAP: VETTEL, 1M34.080S, 131.795MPH/212.104KPH ON LAP 41 • RACE LEADERS: HAMILTON 1-3, VERSTAPPEN 4-27 & 30-56, RICCIARDO 28-29
* 20-PLACE GRID PENALTY FOR USING ADDITIONAL POWER UNIT ELEMENTS

JAPANESE GP

October was far from a great month for Ferrari, as it squandered its opportunities with a truly competitive car, and its failures in Malaysia continued in Japan, allowing Mercedes' Lewis Hamilton to stretch 59 points clear in the drivers' championship.

To fail when your car is not quite on the pace is one thing, but to have poor reliability wreck another race when your cars were competitive is quite another, so one can imagine that there were some extremely uncomfortable debriefs at Ferrari following its Suzuka debacle.

Sebastian Vettel lined up second on the grid behind Lewis Hamilton's Mercedes and was out to make amends for the mess of Singapore and then having to mount a recovery drive at Sepang. Unfortunately, he wasn't able to do so as his Ferrari was afflicted with a misfire, leaving him to tumble down the order to seventh by the end of lap 3 before retiring with a spark plug failure that put pressure on Ferrari's technical department.

Any hopes that Kimi Raikkonen might take the fight to Hamilton were reduced when he qualified only sixth fastest and dropped back to 10th on the grid after being penalised for a gearbox change, and then extinguished on lap 1 when Nico Hulkenberg pushed him off the track and left him to fight back from 15th.

Hulkenberg moved in the opposite direction and was set for points, but a late pitstop brought his Renault back out behind the Haas chargers and Toro Rosso's Pierre Gasly. Then, just as he started to pick them off, his DRS jammed open, making life too hard around the corners to make it worth going on.

While Hamilton was able to resist all that Max Verstappen could throw at him, Daniel Ricciardo lost out to his Dutch team-mate at the start but then held off a back-on-form Bottas to finish third. Raikkonen made it past the scrapping Force India duo to finish fifth, with the Haas drivers also both getting into the points, and Felipe Massa claiming the final point-scoring position as he tried his all to do enough to keep his ride with Williams for 2018.

Lance Stroll, in the other Williams, exited the race in spectacular fashion when his right front suspension collapsed going into the esses. The Canadian was fortunate to avoid the barriers and Ricciardo equally lucky not to be collected by the Canadian's errant car.

SUZUKA ROUND 16

DATE: **8 OCTOBER 2017**

Laps: **53** • Distance: **191.053 miles/307.471km** • Weather: **Warm & sunny**

Pos	Driver	Team	Result	Stops	Qualifying Time	Grid
1	**Lewis Hamilton**	Mercedes	1h27m31.194s	1	1m27.319s	1
2	**Max Verstappen**	Red Bull	1h27m32.405s	1	1m28.332s	4
3	**Daniel Ricciardo**	Red Bull	1h27m40.873s	1	1m28.306s	3
4	**Valtteri Bottas ***	Mercedes	1h27m41.774s	1	1m27.651s	6
5	**Kimi Raikkonen ***	Ferrari	1h28m03.816s	1	1m28.498s	10
6	**Esteban Ocon**	Force India	1h28m38.982s	1	1m29.111s	5
7	**Sergio Perez**	Force India	1h28m42.618s	1	1m29.260s	7
8	**Kevin Magnussen**	Haas	1h29m00.147s	1	1m29.972s	12
9	**Romain Grosjean**	Haas	1h29m01.077s	1	1m30.849s	13
10	**Felipe Massa**	Williams	52 laps	1	1m29.480s	8
11	**Fernando Alonso !!**	McLaren	52 laps	1	1m30.687s	20
12	**Jolyon Palmer !**	Renault	52 laps	1	1m30.022s	18
13	**Pierre Gasly**	Toro Rosso	52 laps	2	1m31.317s	14
14	**Stoffel Vandoorne**	McLaren	52 laps	2	1m29.778s	9
15	**Pascal Wehrlein**	Sauber	51 laps	3	1m31.885s	17
R	**Lance Stroll**	Williams	45 laps/suspension	2	1m31.409s	15
R	**Nico Hulkenberg**	Renault	40 laps/DRS	1	1m29.879s	11
R	**Marcus Ericsson**	Sauber	7 laps/spun off	0	1m31.597s	16
R	**Sebastian Vettel**	Ferrari	4 laps/spark plug	0	1m27.279s	2
R	**Carlos Sainz Jr !**	Toro Rosso	0 laps/spun off	0	1m30.413s	19

FASTEST LAP: BOTTAS, 1M33.144S, 139.460MPH/224.439KPH ON LAP 50 • RACE LEADERS: HAMILTON 1-22 & 28-53, RICCIARDO 23-25, BOTTAS 26-27
* 5-PLACE GRID PENALTY FOR CHANGING GEARBOX;
! 20-PLACE GRID PENALTY FOR USING ADDITIONAL POWER UNIT ELEMENTS;
!! 35-PLACE GRID PENALTY FOR USING ADDITIONAL POWER UNIT ELEMENTS

Lewis Hamilton leads Sebastian Vettel and the Red Bulls into the downhill entry to Turn 1.

For only the second time in 2017, Lewis Hamilton had to pass Sebastian Vettel on the track to win, and he pulled it off with aplomb at Turn 12 on the sixth lap, then controlled proceedings to put himself on the brink of his fourth F1 drivers' title.

When Sebastian Vettel made a brilliant start and nosed his Ferrari into the lead at Turn 1, it looked as though Lewis Hamilton and Mercedes might have to reconsider their strategy. However, Lewis got close enough out of Turn 11 on lap 6 to use his car's DRS to line up a passing move into Turn 12 and, surprised by Vettel's lack of defence, took the lead. From there, victory by 10s was a formality. Even though team-mate Valtteri Bottas wasn't able to challenge the Ferraris, and thus prevent Vettel from claiming the points for second place, Hamilton left Texas with a 66-point lead, and thus hopeful of wrapping up the title in Mexico.

There was extra cheer in the Mercedes camp, as this was the 11th win of the year for the team from Brackley, enough for it to claim a fourth constructors' crown.

Ferrari had to settle for second and third, with Max Verstappen giving chase after a remarkable drive through the field, having started from 16th on the grid after being hit with a 15-place grid penalty. He hunted down Raikkonen, diving past at Turn 17 on the final lap, but was then given a 5s penalty for leaving the track, which most thought was a marginal call at best, and this dropped him to fourth in the results.

Another driver hit with a 5s penalty was Marcus Ericsson, the Sauber driver punished for clipping Kevin Magnussen's Haas when he attempted to pass it as both were lapped by Vettel's Ferrari.

The Force India drivers continued to make their bosses nervous and they refused Sergio Perez's request for Esteban Ocon to let him by when he appeared to be the faster of the pair. They finished sixth and eighth.

There was a new face on the grid, with Brendon Hartley taking Daniil Kvyat's place at Scuderia Toro Rosso. This was a second chance for the Kiwi Le Mans winner, as he'd been on Red Bull's scholarship programme until 2011. He hadn't driven a single-seater since 2012, but did well to finish 13th.

110

CIRCUIT OF THE AMERICAS ROUND 17

DATE: **22 OCTOBER 2017**

Laps: **56** • Distance: **191.634 miles/308.405km** • Weather: **Warm & bright**

Pos	Driver	Team	Result	Stops	Qualifying Time	Grid
1	**Lewis Hamilton**	Mercedes	1h33m50.991s	1	1m33.108s	1
2	**Sebastian Vettel**	Ferrari	1h34m01.134s	2	1m33.347s	2
3	**Kimi Raikkonen**	Ferrari	1h34m06.770s	1	1m33.577s	4
4	**Max Verstappen *!!**	Red Bull	1h34m07.759s	2	1m33.658S	16
5	**Valtteri Bottas**	Mercedes	1h34m25.958s	2	1m33.568s	3
6	**Esteban Ocon**	Force India	1h35m21.971s	1	1m34.467s	6
7	**Carlos Sainz Jr**	Renault	1h35m23.935s	1	1m34.852s	7
8	**Sergio Perez**	Force India	55 laps	1	1m35.148s	9
9	**Felipe Massa**	Williams	55 laps	1	1m35.155s	10
10	**Daniil Kvyat**	Toro Rosso	55 laps	1	1m35.529s	11
11	**Lance Stroll !**	Williams	55 laps	2	1m36.868S	15
12	**Stoffel Vandoorne ** **	McLaren	55 laps	1	1m35.641s	20
13	**Brendon Hartley !!!!**	Toro Rosso	55 laps	2	1m36.889s	19
14	**Romain Grosjean**	Haas	55 laps	1	1m35.870s	12
15	**Marcus Ericsson ***	Sauber	55 laps	1	1m36.842s	13
16	**Kevin Magnussen !**	Haas	55 laps	2	1m37.394s	17
R	**Fernando Alonso**	McLaren	24 laps/engine	1	1m35.007s	8
R	**Daniel Ricciardo**	Red Bull	14 laps/engine	1	1m33.577s	4
R	**Pascal Wehrlein**	Sauber	5 laps/accident	1	1m37.179s	14
R	**Nico Hulkenberg !!!**	Renault	3 laps/oil pressure	0	no time	18

FASTEST LAP: VETTEL, 1M37.766S, 126.140MPH/203.003KPH ON LAP 51 • RACE LEADERS: VETTEL 1-5, HAMILTON 6-19, 23-56, RAIKKONEN 20, VERSTAPPEN 21-22
* 5-SECOND PENALTY; ! 3-PLACE GRID PENALTY FOR IMPEDING ANOTHER DRIVER IN QUALIFYING; !! 15-PLACE GRID PENALTY FOR USING ADDITIONAL POWER UNIT ELEMENTS; !!! 20-PLACE GRID PENALTY FOR USING ADDITIONAL POWER UNIT ELEMENTS; !!!! 25-PLACE GRID PENALTY FOR USING ADDITIONAL POWER UNIT ELEMENTS; ** 30-PLACE GRID PENALTY FOR USING ADDITIONAL POWER UNIT ELEMENTS

Verstappen overtook car after car as he advanced from 16th to third, before being penalised.

MEXICAN GP

Lewis Hamilton equalled Alain Prost in becoming a four-time F1 World Champion, but trailing home in ninth place in Mexico after a recovery drive wasn't exactly how he had hoped to do it, as Max Verstappen easily won the day for Red Bull Racing.

The smallest of taps on his right rear wheel was all it took for Lewis Hamilton's hopes of celebrating the title from up on the podium to be dashed. That the tap came from his title rival Sebastian Vettel was all the more frustrating for the British racer, because it forced him to limp slowly back to the pits for a new tyre, and left him stone last.

When the impact came on the exit of Turn 3 on the opening lap, Max Verstappen had already muscled his way past Vettel's pole-starting Ferrari through the esses and stayed its momentum sufficiently for Hamilton to dive past too. With a bent front wing, Vettel also had to pit and he was joined there by Renault's Carlos Sainz Jr who had clashed with Felipe Massa and spun, flat-spotting his tyres.

As Verstappen tore ever further clear of Valtteri Bottas and Esteban Ocon at the head of the field, the fightback began in earnest for Vettel, who must have understood that his title hopes were all but extinguished.

Hamilton only had to finish in fifth place to secure his fourth F1 title, but this was if Vettel took the 25 points for victory, and there was no danger of that as Verstappen was driving like never before and was totally in control.

Naturally, Vettel did all he could and worked his way through to an eventual fourth, setting the race's fastest lap along the way. Yet, fourth brought only 12 points, and so Hamilton didn't even have to get into the top 10 to claim his fourth F1 drivers' crown. As it was, he made it back up the order to ninth by passing Fernando Alonso's McLaren in the closing laps.

With Ocon running in third place and Sergio Perez fifth, it could have been a great day for Force India, and points were scored, but they fell back behind the Ferraris to end up a lap down in fifth and seventh places at the finish, with Lance Stroll enjoying his best run for a while to take sixth for Williams. Renault also could have been in the mix, but Nico Hulkenberg dropped from fourth when had to retire yet again, this time with electrical problems.

Hamilton (right) is already limping back to the pits after being hit at the exit of Turn 3 by Vettel.

MEXICO CITY ROUND 18
DATE: **29 OCTOBER 2017**

Laps: **71** • Distance: **189.738 miles/305.354km** • Weather: **Warm but cloudy**

Pos	Driver	Team	Result	Stops	Qualifying Time	Grid
1	**Max Verstappen**	Red Bull	1h36m26.552s	1	1m16.574s	2
2	**Valtteri Bottas**	Mercedes	1h36m46.230s	1	1m16.958s	4
3	**Kimi Raikkonen**	Ferrari	1h37m20.559s	1	1m17.238s	5
4	**Sebastian Vettel**	Ferrari	1h37m36.630s	2	1m16.488s	1
5	**Esteban Ocon**	Force India	70 laps	1	1m17.437s	6
6	**Lance Stroll**	Williams	70 laps	1	1m19.159s	11
7	**Sergio Perez**	Force India	70 laps	2	1m17.807s	9
8	**Kevin Magnussen**	Haas	70 laps	1	1m19.443s	14
9	**Lewis Hamilton**	Mercedes	70 laps	2	1m16.934s	3
10	**Fernando Alonso ***	McLaren	70 laps	1	No time	18
11	**Felipe Massa**	Williams	70 laps	1	1m18.099s	10
12	**Stoffel Vandoorne ****	McLaren	70 laps	1	No time	19
13	**Pierre Gasly ***	Toro Rosso	70 laps	1	No time	20
14	**Pascal Wehrlein**	Sauber	69 laps	1	1m19.333s	13
15	**Romain Grosjean**	Haas	69 laps	2	1m19.473s	15
R	**Carlos Sainz Jr**	Renault	59 laps/steering	2	1m17.794s	8
R	**Marcus Ericsson**	Sauber	55 laps/brake by wire	1	1m19.176s	12
R	**Brendon Hartley ***	Toro Rosso	30 laps/power unit	0	No time	17
R	**Nico Hulkenberg**	Renault	24 laps/electrics	1	1m17.466s	7
R	**Daniel Ricciardo ***	Red Bull	5 laps/turbo	0	1m17.447s	16

FASTEST LAP: **VETTEL, 1M18.785S, 122.202MPH/196.666KPH ON LAP 68** • RACE LEADER: **VERSTAPPEN 1-71**
* 20-PLACE GRID PENALTY FOR USING ADDITIONAL POWER UNIT ELEMENTS;
** 35-PLACE GRID PENALTY FOR USING ADDITIONAL POWER UNIT ELEMENTS

This win for Sebastian Vettel, his first since the 11th round, will have given Ferrari a boost, but the real story of the race was Lewis Hamilton starting from the pits and racing through to almost catch Kimi Raikkonen for third place at the finish.

With Ferrari's season having fallen short of its expectations and then the team being criticised after its suggestion that it could even quit F1 if it didn't continue to receive preferential treatment, it needed a good result to redress the balance. Furthermore, after driving into the back of Lewis Hamilton in Mexico, Sebastian Vettel needed to restore his reputation and stop looking as though he was rattled by the Mercedes driver's form.

Mercedes dominated practice, but then Ferrari received a gift when Hamilton crashed right at the start of qualifying, sticking his W08 into the tyrewall at Ferradura. This left Vettel with a great shot at pole, but Valtteri Bottas rose to the challenge of defending Mercedes' honour and claimed the top spot by 0.038s. With no lap time set, Hamilton would have to start from the back. However, the team then elected to fit development engine parts which meant that he'd have to start from the pitlane - making his plight even worse.

Vettel made the better getaway and so had enough momentum to take the lead into the first corner from Bottas, with Daniel Ricciardo one of several to go off after being caught up in an incident with Stoffel Vandoorne and Kevin Magnussen.

Kimi Raikkonen kept Bottas looking rearwards as well as forwards all race, but there was no changing of places.

Hamilton, though, was on the move, tearing through the field and then getting close enough to Raikkonen to have a crack on the final lap, but the Finn held firm. At flagfall, the top four were covered by just 5.4s after a remarkable drive from Hamilton.

Red Bull Racing reckoned having to run on conservative engine modes wrecked its chances and so Verstappen and Ricciardo had to make do with fifth and sixth.

There was a great scrap behind them as Felipe Massa enjoyed his last home race by holding off Fernando Alonso and Sergio Perez for seventh place.

Sebastian Vettel made his return to winning look easy, but it was Hamilton who really shone.

INTERLAGOS ROUND 19

DATE: **12 NOVEMBER 2017**

Laps: **71** • Distance: **190.083 miles/305.909km** • Weather: **Hot & sunny**

Pos	Driver	Team	Result	Stops	Qualifying Time	Grid
1	**Sebastian Vettel**	Ferrari	1h31m26.262s	1	1m08.360s	2
2	**Valtteri Bottas**	Mercedes	1h31m29.014s	1	1m08.322s	1
3	**Kimi Raikkonen**	Ferrari	1h31m30.862s	1	1m08.538s	3
4	**Lewis Hamilton !!!**	Mercedes	1h31m31.730s	1	No time	20
5	**Max Verstappen**	Red Bull	1h31m59.202s	2	1m08.925s	4
6	**Daniel Ricciardo !**	Red Bull	1h32m14.953s	2	1m09.330s	14
7	**Felipe Massa**	Williams	1h32m35.144s	1	1m09.841s	9
8	**Fernando Alonso**	McLaren	1h32m35.625s	1	1m09.617s	6
9	**Sergio Perez**	Force India	1h32m35.762s	1	1m09.598s	5
10	**Nico Hulkenberg**	Renault	70 laps	1	1m09.703s	7
11	**Carlos Sainz Jr**	Renault	70 laps	1	1m09.805s	8
12	**Pierre Gasly !!**	Toro Rosso	70 laps	1	1m10.686s	19
13	**Marcus Ericsson ***	Sauber	70 laps	1	1m10.875s	17
14	**Pascal Wehrlein**	Sauber	70 laps	1	1m10.678s	15
15	**Romain Grosjean**	Haas	69 laps	2	1m09.879s	11
16	**Lance Stroll ***	Williams	69 laps	2	1m10.776s	16
R	**Brendon Hartley !**	Toro Rosso	40 laps/oil leak	1	No time	18
R	**Esteban Ocon**	Force India	0 laps/accident	0	1m09.830s	10
R	**Kevin Magnussen**	Haas	0 laps/accident	0	1m10.154s	13
R	**Stoffel Vandoorne**	McLaren	0 laps/accident	0	1m10.116s	12

FASTEST LAP: VERSTAPPEN, 1M11.044S, 135.676MPH/218.349KPH ON LAP 64 • RACE LEADERS: VETTEL 1-28 & 43-71, RAIKKONEN 29, HAMILTON 30-42
* 5-PLACE GRID PENALTY FOR REPLACING GEARBOX; ! 10-PLACE GRID PENALTY FOR USING ADDITIONAL POWER UNIT ELEMENTS;
!! 15-PLACE GRID PENALTY FOR USING ADDITIONAL POWER UNIT ELEMENTS;
!!! MADE TO START FROM PITLANE FOR CAR BEING MODIFIED UNDER PARC FERME CONDITIONS

ABU DHABI GP

Mercedes was in total control at the final round of 2017, but it was Valtteri Bottas who took pole position, set fastest lap and was first to the finish. Lewis Hamilton tried to pass his team-mate, but Yas Marina offers very few opportunities for that.

With the drivers' and constructors' titles already settled, it was always likely that the Abu Dhabi GP was going to be less dramatic than it can be. And so it proved, as there was no team capable of challenging Mercedes and no way for Lewis Hamilton to find his way past team-mate Valtteri Bottas.

Hamilton gave it a go, but the layout of the circuit offers next to no chance to get past a car that can run at a similar pace. Indeed, Hamilton said afterwards that you need to be around 1.4s a lap faster to find a way past. And he wasn't.

So, that was that and with Ferrari unable to get close, Bottas's third win of the year proved a formality. Sebastian Vettel was the best of the rest, with Ferrari team-mate Kimi Raikkonen coming through to fourth after Daniel Ricciardo's Red Bull pulled off when it was hit with power steering problems. This also cost the Australian fourth place in the points table.

While Mercedes had things taped, there was still great interest and considerable prize money riding on which of three teams would come out on top of the battle to end the year sixth overall, with Toro Rosso, Renault and Haas F1 covered by just six points. Sixth place for Nico Hulkenberg settled the matter in Renault's favour, although the German earned the displeasure of Force India for the way that he nipped past Sergio Perez on lap 1 by shortcutting the Turn 11-13 chicane. Hulkenberg had to serve a 5s penalty at his pitstop, but he was able to open a gap of more than that before he came in. Force India said he should have given the place back rather than serving the penalty. Team-mate Carlos Sainz Jr was also set for points, but a wheel came loose immediately after his pitstop.

As it happened, Toro Rosso was nowhere near the form it needed to keep Renault at bay and Haas F1 simply was not fast enough to challenge, with neither of the teams' drivers finishing in the points.

YAS MARINA ROUND 20

DATE: 26 NOVEMBER 2017

Laps: **55** • Distance: **189.738 miles/305.355km** • Weather: **Sunny & hot**

Pos	Driver	Team	Result	Stops	Qualifying Time	Grid
1	Valtteri Bottas	Mercedes	1h34m14.062s	1	1m36.231s	1
2	Lewis Hamilton	Mercedes	1h34m17.961s	1	1m36.403s	2
3	Sebastian Vettel	Ferrari	1h34m33.392s	1	1m36.777s	3
4	Kimi Raikkonen	Ferrari	1h34m59.448s	1	1m36.985s	5
5	Max Verstappen	Red Bull	1h35m00.331s	1	1m37.328s	6
6	Nico Hulkenberg	Renault	1h35m39.775s	1	1m38.282s	7
7	Sergio Perez	Force India	1h35m46.124s	1	1m38.374s	8
8	Esteban Ocon	Force India	1h35m52.973s	1	1m38.397s	9
9	Fernando Alonso	McLaren	54 laps	1	1m38.636s	11
10	Felipe Massa	Williams	54 laps	1	1m38.550s	10
11	Romain Grosjean	Haas	54 laps	1	1m39.516s	16
12	Stoffel Vandoorne	McLaren	54 laps	1	1m38.808s	13
13	Kevin Magnussen	Haas	54 laps	1	1m39.298s	14
14	Pascal Wehrlein	Sauber	54 laps	1	1m39.930s	18
15	Brendon Hartley *	Toro Rosso	54 laps	1	1m40.471s	20
16	Pierre Gasly	Toro Rosso	54 laps	1	1m39.724s	17
17	Marcus Ericsson	Sauber	54 laps	1	1m39.994s	19
18	Lance Stroll	Williams	54 laps	3	1m39.646s	15
R	Carlos Sainz Jr	Renault	31 laps/wheel	1	1m38.725s	12
R	Daniel Ricciardo	Red Bull	20 laps/hydraulics	1	1m36.959s	4

FASTEST LAP: **BOTTAS, 1M40.650S, 123.436MPH/198.652KPH ON LAP 52** • RACE LEADERS: **BOTTAS 1-21 & 25-55, HAMILTON 22-24**
* 10-PLACE GRID PENALTY FOR USING ADDITIONAL POWER UNIT ELEMENTS

It's a Mercedes double act as Bottas takes the cheers and Hamilton runs to congratulate him.

Abu Dhabi put on quite a show as the Yas Marina Circuit hosted the final round of season, albeit with both the drivers' and constructors' titles already settled in favour of Lewis Hamilton and Mercedes GP.

FINAL RESULTS 2017

POS	DRIVER	NAT		CAR-ENGINE	R1	R2	R3	R4	R5
1	LEWIS HAMILTON	GBR		MERCEDES F1 W08	2P	1PF	2F	4	1PF
2	SEBASTIAN VETTEL	GER		FERRARI SF70H	1	2	1	2P	2
3	VALTTERI BOTTAS	FIN		MERCEDES F1 W08	3	6	3P	1	R
4	KIMI RAIKKONEN	FIN		FERRARI SF70H	4F	5	4	3F	R
5	DANIEL RICCIARDO	AUS		RED BULL-TAG HEUER RB13	R	4	5	R	3
6	MAX VERSTAPPEN	NED		RED BULL-TAG HEUER RB13	5	3	R	5	R
7	SERGIO PEREZ	MEX		FORCE INDIA-MERCEDES VJM10	7	9	7	6	4
8	ESTEBAN OCON	FRA		FORCE INDIA-MERCEDES VJM10	10	10	10	7	5
9	CARLOS SAINZ JR	SPA		TORO ROSSO-RENAULT STR12	8	7	R	10	7
				RENAULT RS17	-	-	-	-	-
10	NICO HULKENBERG	GER		RENAULT RS17	11	12	9	8	6
11	FELIPE MASSA	BRA		WILLIAMS-MERCEDES FW40	6	14	6	9	13
12	LANCE STROLL	CDN		WILLIAMS_MERCEDES FW40	R	R	R	11	16
13	ROMAIN GROSJEAN	FRA		HAAS-FERRARI VF-17	R	11	8	R	10
14	KEVIN MAGNUSSEN	DEN		HAAS_FERRARI VF-17	R	8	R	13	14
15	FERNANDO ALONSO	SPA		McLAREN-HONDA MCL32	R	R	R	NS	12
16	STOFFEL VANDOORNE	BEL		McLAREN-HONDA MCL32	13	R	-	14	R
17	JOLYON PALMER	GBR		RENAULT RS17	R	13	13	R	15
18	PASCAL WEHRLEIN	GER		SAUBER-FERRARI C36	-	-	11	16	8
19	DANIIL KYVAT	RUS		TORO ROSSO-RENAULT STR12	9	R	12	12	9
20	MARCUS ERICSSON	SWE		SAUBER-FERRARI C36	R	15	R	15	11
21	PIERRE GASLY	FRA		TORO ROSSO-RENAULT STR12	-	-	-	-	-
22	ANTONIO GIOVINAZZI	ITA		SAUBER-FERRARI C36	12	R	-	-	-
23	BRENDON HARTLEY	NZL		TORO ROSSO-REMAULT STR12	-	-	-	-	-
24	JENSON BUTTON	GBR		McLAREN-HONDA MCL32	-	-	-	-	-
25	PAUL DI RESTA	GBR		WILLIAMS-MERCEDES FW40	-	-	-	-	-

SCORING

1st	25 points
2nd	18 points
3rd	15 points
4th	12 points
5th	10 points
6th	8 points
7th	6 points
8th	4 points
9th	2 points
10th	1 point

POS	TEAM-ENGINE	R1	R2	R3	R4	R5
1	MERCEDES	2/3	1/6	2/3	1/4	1/R
2	FERRARI	1/4	2/5	1/4	2/3	2/R
3	RED BULL-TAG HEUER	5/R	3/4	5/R	5/R	3/R
4	FORCE INDIA-MERCEDES	7/10	9/10	7/10	6/7	4/5
5	WILLIAMS-MERCEDES	6/R	14/R	6/R	9/11	13/16
6	RENAULT	11/R	12/13	9/13	8/R	6/15
7	TORO ROSSO-RENAULT	8/9	7/R	12/R	10/12	7/9
8	HAAS-FERRARI	R/R	8/11	8/R	13/R	10/14
9	McLAREN-HONDA	13/R	R/R	R/NS	14/NS	12/R
10	SAUBER-FERRARI	12/R	15/R	11/R	15/16	8/11

SYMBOLS AND GRAND PRIX KEY

ROUND 1................. AUSTRALIAN GP
ROUND 2..................... CHINESE GP
ROUND 3......................BAHRAIN GP
ROUND 4...................... RUSSIAN GP
ROUND 5..................... SPANISH GP

ROUND 6...................... MONACO GP
ROUND 7.................... CANADIAN GP
ROUND 8................AZERBAIJAN GP
ROUND 9 .... AUSTRIAN GP
ROUND 10 .... BRITISH GP

ROUND 11 .... HUNGARIAN GP
ROUND 12 .... BELGIAN GP
ROUND 13 .... ITALIAN GP
ROUND 14..............SINGAPORE GP
ROUND 15.................MALAYSIAN GP

ROUND 16 ....JAPANESE GP
ROUND 17........... UNITED STATES GP
ROUND 18 .... MEXICAN GP
ROUND 19 .... BRAZILIAN GP
ROUND 20............... ABU DHABI GP

D DISQUALIFIED **F** FASTEST LAP **NC** NOT CLASSIFIED **NS** NON-STARTER **P** POLE POSITION **R** RETIRED **W** WITHDRAWN

R6	R7	R8	R9	R10	R11	R12	R13	R14	R15	R16	R17	R18	R19	R20	TOTAL
7	1PF	5P	4F	1PF	4	1P	1P	1F	2P	1P	1P	9	4	2	363
1	4	4F	2	7	1P	2F	3	RP	4F	R	2F	4PF	1	3	317
4	2	2	1P	2	3	5	2	3	5	4F	5	2	2P	1PF	305
2P	7	R	5	3	2	4	5	R	R	5	3	3	3	4	205
3	3	1	3	5	R	3	4F	2	3	3	R	R	6	R	200
5	R	R	R	4	5	R	10	R	1	2	4	1	5F	5	168
13F	5	R	7	9	8	R	9	5	6	7	8	7	9	7	100
12	6	6	8	8	9	9	6	10	10	6	6	5	R	8	87
6	R	8	R	R	7	10	14	4	R	R	-	-	-	-	-
-	-	-	-	-	-	-	-	-	-	-	7	R	11	R	54
R	8	R	13	6	R	6	13	R	16	R	R	R	10	7	43
9	R	R	9	10	-	8	8	11	9	10	9	11	7	10	43
15	9	3	10	16	14	11	7	8	8	R	11	6	16	18	40
8	10	13	6	13	R	7	15	9	13	9	14	15	15	11	28
10	12	7	R	12	13	15	11	R	12	8	16	8	R	13	19
-	R	9	R	R	6F	R	R	R	11	11	R	10	8	9	17
R	14	12	12	11	10	14	R	7	7	14	12	12	R	12	13
11	11	R	11	NS	12	13	R	6	15	12	-	-	-	-	8
R	15	10	14	17	15	R	16	12	17	15	R	14	14	14	5
14	R	R	16	15	11	12	12	R	-	-	10	-	-	-	5
R	13	11	15	14	16	16	R	R	18	R	15	R	13	17	0
-	-	-	-	-	-	-	-	14	13	-	13	12	16	-	0
-	-	-	-	-	-	-	-	-	-	-	-	-	-	-	0
-	-	-	-	-	-	-	-	-	-	-	13	R	R	15	0
R	-	-	-	-	-	-	-	-	-	-	-	-	-	-	0
-	-	-	-	-	R	-	-	-	-	-	-	-	-	-	0

R6	R7	R8	R9	R10	R11	R12	R13	R14	R15	R16	R17	R18	R19	R20	TOTAL
4/7	1/2	2/5	1/4	1/2	3/4	1/5	1/2	1/3	2/5	1/4	1/5	2/9	2/4	1/2	668
1/2	4/7	4/R	2/5	3/7	1/2	2/4	3/5	R/R	4/R	5/R	2/3	3/4	1/3	3/4	522
3/5	3/R	1/R	3/R	4/5	5/R	3/R	4/10	2/R	1/3	2/3	4/R	1/R	5/6	5/R	368
12/13	5/6	6/R	7/8	8/9	8/9	R/9	6/9	5/10	6/10	6/7	6/8	5/7	9/R	7/8	187
9/15	9/R	3/R	9/10	10/16	14/R	8/11	7/8	8/11	8/9	10/R	9/11	6/11	7/16	10/18	83
11/R	8/11	R/R	11/13	6/NS	12/R	6/13	13/R	6/R	15/16	12/R	7/R	R/R	10/11	6/R	57
6/14	R/R	8/R	16/R	15/R	7/11	10/12	12/14	4/R	14/R	13/R	10/13	13/R	12/R	15/16	53
8/10	10/12	7/13	6/R	12/13	13/R	7/15	11/15	9/R	12/13	8/9	14/16	8/15	15/R	11/13	47
R/R	14/R	9/12	12/R	11/R	6/10	14/R	R/R	7/R	7/11	11/14	12/R	10/12	7/R	9/12	30
R/R	13/15	10/11	14/15	14/17	15/16	16/R	16/R	12/R	17/18	15/R	15/R	14/R	13/14	14/17	5

It seems a very long time ago now, but this is Fernando Alonso making his F1 debut at the age of 19 for Minardi in the 2001 Australian GP. He finished two laps down in 12th place.

MOST STARTS

DRIVERS

325	Rubens Barrichello	(BRA)	176	Graham Hill	(GBR)	128	Mario Andretti	(USA)
308	Michael Schumacher	(GER)	175	Jacques Laffite	(FRA)		Adrian Sutil	(GER)
307	Jenson Button	(GBR)	171	Niki Lauda	(AUT)	126	Jack Brabham	(AUS)
293	Fernando Alonso	(SPA)	165	Jacques Villeneuve	(CDN)	124	Romain Grosjean	(FRA)
273	Kimi Raikkonen	(FIN)	163	Thierry Boutsen	(BEL)	123	Ronnie Peterson	(SWE)
270	Felipe Massa	(BRA)	162	Mika Hakkinen	(FIN)	119	Pierluigi Martini	(ITA)
256	Riccardo Patrese	(ITA)		Johnny Herbert	(GBR)	116	Damon Hill	(GBR)
	Jarno Trulli	(ITA)	161	Ayrton Senna	(BRA)		Jacky Ickx	(BEL)
247	David Coulthard	(GBR)	159	Heinz-Harald Frentzen	(GER)		Alan Jones	(AUS)
230	Giancarlo Fisichella	(ITA)	158	Martin Brundle	(GBR)	114	Keke Rosberg	(FIN)
216	Mark Webber	(AUS)		Olivier Panis	(FRA)		Patrick Tambay	(FRA)
210	Gerhard Berger	(AUT)	152	John Watson	(GBR)	112	Denny Hulme	(NZL)
208	Andrea de Cesaris	(ITA)	149	Rene Arnoux	(FRA)		Jody Scheckter	(RSA)
	Lewis Hamilton	(GBR)	147	Eddie Irvine	(GBR)	111	Heikki Kovalainen	(FIN)
206	Nico Rosberg	(GER)		Derek Warwick	(GBR)		John Surtees	(GBR)
204	Nelson Piquet	(BRA)	146	Carlos Reutemann	(ARG)	109	Philippe Alliot	(FRA)
201	Jean Alesi	(FRA)	144	Emerson Fittipaldi	(BRA)		Mika Salo	(FIN)
199	Alain Prost	(FRA)	137	Nico Hulkenberg	(GER)	108	Elio de Angelis	(ITA)
	Sebastian Vettel	(GER)	135	Jean-Pierre Jarier	(FRA)	106	Jos Verstappen	(NED)
194	Michele Alboreto	(ITA)	134	Sergio Perez	(MEX)	104	Jo Bonnier	(SWE)
187	Nigel Mansell	(GBR)	132	Eddie Cheever	(USA)		Pedro de la Rosa	(SPA)
185	Nick Heidfeld	(GER)		Clay Regazzoni	(SWI)		Jochen Mass	(GER)
180	Ralf Schumacher	(GER)	129	Daniel Ricciardo	(AUS)	100	Bruce McLaren	(NZL)

CONSTRUCTORS

949	Ferrari	476	Force India (*nee* Jordan then Midland then Spyker)	379	Red Bull (*nee* Stewart then Jaguar Racing)
822	McLaren	443	Sauber (including BMW Sauber)	344	Mercedes GP (*nee* BAR then Honda Racing then Brawn GP)
741	Williams	418	Tyrrell		
613	Renault* (*nee* Toleman then Benetton then Renault II, Lotus II & Renault III)	409	Prost (*nee* Ligier)	230	March
		394	Brabham	197	BRM
567	Toro Rosso (*nee* Minardi)	383	Arrows	132	Osella
492	Lotus			129	Renault

MOST WINS

DRIVERS

91	Michael Schumacher	(GER)		Kimi Raikkonen	(FIN)		James Hunt	(GBR)
62	Lewis Hamilton	(GBR)	16	Stirling Moss	(GBR)		Ronnie Peterson	(SWE)
51	Alain Prost	(FRA)	15	Jenson Button	(GBR)		Jody Scheckter	(RSA)
47	Sebastian Vettel	(GER)	14	Jack Brabham	(AUS)	9	Mark Webber	(AUS)
41	Ayrton Senna	(BRA)		Emerson Fittipaldi	(BRA)	8	Denny Hulme	(NZL)
32	Fernando Alonso	(SPA)		Graham Hill	(GBR)		Jacky Ickx	(BEL)
31	Nigel Mansell	(GBR)	13	Alberto Ascari	(ITA)	7	Rene Arnoux	(FRA)
27	Jackie Stewart	(GBR)		David Coulthard	(GBR)		Juan Pablo Montoya	(COL)
25	Jim Clark	(GBR)	12	Mario Andretti	(USA)	6	Tony Brooks	(GBR)
	Niki Lauda	(AUT)		Alan Jones	(AUS)		Jacques Laffite	(FRA)
24	Juan Manuel Fangio	(ARG)		Carlos Reutemann	(ARG)		Riccardo Patrese	(ITA)
23	Nelson Piquet	(BRA)	11	Rubens Barrichello	(BRA)		Jochen Rindt	(AUT)
	Nico Rosberg	(GER)		Felipe Massa	(BRA)		Ralf Schumacher	(GER)
22	Damon Hill	(GBR)		Jacques Villeneuve	(CDN)		John Surtees	(GBR)
20	Mika Hakkinen	(FIN)	10	Gerhard Berger	(AUT)		Gilles Villeneuve	(CDN)

CONSTRUCTORS

229	Ferrari	17	BRM	3	March
181	McLaren	16	Cooper		Wolf
114	Williams	15	Renault	2	Honda
79	Lotus	10	Alfa Romeo	1	BMW Sauber
76	Mercedes GP (including Honda Racing, Brawn GP)	9	Ligier		Eagle
			Maserati		Hesketh
56	Red Bull (including Stewart)		Matra		Penske
49	Renault* (including Benetton, Renault II, Lotus II & Renault III)		Mercedes		Porsche
			Vanwall		Shadow
35	Brabham	4	Jordan		Toro Rosso
23	Tyrrell				

Niki Lauda pulled Ferrari out of the doldrums in the 1970s and this drive to victory at Monaco was the first of five that helped him to the 1975 title.

Sebastian Vettel races to victory in Singapore in 2013 in his most recent title-winning year when his 13 wins equalled Michael Schumacher's record.

DRIVERS

13	Michael Schumacher	2004	8	Mika Hakkinen	1998	6	Mario Andretti	1978
	Sebastian Vettel	2013		Damon Hill	1996		Alberto Ascari	1952
11	Lewis Hamilton	2014		Michael Schumacher	1994		Jim Clark	1965
	Michael Schumacher	2002		Ayrton Senna	1988		Juan Manuel Fangio	1954
	Sebastian Vettel	2011	7	Fernando Alonso	2005		Damon Hill	1994
10	Lewis Hamilton	2015		Fernando Alonso	2006		James Hunt	1976
	Lewis Hamilton	2016		Jim Clark	1963		Nigel Mansell	1987
9	Lewis Hamilton	2017		Alain Prost	1984		Kimi Raikkonen	2007
	Nigel Mansell	1992		Alain Prost	1988		Nico Rosberg	2015
	Nico Rosberg	2016		Alain Prost	1993		Michael Schumacher	1998
	Michael Schumacher	1995		Kimi Raikkonen	2005		Michael Schumacher	2003
	Michael Schumacher	2000		Ayrton Senna	1991		Michael Schumacher	2006
	Michael Schumacher	2001		Jacques Villeneuve	1997		Ayrton Senna	1989 & 1990

CONSTRUCTORS

19	Mercedes GP	2016		Williams	1993		Renault	2006
16	Mercedes GP	2014	9	Ferrari	2001		Williams	1997
	Mercedes GP	2015		Ferrari	2006	7	Ferrari	1952
15	Ferrari	2002		Ferrari	2007		Ferrari	1953
	Ferrari	2004		McLaren	1998		Ferrari	2008
	McLaren	1988		Red Bull	2010		Lotus	1963
12	McLaren	1984		Williams	1986		Lotus	1973
	Mercedes GP	2017		Williams	1987		McLaren	1999
	Red Bull	2011	8	Benetton	1994		McLaren	2000
	Williams	1996		Brawn GP	2009		McLaren	2012
11	Benetton	1995		Ferrari	2003		Red Bull	2012
10	Ferrari	2000		Lotus	1978		Tyrrell	1971
	McLaren	2005		McLaren	1991		Williams	1991
	McLaren	1989		McLaren	2007		Williams	1994
	Williams	1992		Renault	2005			

MOST POLE POSITIONS

DRIVERS

72	Lewis Hamilton	(GBR)
68	Michael Schumacher	(GER)
65	Ayrton Senna	(BRA)
50	Sebastian Vettel	(GER)
33	Jim Clark	(GBR)
	Alain Prost	(FRA)
32	Nigel Mansell	(GBR)
30	Nico Rosberg	(GER)
29	Juan Manuel Fangio	(ARG)
26	Mika Hakkinen	(FIN)
24	Niki Lauda	(AUT)
	Nelson Piquet	(BRA)
22	Fernando Alonso	(SPA)
20	Damon Hill	(GBR)
18	Mario Andretti	(USA)
	Rene Arnoux	(FRA)
17	Kimi Raikkonen	(FIN)
	Jackie Stewart	(GBR)
16	Felipe Massa	(BRA)
	Stirling Moss	(GBR)
14	Alberto Ascari	(ITA)
	Rubens Barrichello	(BRA)
	James Hunt	(GBR)
	Ronnie Peterson	(SWE)

13	Jack Brabham	(AUS)
	Graham Hill	(GBR)
	Jacky Ickx	(BEL)
	Juan Pablo Montoya	(COL)
	Jacques Villeneuve	(CDN)
12	Gerhard Berger	(AUT)
	David Coulthard	(GBR)
11	Mark Webber	(AUS)
10	Jochen Rindt	(AUT)

CONSTRUCTORS

213	Ferrari
154	McLaren
128	Williams
107	Lotus
88	Mercedes GP (including Brawn GP, Honda Racing, BAR)
59	Red Bull
39	Brabham
34	Renault* (including Toleman, Benetton, Renault II, Lotus II & Renault III)
31	Renault

14	Tyrrell
12	Alfa Romeo
11	BRM
	Cooper
10	Maserati
9	Ligier
8	Mercedes
7	Vanwall
5	March
4	Matra
3	Force India (including Jordan)
	Shadow
	Toyota
2	Lancia
1	BMW Sauber
	Toro Rosso

Lewis Hamilton (right) and Fernando Alonso shared the front row for the 2007 Canadian GP for McLaren, a race that marked the first of Hamilton's record 72 pole positions.

FASTEST LAPS

DRIVERS

76	Michael Schumacher	(GER)
45	Kimi Raikkonen	(FIN)
41	Alain Prost	(FRA)
38	Lewis Hamilton	(GBR)
33	Sebastian Vettel	(GER)
30	Nigel Mansell	(GBR)
28	Jim Clark	(GBR)
25	Mika Hakkinen	(FIN)
24	Niki Lauda	(AUT)
23	Juan Manuel Fangio	(ARG)
	Nelson Piquet	(BRA)
22	Fernando Alonso	(SPA)
21	Gerhard Berger	(AUT)
20	Nico Rosberg	(GER)
19	Damon Hill	(GBR)
	Stirling Moss	(GBR)
	Ayrton Senna	(BRA)
	Mark Webber	(AUS)
18	David Coulthard	(GBR)
17	Rubens Barrichello	(BRA)
16	Felipe Massa	(BRA)
15	Clay Regazzoni	(SWI)
	Jackie Stewart	(GBR)
14	Jacky Ickx	(BEL)
13	Alberto Ascari	(ITA)
	Alan Jones	(AUS)
	Riccardo Patrese	(ITA)
12	Rene Arnoux	(FRA)
	Jack Brabham	(AUS)
	Juan Pablo Montoya	(COL)
11	John Surtees	(GBR)
10	Mario Andretti	(USA)
	Graham Hill	(GBR)

CONSTRUCTORS

243	Ferrari
161	McLaren
133	Williams
71	Lotus
54	Red Bull
	Renault* (including Toleman, Benetton, Renault II & Lotus II)
47	Mercedes GP (including Brawn GP + BAR + Honda Racing)
40	Brabham
22	Tyrrell
18	Renault
15	BRM
	Maserati
14	Alfa Romeo
13	Cooper
12	Matra
11	Prost (including Ligier)
9	Mercedes
7	March
6	Vanwall

MOST POINTS (THIS FIGURE IS GROSS TALLY, I.E. INCLUDING SCORES THAT WERE LATER DROPPED)

DRIVERS

2,610	Lewis Hamilton	(GBR)
2,435	Sebastian Vettel	(GER)
1,860	Fernando Alonso	(SPA)
1,594.5	Nico Rosberg	(GER)
1,566	Michael Schumacher	(GER)
1,565	Kimi Raikkonen	(FIN)
1,235	Jenson Button	(GBR)
1,167	Felipe Massa	(BRA)
1,047.5	Mark Webber	(AUS)
816	Daniel Ricciardo	(AUS)
798.5	Alain Prost	(FRA)
716	Valtteri Bottas	(FIN)
658	Rubens Barrichello	(BRA)
614	Ayrton Senna	(BRA)
535	David Coulthard	(GBR)
485.5	Nelson Piquet	(BRA)
482	Nigel Mansell	(GBR)
469	Sergio Perez	(MEX)
421	Max Verstappen	(NED)
420.5	Niki Lauda	(AUT)
420	Mika Hakkinen	(FIN)
405	Nico Hulkenberg	(GER)
385	Gerhard Berger	(AUT)
360	Damon Hill	(GBR)
	Jackie Stewart	(GBR)
344	Romain Grosjean	(FRA)
329	Ralf Schumacher	(GER)
310	Carlos Reutemann	(ARG)
307	Juan Pablo Montoya	(COL)
289	Graham Hill	(GBR)
281	Emerson Fittipaldi	(BRA)
	Riccardo Patrese	(ITA)
277.5	Juan Manuel Fangio	(ARG)
275	Giancarlo Fisichella	(ITA)
274	Jim Clark	(GBR)
273	Robert Kubica	(POL)
261	Jack Brabham	(AUS)
259	Nick Heidfeld	(GER)
255	Jody Scheckter	(RSA)
248	Denny Hulme	(NZL)
246.5	Jarno Trulli (ITA)	
241	Jean Alesi	(FRA)
235	Jacques Villeneuve	(CDN)
228	Jacques Laffite (FRA)	

CONSTRUCTORS

7,164.5	Ferrari
5,123.5	McLaren
4,221	Mercedes GP (including BAR, Honda Racing, Brawn GP)
3,976.5	Red Bull (including Stewart, Jaguar Racing)
3,559	Williams
2,610.5	Renault* (including Toleman, Benetton, Renault II & Lotus II)
1,514	Lotus
1,279	Force India (including Jordan, Midland, Spyker)
854	Brabham
810	Sauber (including BMW Sauber)
617	Tyrrell
439	BRM
424	Prost (including Ligier)
418	Toro Rosso
333	Cooper
312	Renault
278.5	Toyota
171.5	March
167	Arrows
155	Matra

Juan Manuel Fangio raced to five F1 titles in the 1950s and no drive was more imperious than his pursuit of the Ferraris in Germany in 1957.

MOST DRIVERS' TITLES

7	Michael Schumacher	(GER)		Alberto Ascari	(ITA)		Denis Hulme	(NZL)
5	Juan Manuel Fangio	(ARG)		Jim Clark	(GBR)		James Hunt	(GBR)
4	Lewis Hamilton	(GBR)		Emerson Fittipaldi	(BRA)		Alan Jones	(AUS)
	Alain Prost	(FRA)		Mika Hakkinen	(FIN)		Nigel Mansell	(GBR)
	Sebastian Vettel	(GER)		Graham Hill	(GBR)		Kimi Raikkonen	(FIN)
3	Jack Brabham	(AUS)	**1**	Mario Andretti	(USA)		Jochen Rindt	(AUT)
	Niki Lauda	(AUT)		Jenson Button	(GBR)		Keke Rosberg	(FIN)
	Nelson Piquet	(BRA)		Giuseppe Farina	(ITA)		Nico Rosberg	(FIN)
	Ayrton Senna	(BRA)		Mike Hawthorn	(GBR)		Jody Scheckter	(RSA)
	Jackie Stewart	(GBR)		Damon Hill	(GBR)		John Surtees	(GBR)
2	Fernando Alonso	(SPA)		Phil Hill	(USA)		Jacques Villeneuve	(CDN)

MOST CONSTRUCTORS' TITLES

16	Ferrari			Red Bull	Brawn
9	Williams		**2**	Brabham	BRM
8	McLaren			Cooper	Matra
7	Lotus			Renault	Tyrrell
4	Mercedes GP		**1**	Benetton	Vanwall

NOTE: To avoid confusion, the Lotus stats listed are based on the team that ran from 1958 to 1994, whereas the those listed as Renault* are for the team based at Enstone that started as Toleman in 1981, became Benetton in 1986, then Renault II in 2002, Lotus II in 2012 and Renault again in 2016. The Renault listings are for the team that ran from 1977 to 1985, the stats for Red Bull Racing include those of the Stewart Grand Prix and Jaguar Racing teams from which it evolved, and those for Mercedes GP for the team that started as BAR in 1999, then ran as Honda GP from 2006 and as Brawn GP in 2009. Force India's stats include those of Jordan, Midland and Spyker, while Scuderia Toro Rosso's include those of its forerunner Minardi.

Ferrari failed to win on home ground at Monza in 2017, but that didn't stop the team's passionate fans, the *tifosi*, from showing their true colours. Maybe they will have more to cheer about in 2018?

2018 FILL-IN CHART

DRIVER	TEAM	Round 1 – 25 March AUSTRALIAN GP	Round 2 – 8 April BAHRAIN GP	Round 3 – 15 April CHINESE GP	Round 4 – 29 April AZERBAIJAN GP	Round 5 – 13 May SPANISH GP	Round 6 – 27 May MONACO GP	Round 7 – 10 June CANADIAN GP	Round 8 – 24 June FRENCH GP	Round 9 – 1 July AUSTRIAN GP
LEWIS HAMILTON	Mercedes									
VALTTERI BOTTAS	Mercedes									
SEBASTIAN VETTEL	Ferrari									
KIMI RAIKKONEN	Ferrari									
DANIEL RICCIARDO	Red Bull									
MAX VERSTAPPEN	Red Bull									
SERGIO PEREZ	Force India									
ESTEBAN OCON	Force India									
LANCE STROLL	Williams									
SERGEY SIROTKIN	Williams									
PIERRE GASLY	Toro Rosso									
BRENDON HARTLEY	Toro Rosso									
NICO HULKENBERG	Renault									
CARLOS SAINZ JR	Renault									
ROMAIN GROSJEAN	Haas F1									
KEVIN MAGNUSSEN	Haas F1									
FERNANDO ALONSO	McLaren									
STOFFEL VANDOORNE	McLaren									
CHARLES LECLERC	Sauber									
MARCUS ERICSSON	Sauber									

SCORING SYSTEM: 25, 18, 15, 12, 10, 8, 6, 4, 2, 1 POINTS
FOR THE FIRST 10 FINISHERS IN EACH GRAND PRIX

Round 10 – 8 July BRITISH GP	Round 11 – 22 July GERMAN GP	Round 12 – 29 July HUNGARIAN GP	Round 13 – 26 Aug BELGIAN GP	Round 14 – 2 Sept ITALIAN GP	Round 15 – 16 Sept SINGAPORE GP	Round 16 – 30 Sept RUSSIAN GP	Round 17 – 7 Oct JAPANESE GP	Round 18 – 21 Oct UNITED STATES GP	Round 19 – 28 Oct MEXICAN GP	Round 20 – 11 Nov BRAZILIAN GP	Round 21 – 25 Nov ABU DHABI GP	POINTS TOTAL

127

Four fingers for four F1 world championship titles for Lewis Hamilton. He appears to be the main man in car racing right now, unquestionably making the most of being with the top team, and he certainly sets the standards for his rivals to aim at.

The publishers would like to thank the following sources for their kind permission to reproduce the pictures in this book.

LAT Photographic: 17, 49, 61T, 103, 119; /Sam Bloxham: 26, 99, 106; /Charles Coates: 3, 21, 22, 23, 25, 27, 38, 52, 55, 62C, 64-65, 96, 121; /Glenn Dunbar: 6-7, 20, 28-29, 32, 34, 62TL, 72-73, 101, 104, 108, 114-115; /Steve Etherington: 10, 13, 14-15, 35, 58TR, 92-93, 95, 97, 102, 105, 118, 128; /Andrew Ferraro: 39, 53; /Andrew Hone: 16, 18, 19, 30, 37, 40, 45, 46, 58B, 98, 107, 109, 120, 124-125; /Hoyer/Ebrey: 12; /Zak Mauger: 33, 41, 48, 54, 56-57, 62B; /Tony Smythe: 123; /Steven Tee: 5, 8-9, 11, 24, 36, 42-43, 44, 47, 50, 51, 58TL, 61B, 90-91, 94, 100, 110; / Diederik van der Laan/Dutch Photo Agency: 61C

Sutton Images: 31, 62TR; /Mirko Stange: 87, 111

Every effort has been made to acknowledge correctly and contact the source and/ or copyright holder of each picture and Carlton Books Limited apologizes for any unintentional errors or omissions that will be corrected in future editions of this book.